RULERS OF MECCA

RULERS OF MECCA

by

GERALD de GAURY

DORSET PRESS
New York

This edition published by Dorset Press,
a division of Marboro Books Corporation.
1991 Dorset Press
ISBN 0-88029-666-6

Printed in the United States of America

M 9 8 7 6 5 4 3 2 1

PREFACE

ECCA IS STILL A FORBIDDEN CITY, THE LAST IN THE WORLD, whither none but Muslims may go, and where others enter only at their peril. The present authorities, the officials of the Saudi Arabian Government, it is true, would be loath to see foreign blood spilt there, but in the multitude of pilgrims drawn from all the Muslim world some are fanatics, and a non-Muslim being detected by them might become a sacrifice, be done to death by pilgrims in exalted mood, before he could be rescued. A few Christians have been there in disguise and returned safely; fewer still have renounced their faith with proper and previous formality, and visited it as Muslims; thus Mecca remains sacrosanct and almost unknown, the difficulty for a Christian author concerned with its story being thereby increased.

From among many who have helped me in one way or another it is embarrassing to single out individuals for mention, but it should be explained that the medieval history is largely taken from a manuscript book lent me with confidence, in spite of its value, by a Christian notable of Baghdad, Yacoub Sarkis. It will be found listed in the bibliography under the name of its author, Al Hussaini, and is believed to be the only copy of the original book, now lost. Thus the contemporary copy of Al Hussaini's work and the printed histories by Ibn Zaini Dahlan, a one-time Mufti in Mecca, furnished most of the material for the medieval period, and are the sources where no other references are given. As their works, like those of most Arab historians, are arranged chronologically, often under "the events of the year ——," or having the years in the margin, a multiplicity of page references has been avoided.

The well-provided library of the genial and learned Rauf al Chadirchi, of Baghdad, was placed at my disposal and frequently made use of for the culling of material from Turkish military history in Arabia.

Sayid Hussain Taymur, of the British Embassy staff in Baghdad, was most diligent in translating and in voluntary secretarial work, in spite of being free to undertake such work only in the heat of the afternoon; that he did so in the climate of Iraq was a feat for admiration.

Many other notables and officials offered their help and advice, which is very gratefully acknowledged.

I have also to thank the Sherifs Abdul Majid and Muhiyidin Haidar for their advice, and the Sherif Hazim ibn Salim Pasha, brother-in-law of the Regent of Iraq, and Sherif Muhammad Amin Haidar, both of whom generously made their knowledge and their libraries available to me and courteously followed up inquiries.

The illustrations for a book on the Meccan rulers present difficulty because the portrayal of the human figure—or of any creature or object which might thereby lend itself to idolatrous affection—was for long anathema to the Muslims, and still is hateful to the puritanical; so that there were no portraits made of the rulers until recently.

In Ankara and Istanbul I received the help and advice of Turkish and British officials and civilians, for which I am most grateful; and a note on the Imperial Ottoman Archives will be found in Appendix I.

The Astronomer Royal of England very kindly compared the dates of some of the phenomena recorded[1] by Al Hussaini with those of known date, with which in more than one case they accord excellently, thus helping to confirm Al Hussaini's accuracy. While the Regent of Iraq, son of the last Grand Sherif, most generously lent me the Qasr al Melik Ali, in Baghdad, the house in which his father had lived after leaving the Hijaz, so presenting me with an *ambiance* perfectly suited to the theme.

It was my intention to bring to light the unknown medieval history for the English-reading public, and in doing so I am conscious that I may not have stressed what in Muslim minds should be stressed; for I have not enlarged upon recent happenings or political history, which is comparatively well known to us, and in particular they may feel that this is the case in regard to my treatment of the days of the Prophet Muhammad;

[1] See Appendix II.

for that I beg their indulgence on the grounds that my motive in doing so was to present the whole secular history of the house of Hashim, without touching, except in so far as might be necessary for the purposes of continuity, on the ethics of Islam or the life and teachings of Muhammad, on which numerous and lengthy volumes have been written in many languages.

Although descent from the Prophet chiefly accounted for the prestige of the rulers of Mecca, it is remarkable that the same clans were able to hold the rulership of a city without material resources other than the income from the pilgrimage for so long and in the midst of ambitious neighbours.

The clans were constantly at loggerheads, but each in turn when it achieved the rulership maintained its unity against the deposed clan, and especially during the Middle Ages the ruler was supported by two, three, or even four co-partners from his family. This perplexing way of ruling, with constant deference to family feeling and perpetual fear of the opposition clan, with behind it, on the one hand, the pride and prestige of descent from the Prophet, and, on the other, the simple democracy of the desert-dwellers who surrounded them and from whom they themselves were descended, nevertheless succeeded until a quarter of a century ago, when the Meccan mantocratic state at last fell to an Arab invader.

In presenting this story the writer must make one final expression of thanks, to those long-dead Orientals, and more recent Orientalists, to whose works he is indebted.

GERALD DE GAURY

CONTENTS

ILLUSTRATIONS

CHRONOLOGIAL TABLES

PEDIGREES

RULERS OF MECCA

Here the elders and chief citizens and strangers and his kinsmen, are daily assembled with the Sherif; for this is the Mejlis, and coffee parliament of an Arabian prince; who is easy of access and of popular manners, as was Mohammed himself.

CHARLES DOUGHTY, *Arabia Deserta*, chapter xvii

Les Chérifs constituent la seule aristocratie du sang qui existe dans les pays musulmans.

CHARLES DIDIER, *Séjour chez le grand-chérif de la Mecque*, chapter viii

Chapter I

THE FOUNDING OF MECCA

GREAT ARABIA WAS HEAVED UP FROM BENEATH THE waters in the ultimate writhing of the earth, and, save for the fertile southern corner, fed by monsoon rain, and for its thorn-covered plains and bushy hollows, is until now utterly barren. Along its western side are lava-strewn mountains, old volcanoes, and all its length from north to south a steep declivity marking how the surface sundered to the furnace of the globe. Into such a land only the fiercest men ventured from their foothold in the south, searching for gullies where water lingers or as parasites to camels in the waste. So peninsular Arabia was a land of myth and dread, most awesome to the ancients, mournful and mysterious beyond compare.

An early author, Al Tabari, wrote, "The mountains of Kaf encircle the world like a rim, being emerald in colour; the blue we see in the sky being reflected from them."[1] There are, he says, two inhabited places belonging to Kaf, "Sabouka and Jaboulsa." The inhabitants do not even know the name of Adam, live on herbs, and wear no clothes. They do not want to have children because they are all males. Some say that they live beyond where the sun sinks and that the two-horned one, great Alexander of Macedon, "would have had to march another two months into the shadows to reach that land."

There are still mountains called Kaf in Central Arabia. The story of the all-male inhabitants may have arisen from a traveller's tale of the pre-Islamic Arab custom of stifling nearly all females at birth, or, more probably, from the annual absence from the islands off the southern coast, for half the year, of all the men and youths to harvest, unpolluted, the frankincense-trees on the terraces of the main; whence they dispatched incense to the temples of the Occident.

Great caravans came northward from the South Arabian

---

[1] *Tarikh al Umam wa al Muluk al Hussainiya*, vol. i, chapters vi and vii.

incense-land,[1] and to their cargo was added other merchandise, precious stones, cinnamon, pepper and luxuries from the Indies, slaves from Abyssinia, and whatever might tempt the Western world. In South Arabia there grew up rich entrepôts, with temples, like those at Shabwa and that to the sun-god or -goddess on Socotra Island, in the Indian Ocean off the Horn of Africa. For South and South-western Arabia was the landfall and link between the Orient and the markets in the West, and so prospered, developed kingdoms, whose caravans must needs pass across or along the wild valleys which drain the surface-running rainwater from the Arabian plateau all the length of the Red Sea—the Hijaz, or 'barrier' country.

On the swiftest dromedary a rider cannot reach Gaza, on the Mediterranean coast, from Aden, on the Indian Ocean, under a month, and a slow-moving caravan takes three times as long. There would be halts for rest and refitting, for changing here and there of an exhausted animal. In the midway marches the mountains, which to the north and south reach ten thousand feet and more, are only some three thousand feet above sea-level, and beyond them, inland, is grazing, where bedouin may prosper.

This access to the tribes of Central Arabia, furnishers of desert guides and of camels, if it were a benefit to the passing caravans was offset by the truculence of the nomads, only to be subdued by making with them a concord much to their advantage, and by the inhospitable nature of the country beneath the mountains, the middle Hijaz. Farther north, some days ahead of the caravans, the upland plain spills out towards the sea, but hereabouts is nothing save a nightmare of gaunt, glittering hills and labyrinthine gullies, in one of which is Mecca. The heat is stifling in winter, and almost insupportable, even by Arabs, in summer.

On the plain above the Hijaz the rapacious nomads, fiercely stimulated and made quarrelsome by the dry heat, were masters of the few desert water-holes and wells; while the sea was dangerous near the shore, because of innumerable shallow reefs of coral, and farther out men feared to go, for dread of being buffeted by winds in the northward passage.

---

[1] Genesis xxxvii, 25: "... a company of Ishmaelites ... with their camels bearing spicery and balm and myrrh."

Moreover, the open coastal plain by the seashore is soft, salty ground, where animals sink and tire as they plod, and so an inland road between coast and plateau would have to be endured.

MECCA AND ITS SURROUNDINGS

This Hijaz, or 'barrier' country, part of a gruesome rent in the earth's surface, is a naked land with few hollows decorated with palms and thickets, where man can lead a settled life. Every fifty miles or so in the valleys, and above on the plateau, are wide rings of lava, collars to old volcanoes, blocks of basalt tumbled out on the plain, or down the hillsides, black as iron; doubly fearsome to the early Arabs, for in those days the volcanoes still erupted.

Between the hot and dry Central Arabian atmosphere and the humid air from the Hijaz electric storms are quickly generated, and day after day and night after night, from mountain-top to mountain-top, lightning plays, without ceasing for many hours. And now and then in winter there is a cloud-burst in that otherwise almost rainless land, and spates rush down the gullies, sweeping away men and animals. Nowhere else on earth is there so great a contrast in climate—nowhere, unless it be between the hot, humid depths of the Dead Sea and the dry, harsh mountain-sides above it that tower over Jordan, the inland part of Palestine; but the heat is less stifling in Lower Jordan than on the rotting coral shore of the Hijaz.

In such a country man is wrought to an unusual tenseness by the climate and his surroundings, and, aspiring to propitiate the elemental forces, invents or imports and then becomes a slave to gods and ritual; thus long before Mecca became a populous and settled station on the caravan route it was, like Taif, its sister city on the plateau edge, a sanctuary and temple.

The Arab author Al Azraki, among others, gives the later Muslim legend of Mecca as a sanctuary. Once upon a time a southward-bound caravan of the Bani Jurham tribe noticed a spring of water where none of them had known that there was water. The caravan was halted, and two men were sent to examine it. They found a woman and a male child beside her. She said that her name was Hagar and that the well belonged to them, so with her permission the tribe camped there, and from then onward began to use the well and set up their shelters about it.[1] The spring was called Zemzem, and is the well now enclosed in the sanctuary of Mecca.[2]

---

[1] See note at end of chapter for list of known princes of the Bani Jurham, beginning, however, very much later than Abraham's day, which Sir Leonard Woolley in his *Abraham* gives as about 2000 B.C.

[2] Al Maqdisi, the tenth-century geographer, says that at his first visit he tasted the water of Zemzem and found it detestable. At his second visit he found it excellent. The opinions of more recent travellers have varied one from another. Ali Bey al Abbassi wrote of the water that "notwithstanding the depth of the well, and the heat of the climate it is hotter when first drawn up than the air. It resembles warm water, which proves that there is at the bottom a particular cause of vehement heat." The water is sold to pilgrims in flasks for them to take away, as is the water of the Jordan to Christians. The word 'Mekka' appears to be connected with the Arabic root-word meaning 'what is sucked dry.' 'Bekka,' its alternative name, means 'a well with little water.' 'Zamzam,' of a well, means 'to resound or burble.'

Hagar's son Ishmael grew up with the Bani Jurham, a South Arabian tribe, and was given a bride by them and lived by hunting. Then Abraham came down from Damascus to look for his wife and child, but happening to arrive when Ishmael was away hunting, and being off-handedly received by Ishmael's wife, he left a message with her that Ishmael might understand, that "the lintel of his door pleased him not." So Ishmael[1] the hunter took another bride from the Bani Jurham, and Abraham was pleased, and when he came the third time he found Ishmael sharpening arrows near the well, and he said to him that there, to please God, he would build a house to Him, and they chose a rise and built it. Tubba Asad al Himyari, a historical figure and King in the Yemen, whose people became converted to Judaism, his successors formally adopting it, made a door for it with locks, and the angel Gabriel brought the Black Stone for it. The stone was on Jebel Qubais, immediately above Mecca, and at that time it was glittering and bright, "only becoming black later when, in the times of 'ignorance,' there was a fire begun by an old woman who upset an incense burner. . . ."[2] The Qoraish, the successors of the Bani Jurham in Mecca, then rebuilt the house. It was formerly covered with skins, but afterwards the rich pilgrims, when they stripped off their clothes on the morning of the sacrifice, gave their silks to the guardians to make a covering for the house.

According to Abu'l Feda, there was a statue of Abraham in Mecca, and there are other and numerous versions of the story of Abraham in Mecca, but this one is the core of most of them.

Al Maqdisi relates that in the early days of the Bani Jurham it became customary for the tribesmen and travellers to take away and to carry round with them pieces of the stone of the House, of that House of God "built by Abraham," which they used to circle in veneration. "So gradually they began to worship stones, and then idols were permitted, and they worshipped idols," he adds.

---

[1] Ishmael is also said by the Arabs to have been the first man to tame a wild mare for riding.

[2] The stone has been believed by qualified observers to be of meteoric origin. It is fixed, by means of a silver band, in the outer wall of the Ka'aba so that it can be kissed by pilgrims as they pass it.

Visiting tribesmen, passing travellers, and caravaneers all found there or left there something of their own cult, until Mecca became a pantheon. Judaism had been professed in the Yemen, in Nejran, where there still are Jews, and at Khaibar and Medina, in the Hijaz, to the north and south of Mecca. Christianity was accepted by some of the Rabia tribes, in Eastern Arabia, and about Dumat al Jandal in Northern Arabia, and later was to be introduced from Abyssinia into the Yemen. But most of the tribes and many of the people of the oases, in the heart of Arabia, were pagan. The gentle moon-god, Wadd, or 'love,' was in their high favour and took precedence among them over the sun. Some of the Arabian nomads to this day hold that their life is regulated by the moon, which condenses the water-vapours and distils the beneficent dew on the pastures, and by the Pleiades, or Tharaya, which bring the rain. On the other hand, the sun, a female goddess popular in agricultural settlements, would like, as they believed, to destroy the bedouin, as well as all animal life, and is fierce and cruel. Thus the Kinana ancestors of the Qoraish tribe of Mecca worshipped the moon and Aldebaran, while the Lakhim and the Jurham tribes preferred Jupiter; some, like the Bani Asad, Mercury, or, as the Tay and others, Canopus and Sirius. A few believed that death ended all, and others held that there was a resurrection and that the soul flew off in the form of a bird, which they called Hama or Sada, that came fluttering and somersaulting near the tomb with phantom cries and reported to the deceased what his sons were doing. But from remote times nearly all the Arabs seem to have held that Allah was a dominant god or being with whom their own particular deity could intervene for them.

One of the first Europeans to describe the Red Sea coast and mention the Meccan sanctuary was Diodorus of Sicily. He says:

This coast has very few harbours in it by reason of the many vast mountains that lie all along as they sail; from whence is presented to the view such variety of colours, that they afford a most wonderful and delightful prospect to the passengers as they sail along. The promontory of the Alainites next salutes them that sail on forward, full of towns and villages inhabited by the Arabians called Nabatæans: they possess a large country all along the sea-coast, and so far likewise up into the land: this tract is very populous, and exceeding rich in cattle. Once they lived justly and honestly, content with the sustenance they had from their flocks and herds; but after that the Kings of Alexandria allowed liberty to merchants to traffick in the Red Sea, they not only robbed them that were shipwrackt, but provided little skiffs, and acted Pyrats, and spoil'd all other merchants that traffickt in those seas. . . . But afterwards being beaten in a fight at sea by some gallies sent out against them, they were punish'd according to their demerits.[1]

"After passing of these tracts," says Diodorus, "is a flat champain country . . . that abounds in rich pastures, and produces great plenty of medica and lotus, as high as a man."[2] Continuing, he describes the next most southerly people as being "called Bizomenians, and they live upon wild beasts taken in hunting. Here's a sacred Temple in high veneration among all the Arabians."

Herodotus[3] says that the Arabs worshipped Orotal and Alilat, the first being, he explains, Bacchus[4] and the second Urania. Orotal is doubtless Allah taala, as the Almighty is yet called by the Arabs, and Alilat is the goddess Allat, whose centre was at Taif on the edge of the plateau, not far east of Mecca. He describes the oath-binding or uniting of two Arabs, still in practice in some tribes.

When two men would swear a friendship they stand on each side of a third, who with a sharp stone makes a cut high up the inside of the wrist below the middle finger and taking a piece from their dress, dips it in the blood of each and moistens therewith seven stones lying in their midst, calling the while on Bacchus and Urania.

"The Arabs keep such pledges more religiously than almost any other people," he adds; and taken in Mecca itself these oaths were doubly binding.

---

[1] *The Historical Library of Diodorus the Sicilian*, Book III, chapter xxxi. Diodorus Siculus died soon after A.D. 57.

[2] The Harb tribesmen who to-day inhabit this country are still known by their northerly neighbours as 'gum-eaters,' because they chew the gum of trees and feed their camels on the leaves, which they believe have remedial properties.

[3] *The History of Herodotus*, edited by G. Rawlinson, book iii, chapter 8.

[4] The Koran forbids 'intoxicating' liquor. Vines grow at Taif and in its neighbourhood. Wine was made there in the early nineteenth century—*see* J. L. Burckhardt and others.

Such are some of the few glimpses we have of Mecca and of Arabian worship in those early days. Ptolemy calls Mecca Macaraba, and *macuraba* means 'sanctuary' in the language of the Sabæan Arabs, who dominated Southern Arabia and Arabian trading in the last millennium before Christ.

To it was made an annual pilgrimage at a fixed time in the autumn, and, by mutual consent, at that time fighting was forbidden. The Arabic names for the months, in use before Islam, confirm this practice, one of them still being called the 'forbidden.' In those days the lunar months were kept to their solar setting by periodically inserting extra days, a practice abandoned by Muhammad.

Approaching the House of the God, or Ka'aba, at Mecca the pilgrims stripped off all covering, in sign of humility. They compassed it, kissed the Black Stone, ran between the hillocks of Marwa and Al Safa, threw stones near Muna, and made a sacrifice, exactly as they do to-day.

When these practices were confirmed by Muhammad and the pilgrimage enjoined upon Muslims he seems to have preferred them to be clothed, in a loincloth,[1] and he spoke disparagingly of the pagan custom of "clapping hands and whistling through the fingers," which he desired should be replaced by a uniform and more subdued method of praying. Until his day it had been habitual to go naked in the dark of dawn to the leather-covered Ka'aba for the rites of absolution, which were ended in joyful ecstasy under the noonday sun. To-day it is still customary to reply to one who says that he intends to make the pilgrimage, "It is a guilt-removing endeavour."

While altering the form of worship Muhammad was to retain the pilgrimage as one of the five cardinal precepts of Islam, the others being prayer, cleanliness, charity, and fasting. Of the pilgrimage he said:

> Verily the first house appointed unto man to worship in was that which is in Becca [an alternative name for Mecca], blessed and a direction to all creatures. There are manifest signs: the place where Abraham stood: and whoever entereth therein shall be safe. And it is a duty towards God, incumbent on those who are able to go thither to visit this house: but who-

[1] The Koran, chapter vii. The words used are not categorical.

soever disbelieveth, verily God needeth not the services of any creature.[1]

In verse 82 of the ninth chapter of the Koran he followed up the last saying by this revelation: "Verily the idolators are unclean: let them not come near unto the Holy Temple after this year." The year in question was the eighth of the Hejira or Muslim year, the year A.D. 629. Mecca was ever afterwards to be a forbidden city for all but Muslims. Until that revelation to Muhammad all might come and go to Mecca of whatever creed, except that in pagan days women did not frequent the sanctuary. Their abstention was probably not from a want of right to do so, but from a sense of fitness; for propitiation of the gods, and the feeling of guiltiness before them, would be men's affair, a matter for the male adventurer, traveller, and hunter.

Woman had not then attached herself to the husband or lord under that system called ba'al marriage, which came into general use in Arabia only a little time before Islam, and even when it did so the older, freer system was still practised. Under the former, woman remained in the tribe with her own people, and retained the children, who became members of her totem, and she formed only a temporary union, which she could dissolve at will. By Muhammad's time matches of this kind had gradually come to be regarded as discreditable, and the women who made them were beginning to be regarded as harlots or were found only in ignoble tribes. A Meccan woman of good birth by then had come to pride herself on her chastity: the restraint which was originally imposed on captive women and slaves by their lords being accepted by the wife herself as a point of honour.[2] This change is ascribed to foreign influences, to the customs of the north and of the world beyond Arabia becoming known through trade and the settling of foreigners in Arabia. The saying, "The children are to the bed," which is still extant, dates from the days of this former system, which is in use to this day among the Shiah Arabs and, indeed, by most Shiah Muslims of whatever race. Known as mita', it permits a man to marry for a short period, and is often adopted by pilgrims, sailors, and caravaneers, or whoever are travelling without their wives. However strange

---

[1] The Koran, chapter iii.
[2] L. de O'Leary, *Arabia before Muhammad*, p. 191 *et seq.*

this early form of marriage contract may seem to-day, it worked admirably for many centuries, and under it was born chivalry itself, copied by the West from Arabia, while it is a fact that from the subsequent system of *ba'al* marriage, whereby the man is lord, there gradually came into being the 'harem' system and its abuses. When we deplore the harem system it should be remembered that it arose after adoption of a foreign form of marriage, found in course of time to be unsatisfactory as it stood, and which is itself not likely to be the final arrangement for generating and perfecting children. In any case it was under the temporary form, whereby woman remained in the tribe among her own people, that chivalry was born. The Arab poets before Islam sing of knights-errant and their adventures, and it is before Islam and in its early days, before the harem, more often than in later history that there are tales of wise, witty, beautiful women playing their open part in the life of the race and even ruling states or cities.

Sanctuary, the very essence of chivalry, was not confined to Mecca then any more than it is to-day, when still every man may give to another, to the best of his ability, protection in case of need, and, his honour being engaged, may lay down his life in doing so, even if the man is a stranger or undeserving, once the word whereby he promises sanctuary has been given. Every tribal sheikh gives his protection in a just cause, and even in an unjust one would give it for three days and do his best to help the fugitive escape from his sanctuary with a fair chance of making away unharmed.

Every noble, too, kept his round, red-leather tent as a symbol of chivalry, the traditional tabernacle and tribal sanctuary for guests and refugees,[1] where in some cases a piece of the Ka'aba stone or other sacred object was reverently guarded.

The camel-borne ark, until recently carried by the Ruwala bedouins of the Syrian desert, was perhaps the lineal descendant of the red-leather tribal sanctuaries of the pagan Arab.[2] The nobles of the Qoraish tribe, successors of the Bani Jurham as masters of Mecca, were well known for the fondness they displayed for these signs of honour, which they erected beside their own tents.

---

[1] H. Laemmens, *La Mecque à la veille de l'hégire.*
[2] Professor Hitti in his *History of the Arabs* suggests another origin.

Such were some of the customs of the early Arabians, from among whom there were annually drawn barefooted pilgrims, padding softly onward in gathering throngs, augmented from district to district and tribe to tribe by more and more companions bound for Mecca, in hope of absolution by compliance with an enjoyable, sanctified ritual in the great sanctuary. A guiltless, perfectly amoral people, ordinarily at large in the deserts, they were devoted to this annual gathering and ceremony of propitiation of the life forces by circulating naked before the gods, kissing those that were kissable, their senses being further titivated by the burning of quantities of frankincense; and as the shapes of the gods were many and their significance wide there was something to please and comfort every one of them.

The pilgrimage time being customarily in the autumn, when the nomads were in any case obliged to send their caravans to the markets to restock ready for the winter migration in search of grazing, there was for all the central Arabian bedouin a fair held annually at Ukaz, between Taif and Mecca, and three short marches from the latter, in an oasis of palms. Here they diverted themselves before the pilgrimage with the recitation of poems, and here came traders with goods from the poor valleys of the plain, from the fertile valley of Marr, north of Mecca, from the fields of Taif itself, and from the port of Shuaiba, the predecessor of Jedda.[1] There is no tale of a sanctuary at Ukaz, and it was not the gathering of the tribesmen and merchants for trade that brought into being *a priori* the sanctuary and harbour for gods at Taif and Mecca. Whoever searches for a reason other than those in the Arab legends for the use of Mecca as a sanctuary can find nothing material to put forward.

There is in the Arab legends a core of truth, often overlaid with a characteristic and ingenious lacquer of invention to cover what has seemed distasteful or incomprehensible to later generations. When Meccan history opens it was a pagan temple and sanctuary without permanent habitation, where indeed man feared to build and even refrained from cutting down trees lest he might be guilty of desecrating its holiness.

[1] Jedda was made a port by the third Caliph in A.D. 646. Wadi al Marr is to-day known as Wadi Fatima.

Its second phase begins about the fifth century A.D. with the settling of merchants from South Arabia. From then onward it grew to be a great trading centre, the most important commercial city in Arabia, and remained so until the days of the Prophet Muhammad—that is, up to the middle of the seventh century. Before the Prophet it had had some two hundred years of commercial success and fame, but they were the last years in which the Arabian caravans were to come to the West with the riches of the Orient, the last when they would be awaited with impatience by merchants and princes of the Byzantine Empire; as had waited for them their forerunners in Rome, of Greece, ancient Egypt, and Babylonia.

In this last period a move to Mecca was forced upon the merchants of Aden and of Southern Arabia because of the loss of their middlemen's monopoly with India, a decline in the incense trade, and a reluctance of the West to trade with a country which was in little need of imports in return. The West was still, however, in need of Arabian gold, of Arabian skins for warriors' coats—useful too for harness and hangings —and of camels, which the Roman commissariat had introduced into North Africa. And from some half-way point in the Hijaz the marshalling of Central Arabian trade, and of such of it as remained to them from the south, might be more expeditiously managed. In any case behind them Abyssinia, the Kingdom of Axum, was closing in, was already astride the Red Sea. The new settlers, either unconscious of their approaching doom as caravan traders with the West or perhaps aware, and so the more readily urged by it, organized their caravans with crafty ability. Not for them, more often than they could help it, were the dangers of the road. They placed their caravans in charge of men who had nomad relatives, kin to sheikhs. In guaranteeing safe passage to the caravans these men acted in some sort as insurers, with their nomad allies and cousins as reinsurers who stood to lose their honour if the caravans were attacked and their oath to protect them broken.

As guards the caravans had, like the persons of the merchants and their houses in the rich Al Batha quarter of Mecca, black Abyssinians, for Mecca had already become in these days a paradise for military adventurers, and the mountaineers of Abyssinia were the Swiss Guard of the peninsula. The poets spoke of them as "the crows of the Arabs" and as "erect, immobile, lance in hand." Ibn Diba wrote of "these thousands of soldiers, dark as thunder in the sky, their war-cries alone deafen the horses and hold off an enemy . . . demons innumerable as grains of sand in a storm. . . ." Another, speaking disparagingly of the Meccan merchants, says, "Great square-shouldered negroes you send in regiments instead of you"; but these, unlike the Abyssinians, were African slaves brought to Arabia through, and not from, Abyssinia, the land of ivory and slaves.[1]

The charge on goods made by the caravaneer bankers was 100 per cent., but as the caravan might be away many months, and as they stood on occasion to lose all, their charge was perhaps not so excessive as at first it sounds. For safety, no large sum was carried and bankers at either end of the journey were needed, so every Meccan banker had his partner in desert ports. Some of them found it wise to have foreign secretaries and agents, perhaps Græco-Syrians, like the partner-agent of the famous millionaire banker of Mecca, Ibn Jadaan, or able sons of Ulysses, like those to be found to this day in the ports of the Red Sea and the Mediterranean, or indeed nowadays almost everywhere; and there were colonies in Mecca from all the neighbouring countries, Jews and Christians entering it freely.

In summer the caravans went to Syria and in the winter to the Yemen. It is difficult now to imagine the fascination which Arabia and its merchandise held for the West, with what impatience the annual cargo of gold-dust, aromatics, perfumes, Negro slaves, skins, ivory, aloes, and myrrh was awaited.

At Palmyra there were statues erected in gratitude and admiration to Arabian caravan leaders, and when a caravan neared its destination the leader sent ahead a courier, who if all was well would be received by prolonged rolling of drums, fêted, and rewarded lavishly. To be selected as the herald of a safely come caravan from Arabia was to be made for life.

It was quite otherwise if the news was bad. In a piteous attempt to fend off punishment the courier would slit the ears of his camel so that they streamed blood, tear his clothes before and behind, reverse his saddle, and, as he passed into the city,

[1] H. Laemmens, *Les Ahabis et l'organisation militaire de la Mecque au siècle de l'hégire.*

shout again and again, "I be your agent, stripped of all. Oh, misery, Oh, evil surprise, stripped of all, stripped of all!"[1] Wise merchants here and there, with stocks concealed, would doubtless profit and could count their gains gleefully as prices rose, but it was sad news to be whispered to their lords and mistresses by the dusky slaves of Byzantium and Egypt.

Strabo, historian of the abortive Roman expedition to Southern Arabia in 24 B.C., who saw a Meccan caravan arriving at Petra, compares it with an army, and Al Tabari speaks of one with two thousand camels. At these times they entered Byzantine territory at Ailat (Elpath of the Bible), on the Gulf of Akaba, where there had been a station of the Tenth Legion during the Roman occupation of Nabatæan Arabia since A.D. 105, with a detachment and barracks at Al Hawara, the port of Medina, of which there are some little remains to be seen to-day. Ailat in these later days was a Byzantine frontier town of importance and the seat of a bishop. Many of his flock were far afield and there were monasteries and hermitages in the Wadi al Qura, along which the caravans passed. Their inhabitants were famous for their welcoming of passers-by, whether bedouin or merchants, offering them water from their wells, and wine; while at night the lamps of hermits engaged in their night-long vigils were a guide which gave encouragement.

Near Ailat, or formerly Petra itself, the caravans divided, those bound for Gaza made westward and those for Damascus north towards Bosra and Mazarib, in Hauran. At Damascus and Gaza the Meccan camels, kneeling to be unloaded, gave their self-pitying groans for their obedience to man for the fiftieth or more time since Mecca. But their quiet grazing was never for long, and the return-loads for Arabia of olive-oil, cereals, wine, arms, and armour waited. The sturdy Abyssinian militia, the negro slaves and mercenaries, the merchant adventurers, Greek scribes, brides-to-be, wild, sun-darkened bedouin guides—all were ready for the journey into the land of mournful solitude and romance. The first day's march was only for an hour or two, so that late-comers might catch up and things forgotten be retrieved, and for the same reason they customarily left towards the full-moon night, for thus the

[1] H. Laemmens, *La Mecque à la veille de l'hégire*.

passengers and soldiers might more easily know their own divisions, make repairs to slipping packs, replace or alter ropes and loads; so, in the moonlight, come to know their fellows and their whereabouts, be done with that inquisitive coming and going of travellers on the first setting-out. For such was the practice from time immemorial, which would be followed by their descendants with pilgrims, or with less romantic merchandise in other deserts, for another thousand years or more.

And at Mecca the prudent, opportunist bankers waited. About them had grown up foreign colonies; Jews, Christians, pagans were free to come and go, and from a lonely shrine Mecca was become a great metropolis. Besides a nobility of birth, of ruling clans, it had developed from them a nobility of commerce, as well as that of hereditary office in the sanctuary.

A council of elders, chosen from among the settled nobility, delivered the customary law, but, jealous of their privilege, watched each other with habitual concern for another's pretensions, the more so for nature herself had imposed democracy on their desert-dwelling ancestors in exchange for their survival. A generous hospitality; an equal division of their means of life with wayfarers; their conception of every man's right to water, to the serving in case of need and without requitement of cattle and mares, and, above all, to sanctuary —these arise, like their directness of manners and spoken solicitude, out of the nature of desert life from the narrow margin between them and death, and have their origin long before the revelation of Islam. To break these ancient rules was, for them, to break laws of survival, and of Nature herself.

So again and again there were to be instances of the calculated humility of ardent and self-willed Meccan Arabs who, if they ruled a quarter of the civilized world, would ride pillion with their guide or man-at-arms to take the submission of an army or of a city, who took care to receive ambassadors in the simple dress of the desert, who would habitually seat themselves on the ground, and by calling their men to prayers in person, by having plain undecorated outer walls and doorways to their houses, and by suchlike evidence of their modesty would stave off the shafts of envious anger and give to power an everyday guise. This was the democratic habit of the pagan magistrates and wardens of the Qoraish tribe in Mecca and of their early

Caliphs of Islam in Medina, a modesty practised and annually renewed at the pilgrimage by a ceremonious humility and abasement.

It was a departure from this simplicity, and from deference to their fellows of Arabia, that later was to bring about the great schism in Islam, and give birth to a quarrel which endured for centuries. It was the descendants of the Meccan bankers, ruling in Syria as military captains of the Islamic armies, who struck the first blow, but it was the spiritual lords, descendants of the wardens of the holy sanctuary, who in the end survived.

No one claims to be, or knows to-day where are, the children of Abu Sufyan the banker, of his offspring the Caliphs—by right of might—of Damascus and Cordova; but the descendants of the wardens of Mecca, children of Muhammad by Hassan, his grandson, still rule Arab lands.

THE PRINCES OF THE BANI JURHAM

Jurham ibn Jahla	74 B.C. –	44 B.C.
Abd Yalil ibn Jurham	44 B.C. –	14 B.C.
Jurham ibn Abd Yalil	14 B.C. –	16 A.D.
Abd-al-Madan ibn Jurham	A.D. 16 –	A.D. 46
Bakila ibn Abd-al Madan	A.D. 46 –	A.D. 76

Abd-al-Masih ibn Bakila
 (believed real name Amr, and   } *dates uncertain*
 Abd-al-Masih a style)

Mohadh al Akbar ibn Amr Abd-al-Masih   A.D. 106 – A.D. 136

Amr ibn Mohadh   } A.D. 136 – A.D. 170
Harith ibn Mohadh

Amr ibn Harith[1]
Bishr ibn Harith
Mohadh al Asghar ibn Amr ibn Mohadh } A.D. 170 – A.D. 206
 (cousin of the two preceding rulers)

Defeat and dispersal of the Bani Jurham, A.D. 207.

Note: Yalil and Madan were idols and Abd means 'devotee.'
'Masih' means 'messiah.'

Sources: A. P. Caussin de Perceval, *Essai sur l'histoire des Arabes,*
iii, p. 95, and Ibn Khaldun, *Kitab al 'ibar wa diwan al mubtada wa al
khabar fi ayyam al Arab wa al barbar.*

---

[1] Ibn Khaldun asserts that Amr ibn Harith was a chieftain not of the Bani
Jurham, but of the Khozaa, who supplanted them. Amr ibn Lohay is generally
accepted as the first chieftain of the Khozaa to supplant the Bani Jurham but
whether he is identical with Amr ibn Harith is uncertain. He is said to have
brought the idol Hubal from Syria or Iraq to Mecca. His succession is obscure.

Chapter II

EARLY RULERS, AND THE PROPHET MUHAMMAD

ACCORDING TO THEIR TRIBAL TRADITIONS HANDED DOWN
by word of mouth the Arabs are divided into three: the
Arabs of the Arabs; the Arab al Muta'ariba, or those
become Arabs; and, thirdly, the Arab al Musta'ariba, or those
who wished to become Arab.

The first are extinct, while the second are the Arabs of the
Yemen, descendants of Qahtan, the Joktan of Genesis. The
last, the Arab al Musta'ariba, descended from Ishmael, son of
Abraham, lived in the Hijaz and built the Ka'aba at Mecca.

The Meccan nobles of the Qoraish tribe are thus traditionally
descended from those who "wished to become Arabs"—
from Ishmael.

The Bani Jurham, their early predecessors, from whom
Ishmael is said to have taken a wife, were from the southern
people, from the Qahtan, or those who had "become Arab."
They settled at Mecca as owners of the well until they were
driven out by the chief of the Khozaa tribe, Amr ibn Lohay
al Harith, about A.D. 207, as a result of a migration from the
Yemen.[1]

In Arabia there is a difference in appearance and character,
often very marked, between the present-day Ishmaelites and
the Qahtanites.

In the north round the fertile crescent of Jordan, Syria, and
Iraq are tribes counting their descent from both groups, but
there, as might be expected, the difference is no longer visibly
evident.

The impression received from Arab tales is that they embody
and preserve, in embroidered and partly altered form, the
history of the meeting of two distinct peoples over a long
period and of the early coming of Abraham's monotheistic
religion as far south as the Hijaz, brought there by returning

[1] A. P. Caussin de Perceval, *Essai sur l'histoire des Arabes.*

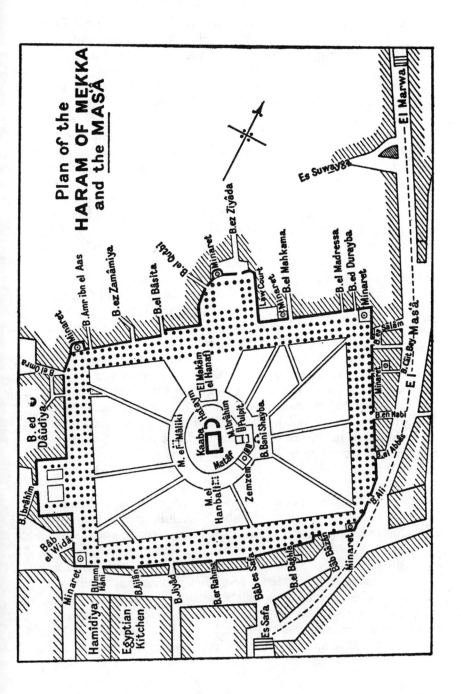

Plan of the
HARAM OF MEKKA
and the MAS'Á

El Marwa.

Es Suwayga.

B.ez Ziyáda.

B. el Qutbi.

Minaret.

B. el Mahkema.

Law Court.

Minaret.

B. el Madressa.

B. ed Dureyba.

B. el Básita.

B. ez Zamámiya.

B. Amr ibn el Aas.

Minaret.

B. es Salám.

Minaret.

B. el Ómra.

B. ed Dáúdíya.

B. Ibráhím.

Báb el Widá

Minaret.

Hamídíya

Egyptian Kitchen

B. Umm Háni

B. Ajlán

B. Jiyád

B. er Rahma

Báb es Safa

B. el Baghla

Báb Bázán

Minaret.

Es Safa

El Mekám el Hanafi

Kaaba Haram

M. el-Máliki

M. Ibráhím

Pulpit.

B. Bani Shayba.

M. el Hanbali

Matáf

Zemzem

B. Ali.

B. el Abbás.

B. en Nabi

Minaret.

El Git Bey-Mas'á

caravaneers and where, after some initial setback, it did for a time take root, only to be repelled or weakened by non-Ishmaelite pagans coming and going from their homeland in the south.

Thus it seems that the Bani Jurham, the first of the non-Ishmaelites to have been converted, were ejected from their tent settlements about Mecca, and full-blooded paganism once more took hold in the Hijaz, remaining strongly entrenched, in spite of a later percolation of Judaism and Christianity both to the south and north of it, until Ishmaelism came again in a different form to have at last, after a period of economic stress, an almost immediate, overwhelming, and permanent success.

In Bani Jurham days the House of God, or Ka'aba, was built, according to Al Azraki, on a rise, in order to avoid flooding by spates. As the present Ka'aba is in low ground and the Haram has frequently been flooded, Al Azraki is either incorrect or the original site was a different one. The Bani Jurham themselves lived on the slopes of Jebel Gaygaan, the western wall of the valley, with a primitive rallying point or fort on the shoulder of the hill above them, presumably on the point where is the modern fort, or *Qalaa*, of Jebel Hindi. Below them curled the track to Wadi Fatima, then called Wadi al Marr, and to Jedda. Opposite to them was the Jebel Qubais, where was found, or was transported, the Black Stone incorporated in the Ka'aba, and past it, leading eastward was the re-entrant of Al Jiyad, in which lived the Amalekites, and the track to the Yemen. The third exit from the valley ran northward towards Jebel Arafat and the place of sacrifices. The narrow valley, with few ways into it, thus formed a natural refuge.

The Meccan Ka'aba itself was originally a simple cube (Arabic, 'ka'aba'; Greek, 'kubos'; English, 'cube'), and it was for a time to have a rival at Sana, in the Yemen, and the Black Stone a counterpart at Petra, while Taif and other places had stones as idols. From time to time the cube was rebuilt and improved, roofed, given a door, and covered respectfully with the skins of animals sacrificed at the pilgrimage. The Bani Jurham guardians and the Amalekites were displaced in A.D. 207 in circumstances unknown by the Khozaa tribe, and they in turn after A.D. 400 were displaced by the Kinana clan of the

Qoraish tribe, the direct ancestors of the present nobles of Mecca. They were to be guardians for fifteen hundred years, and their offspring were to have among their number the Prophet Muhammad and the Caliphs in Damascus, Cordova, Baghdad, and Cairo, the rulers of North Africa, the Yemen, Iraqi, Jordan, and countless smaller states, the tribe still having nomad branches outside Mecca, as well as settled clans in the city.

It was they who chiefly embellished the Ka'aba and they who first built permanent habitations in the Meccan valley. The simple story of the advent of the Qoraish is told by Qutub-al-din al Hanafi. He says:

> The Khozaa ruled Mecca and guarded the Ka'aba well and intelligently, without any pretentiousness which might disturb relations among the people, down to the time of Qossay ibn Kilab ibn Murra, who was the first of the Kinana clan to achieve the rulership, and who united his tribe the Qoraish.

He was given the nickname of "Al Mujamma" ("the Unifier"), although also called Zaid, Qossay being an earlier nickname given him because he came from far away, his widowed mother having returned with him while he was still a child, after his father's death, to her home in Syria, where she married again. When Qossay was grown he quarrelled with his stepfather's family, and, being told that his father's family lived beside the temple in Mecca, he set out to rejoin them, finding a cordial welcome because of his kinship and agreeable manners. The then ruler Khalil, or Hulayil, ibn Jaish al Khozaai gave his daughter Hubba, or Hai, to Qossay in marriage, and they had numerous children and soon became rich and powerful. When Khalil died he gave the key of the Ka'aba to Hai, who bestowed it on her relative, of the Khozaa, one Ibn Ghubshan. Ibn Ghubshan was, however, much addicted to wine and for a flask of it sold the key of the Ka'aba to Qossay. The Khozaa clan were not disposed to let the key and guardianship pass out of their hands as easily as had their sottish chieftain, and taking up arms they prepared to defend and recover their patrimony. Qossay, however, had already forewarned the Qoraish, who overbore the Khozaa and turned every one of them out of Mecca.

This tale seems to embody, with fanciful addition, the story of a newly arrived and vigorous tribe overcoming in a generation and supplanting an effete clan until then in possession of the sanctuary. Qossay is believed to have died about A.D. 490. Until that time the respect borne to the Ka'aba and to its area was so great that it had long been customary for both the guardians and pilgrims to leave it at sundown. None dared live and none were allowed to die within the sacred area. No funeral and no grave-digging were permitted in it, and no man would pleasure his wife or commit adultery within it.

Qossay, of the Qoraish, however, assembled his clan and persuaded them to build their houses and live within the sacred area. When they had done so he explained that they would be singularly respected, so that no other Arabs would dare attack them or turn them out of it.

It is said that he himself cut down the first tree and laid the first stone of a permanent house in the sacred area, for without his leadership no man would have had sufficient courage. This must have been about the year A.D. 480, for Muhammad the Prophet was born in about A.D. 571, and he was the fifth generation from Qossay.[1]

He restored and improved the Ka'aba and altered the position of the idols, ordering some of them to be brought inside the pantheon from afar, gathering together the gods as he had gathered together his people, and building a council chamber and hall of ceremonies, called ever afterwards the Dar al Nadwa. Members of the council were to be at least forty years of age, except for his own sons, who were admitted as soon as they came of age, which they would probably be considered to have done about fourteen. Their houses are said to have completely surrounded the Ka'aba and the present numerous entrances—there are twenty-four—to have been on the site of the passages left between their houses, by which the pilgrims entered the court for their tour of the pantheon.

He gathered into his own hands the various offices about the sanctuary, including the important rights known as *hajaba*, or the stewardship; *saqaya*, or the right to provide the pilgrims

---

[1] Marriages habitually took place very early in Arabia and countries where there was no artificial restriction, and twenty years may be allowed for each generation. The event was probably in Qossay's middle age.

with water and date juice; *rafada*, or the right to supply them with food; *nedwa*, or the headship of the council; *liwa*, or the right to raise the war standard and assemble the clansmen for an expedition; and *qiyada*, or the right to command in war.

About the time of Qossay's birth there had been a new move of South Arabian tribes, popularly connected with one of the disasters at the great Marib dam, in the Yemen, which carried some to Iraq and some to Syria, and resulted also in augmenting the earlier, South Arabian, settlements in Abyssinia; for along the whole coast of East Africa there was an infusion of Arabian blood of far earlier origin than the Muslim invasion. The beginnings of the city of Aksum, whose ruins littered with fallen pagan emblems still stand, an original nucleus of later Abyssinia, belong to the earlier period, to the first century A.D.

There was, it may be assumed, an immediate economic effect on Arabian trade in the first century owing to the discovery of the sea-route to India by the Romans and then a protracted decline in Arabian trade, which reached a climax in the fourth century, when the water broke the Marib dam, and a final catastrophe when the dam was ruined, never to be repaired, between A.D. 542 and 570, an event alluded to in the Koran. Later, imagination of the Arab seized upon the spectacular breaking of the Yemen dam to explain an age-long process of decline and decay in South Arabian trade, agriculture, and national life, a decline in fact due to the entry of Roman shipping into the Red Sea, the influence of new religions, and of the foreign policy of Western empires. The story of the 'bursting of the dam' may be a dramatic retelling of a long history of economic and social causes that led to the breakdown of South Arabian society.

So, with what appears to be a subtle appreciation of the intangible quality of the true causes leading up to this tragedy, some of the chroniclers report that a rat overturned a stone which fifty men could not have lifted and thus brought about the collapse of the dam.[1]

There were thus three crises of disturbance and of exodus, the original in the first century, when the exodus appears to

---

[1] P. K. Hitti, *The History of the Arabs*, pp. 64–65.

have been mostly overseas, to Abyssinia on the one hand and to the Persian Gulf on the other, use being made of the ships which could no longer profitably engage in trade, and bringing to an end a maritime commonwealth of which little is known. The second exodus took place in the middle of the fifth century; in this Qossay and the Qoraish tribe rose to power, appreciating or sensing that the only means of surviving was to shift the centre of trade farther north, in order to exploit Arabian resources rather than depend upon export of incense and Indian goods. The last exodus followed the final collapse of the foreign market and the revelation of Islam in the middle of the seventh century, the invasion and overrunning of the Roman west by the Muslims being the conclusion of a long process begun as a consequence of Roman interference with Arab economic life six centuries earlier.

Both Qossay's reform and Islam, from one point of view, may be seen as the consequences of heart-searching following economic stress and the remarking by a physically virile people of the material success of the foreign nations with whom they were trading under difficulty. The recent Wahhābi revivals and warlike excusions into the green belt outside the peninsula proper, before the granting of oil concessions, were a small, new turning of an old wheel.

Qossay was as wise in his senility as in his vigour, and transferred his powers to his eldest son, Abd-al-Dar (the 'devotee, or slave, of the temple'), in the hope that he might secure and maintain his position after his death; but hardly had Qossay died than his other sons began to demand a share of the profitable pilgrimage rights. Often in the history of Mecca the ruler was to abdicate in favour of a son in the hope of securing the succession to his favourite child, and almost as often the ruse was to be unsuccessful. Abd-al-Dar did indeed manage to retain his rights, but after his death his sons were despoiled by the sons of a more virile brother, Abd-al-Manaf, and by other notables of the Qoraish. Thus the keys of the Ka'aba passed into the hands of the Shayba family, who are mentioned in the Koran as holding them, and who hold them to this day. Similarly Amr-Hashim, son of Abd-al-Manaf, obtained the right of watering and feeding the pilgrims, and he it was who regularized the departures of caravans, in the winter to the south, and in the summer to the north, and, having hastened their turn-round, singularly prospered. Unlike so many of the later Meccans, Amr-Hashim often personally accompanied the caravans, and it was on one of his expeditions that he died, at Gaza, on the Mediterranean Sea, at an early age.

The Prophet's grandfather, Abd-al-Muttalib ibn Hashim, was born and brought up in Medina, his mother having borne him after a marriage made there by Amr-Hashim on his last journey. It was not until some years later, hearing of the boy's intelligence and promise, that an uncle, Muttalib, reclaimed the child and brought him to Mecca; this adoption explains the name by which he became known, Abd, or 'devotee,' of Al Muttalib.

The uncle himself died in the Yemen, and Abd-al-Muttalib, the only and orphan son of Amr-Hashim, succeeded to his property and bore numerous sons, of whom one, Abdulla, died while still young, just before the birth to him of Muhammad, in or about A.D. 571. Thus Muhammad's upbringing, like his grandfather's, devolved on an uncle, one Abu Talib.

The descendants of Qossay had divided the heritage so that some devoted themselves to the conduct of the sanctuary; others, like the branch of Amr-Hashim, had right of supplying the pilgrims, and traded abroad at the same time; and some specialized in trading only, like the offspring of Amr-Hashim's brother, Abd-al-Shams, who were to become famous bankers and, later, governors of the western Arab world.

The council of elders of the republic of Mecca were jealous of their privileges, and when one of their number, Uthman ibn Huwarith, took it upon himself to visit Cæsar and to propose an agreement for the safety of the Meccan caravans going into Damascus, in return for a payment of a trifling annual tribute in kind and recognition of his authority over Mecca, he was immediately denounced, upon adoption of the kingly title, by his fellow nobles of the city.[1]

It was about A.D. 600—before Islam—that the Qoraish once more rebuilt the Ka'aba, widening the area of the court and heightening and enlarging the building itself. They were

[1] A. P. Caussin de Perceval, *Essai sur l'histoire des Arabes*, p. 333; and Ibn Khaldun.

brought to that decision following a flood which had partially destroyed the Ka'aba and had actually entered the holy of holies, so that they wished to raise the door and prevent a similar event in the future. Moreover, an opportunity had presented itself in the wrecking of a Greek ship near Jedda on its way to Abyssinia from Egypt. A Qoraishi noble was dispatched to Jedda to find the master, one Bakoum, and purchase from him the wood of his wreck: an Egyptian master-carpenter in Mecca, together with Bakoum, using his ship's ropes and spars, undertook the work on a grander scale than had ever been before, the door of the Ka'aba being built above the level of the court to prevent spates entering it.

The Ka'aba has since been rebuilt and repaired several times, and it had been altered more than once before this enlargement, but its present scale and arrangement date from that time, and the Ka'aba and its court, as seen to-day, has therefore been unchanged in essential appearance for the last thirteen hundred and fifty years.

Somewhere about this time Muhammad, a man of twenty-five or so, married a wealthy and high-minded widow of Mecca, one Khadija. He had undertaken for her the conduct of caravans to the north, furnished with her capital, but now his marriage gave him leisure and enabled him to pursue his own inclinations.[1] He joined, and took very seriously the oath of allegiance to, the Union of Grace, known as the Hilf al Fadhoul, a reforming society to which the distressed resorted for assistance, and it is related that he frequented at this time a little cave on a hill outside Mecca called Al Hira, secluding himself there to engage in meditation.

Anxiety for his patron's goods before his marriage, and for his own afterwards, directed Muhammad's attention to the precarious nature of Meccan prosperity. The town was depending for its wealth on the caravan trade, for its food supply and the safety of the pilgrims on the mercy of tribes outside its control. One of these, the Hawazin, ancestors of the great modern tribe of Harb, was at feud with the Meccans, and raided up to their walls during his earlier years as a settled citizen. How soon this danger and other material, as well as spiritual, considerations directed his thoughts towards

[1] The Koran, chapter xciii, 6, 9.

religious reforms and a return to monotheism is unknown; but certainly before his thirty-ninth year Muhammad had formed some plan to reform and unify religion.

There had been apostles of monotheism to instruct him in the possibility—not only the Nejdean teacher, Maslama, but a local iconoclast, Zaid ibn Umr, who preached abhorrence of meats offered to idols; and he is said to have listened, at a fair, to a Christian bishop from the Yemen.[1]

His own words in the older part of the Koran speak of his early intercourse with Judaists.

Though he could not read their sacred book for himself, being more or less illiterate until late in life, and the Meccan Jews are unlikely to have been able to explain its spirit, he could not have failed to hear of the reiterated promise that the One God gives the Kingdom to whosoever will worship him in singleness, for Mecca itself was the seat of an Abyssinian, presumably Christian colony.[1]

Bilal, who became the Prophet's muezzin, was himself an Abyssinian Negro. In any case, Christian Abyssinia was contesting the Yemen with Zoroastrian Persia in the century preceding Muhammad, and in about the year of his birth one of their expeditions under a Viceroy in Arabia, Abraha, fortified by a division of elephants, had marched on Mecca, and was only defeated by an outbreak of smallpox among the troops. Jewish colonies flourished in Medina and in various oases of the northern Hijaz, while in the Yemen Judaism had reached the dignity of a state religion.

Dissatisfied Arabs known as 'hanifs,' who developed vaguely monotheistic ideas, were becoming more numerous in Central Arabia, and the anarchy prevailing in the political field inevitably brought a falling away in respect for the pagan gods, who, most of them nothing but stones, had never claimed any qualities except what man had claimed for them, but were now to be blamed and abandoned. Since the reforms of Qossay, who had brought them all to Mecca, they had become very numerous, sheltering for strength, as it were, one against the other.

If the promise of the Kingdom to the people of the One

[1] D. G. Hogarth, *Arabia*.

God had seemed slow of fulfilment to the Jews, Muhammad could not have failed to notice that Jehovah had not failed the peoples of the Book in Syria. For that matter, a less keen intelligence than Muhammad's would have discerned that one way to end the tribal peril lay in blending Mecca and the tribes into one polity, and that if this were to be done it could only be through absorbing all the attributes of the gods into one.

His choice of one god to absorb all could not be in doubt. Allah already had the allegiance of his own, the Qoraish tribe, the dominant civic class. In whatever measure, however, Muhammad's meditations may be explained reasonably, spiritual motive in himself and spiritual aspiration in his hearers must be allowed. Like most apostles before and since, he addressed himself at the outset to those for whom the existing order did so little that promises in another world of all that was being denied them in this would be likely to make a strong appeal. With such he relied chiefly on equality in this world and a revelation of life after death.[1] Progress was slow. A year brought but three converts. Muhammad met them at first in many places, seldom in his own home, until a hut on the hillock of Al Safa became an habitual meeting-place. By the close of A.D. 613 he had at the most some six hundred converts, and the secret now being out he was beginning to meet strong opposition. Attempts to induce the Hashimite clan of the Qoraish to exclude Muhammad from the tribal pale broke against the opposition of his rich and influential uncle, Abu Talib. His less well-protected followers, however, began to become uneasy and a number migrated to Abyssinia, where the Christian Negus welcomed them and rejected the embassy and presents sent to him from Mecca with the request that he would return the emigrants to the Hijaz. Thus the mischief was made worse. Malcontents had the ear of a monotheistic power, and Muhammad became a person in favour with an alien king. Persecuted in Mecca, he left it for Taif, but made no headway. The town of Yathrib, or Medina, as it was later called, was more encouraging. Rumours that he had been invited to Yathrib began to circulate in Mecca, and the Meccan nobles decided that for the good of the whole he must be destroyed. When the executioners reached his

[1] D. G. Hogarth, *ibid.*

house he had already, but only just, fled with one of his first converts, Abu Bekr, reaching Medina on September 24, 622, from which date the Muslims reckon their calendar.

At Medina Islam was to become a combatant polity, wielding the sword of Allah, of the former Qoraishi god. Such had not been its founder's original ideal. A Meccan, reluctant to shed blood, he had hoped, before his banning by the nobles, to win the city by peaceful means. After the flight to Medina, he was forced to muster troops to resist the attacks of the Meccans led by his rich clansman cousin, Abu Sufyan, the banker. Several years of raids and attacks, of more than one famous battle, of consolidation of his power, of ultimatums to the Jews of Medina and the neighbouring tribes and oases brought his power, if not without some setbacks, to a pitch when many Meccans began to desert to him, in spirit if not in person; and after a compromise agreement he was finally able to go to Mecca for the pilgrimage, first on sufference for three days, and finally on his own terms. In the end, as he approached Mecca only a knot of diehards had to be brushed off a near-by hilltop before Abu Sufyan himself came out with the city's surrender. The keys of the Ka'aba were left with their holders, the Shayba family, and Muhammad came into his own.

Consecrating the whole town a sanctuary, he decreed the abolition of the blood-feud, forbade torture or mutilation—although, as he himself twice ordered the cutting off of the hands of criminals, this practice is still in force in parts of Arabia—prohibited the infanticide of females, and destroyed the idols. At the same time he confirmed the ritual of the pilgrimage and the existence of countless supernatural beings below the One God, whose single worship he harmonized. To the pilgrimage of A.D. 631 he was unable to go himself, being engaged in the consolidation of his gains, the overcoming of the people of Taif and of the Hawazin tribe, but in A.D. 632 there was a purely Muslim pilgrimage which he led in person. In the same year, overtaken by some disease unidentified, marked by increasingly severe fevers, he died, on Thursday the 4th of June.

Unanimous authority gives Muhammad the sole credit for the establishment of Islam, but the Prophet had been wont always to couple with his name those of Abu Bekr and Omar.

Whenever he desired to reinforce his authority he used the
formula, "I, Abu Bekr, and Omar . . ." So, from the very
beginning, there had been that triumvirate, that family partner-
ship in ruling, which was for centuries to be customary in
Mecca.

Muhammad had been, as it were, king, but king of a republic,
and Muhammad was unique. In the absence of a grown male
heir of his blood, he was succeeded by Abu Bekr, who was
elected as his successor, using the style of Caliph, but not
without opposition at the time, and later, throughout the
Prophet's dominions.

Abu Bekr had to take quick action to suppress rebellion.
The tribes of Bahrain were reverting to Christianity, and tribes
of the Yemen were reasserting the power of tribal gods.

But only in Central Arabia, an old seat of monotheism,
was there serious fighting. There Maslama, the 'little prophet,'
had outlived the Great, and with his faithful Bani Hanifa, and
the villagers of Al Yamama, would not brook a successor to
Muhammad. He made some headway against the first
columns sent against him, but lost a hard-fought battle with a
larger army, and in a riot of massacre and plunder the glory
of Al Yamama, 'the granary of Arabia,' which the poets of
pagan days had sung, perished. Within a year and a few
months the peninsula was once more brought within the
secular and religious discipline of Mecca.

The Muslim army, in which there were many bedouin and
adventurers, for whom fighting and rapine were worth apostasy,
was already a fearsome weapon, for which constant employment was required. Now that all the peninsula had returned
to Islam there was nowhere left for it to turn except the outer
world; thither Abu Bekr hastened to direct the armies to the
north and north-east before the close of the year 633.[1] Probably
he had no idea of anything beyond raiding and return, but
both the Byzantine and Persian kingdoms were weak and his
armies were on the point of discovering what the barbarians
on the western frontier of the Roman Empire had discovered
about Rome three centuries earlier.

Whether Abu Bekr ever received the startling news of great
promise is unknown, for he died towards the end of August in

[1] All dates are A.D. unless otherwise stated.

the modest hut in which he had long lived, first and last of the Medinese Caliphs to pass in peace. The Muslim state had already entered a period of rapid and uncontrollable change —change caused to a great extent by physical and social conditions outside Arabia, so that the days of direction from Mecca or Medina were numbered.

The history of the rulers of Islam was to become, not the story of a city in Arabia, but that of a people on the march across the remains of the Roman and Persian empires, with new camps and capitals far beyond the peninsula. Omar, the successor of Abu Bekr, tried for a time to retain the control for Arabia, issuing an edict that believers might not acquire property in territory conquered from unbelievers, but a few years were to prove the impossibility of maintaining it.

Because the imperial expansion had passed beyond Meccan or Medinese control, it fell to Omar to adapt uncodified ordinances, made for Meccan society, to the needs of a vast cosmopolitan state and of armies living under all sorts of conditions. His first task was to commit to writing the revealed ordinances of Allah to Muhammad, and the second to provide that the resultant canons should be capable of application to conditions not considered at the time of revelation.

So came into being the written text of the Koran, the written book of revelations by God through Gabriel to Muhammad, held by Muslims to be the very words and letter of God, their law and religion in one.

While the ever-increasing armies of Islam were expanding northward and westward, and the Caliph's seat was in Medina, the rulership of Mecca itself was of secondary importance. The Prophet had appointed one Attab ibn Usaid ibn Abi al As,[1] a kinsman and great-grandson of Ummaya, to be his Wali[2] in Mecca. Attab was now succeeded by various other members of the same branch of the Hashimite family, selected from time to time by the Caliphs.

It was under the Caliph Omr that Jedda, as being nearer to Mecca, was substituted for Shuaiba as a port, and that in A.D. 638 for the first time a low, protecting wall was built

[1] See the dictionaries. It was after Attab that a quarter of Baghdad was named in which the watered silk known as 'attabi' was made, from which was derived the word tabby, used for watered silks and brindle cats.
[2] See glossary.

round the Ka'aba, at a short distance, as a measure towards controlling the pilgrims who now came in greater numbers than ever before. It must have then seemed quite unlikely that Mecca would suffer attack now that the Muslim armies and front line of Islam were so far afield, but it was from them that attack was in fact to come.

On the death of the Caliph Omr, slain by a Christian slave of Iranian origin, six companions chosen by him on his death-bed elected one Uthman ibn Affan, great-grandson of Umayya and nephew of Abu Sufyan, a member, that is, of the great banker branch and not of the branch of the guardians of the sanctuary.

Ali, son-in-law and cousin of the Prophet had asserted ever since Muhammad's death that he only had been named the successor, and now gradually a party in his favour began to form. A vast number of those outside Arabia who had accepted Islam were used to the incarnation theory and craved for a visible manifestation of God in such flesh as their own. The disintegrating ideas spread into Arabia from both Byzantine Christendom and from Iran, but mostly from Iran, the complete conquest of which was to take place under the third Caliph. The culture which the Arabs encountered there exerted ever-increasing influence on them, and the doctrines of incarnation and of the divinity of rulers began to spread in Islam as it had in the long past spread from there to Greece and Rome.

But before this occurred Uthman, already conscious of a dangerous disaffection among leading Hashimites in Medina, turned to Mecca. Himself a member of the Umayyad clan, who had inherited a fortune in early life and passed as a man of fashion, he addressed himself now to his kin and put its members into the more important posts throughout the Empire.

The split among the nobles of the Qoraish was now open——between Ali, cousin and son-in-law of the Prophet, and his kin, on the one hand, and, on the other hand, the Umayyad clan, the merchant-adventurer and banker side of the family, which had originally under Abu Sufyan disputed Mecca with Muhammad.

The old feud was renewed. The Umayyads established themselves in Damascus while Ali, finding support in the eastern half of the Empire, was drawn to Iraq.

By June 656 the increasing disaffection was brought to a head by the killing of the Caliph Uthman in Medina by Muhammad, son of Abu Bekr, who had been the Prophet's friend and Uthman's predecessor. Muawiya, son of Abu Sufyan, now came out as their champion and as the Umayyad Caliph in Damascus. He exhibited the bloodstained shirt of Uthman in the mosque at Damascus and with heated eloquence endeavoured to play on Muslim emotions. Meanwhile Ali had left the Hijaz, never to return, bound for Al Kufa, in Iraq, where five years later he in turn was murdered. To his partisans and descendants Ali became at once, by his martyrdom, pre-eminently the saint of Islam. Though lacking in some of the qualities which make a leader, he had been wise in counsel and brave in battle, true to his friends and magnanimous to his foes. He was to be for ever the paragon of Muslim nobility and chivalry, and his sword—that which the Prophet himself had carried—has been immortalized in the words of the verse to be found engraved on many Arab medieval swords, "No sword can match the Cleaver and no young knight can compare with Ali," and all the later Arab chivalry took Ali for its model. The throngs of pilgrims who still flock to his tomb at Nejef and to that of his son Al Hussain, who was later to be killed by Umayyad forces at Kerbela, in Iraq, testify to his standing among the Muslims and in particular among the Shiahs, who were to be his especial followers, supporters of Caliphal legitimacy and of Ali's descendants, fanatically opposed to the supporters of the Umayyads and all non-Alid dynasties.

From the moment of Muawiya's accession, at Damascus in A.D. 660, Arabian history sinks back into the peninsula. It had sent its spirit and blood into other lands, but henceforth its part in history was to be secondary to that of the dynasties which had sprung from it and had by now established their own capitals. Nevertheless Arabia made an effort to establish her primacy. She set up a Caliph of her own, Abdulla ibn Zubair, against the secular usurper of Syria and held out for a generation, even at one moment securing Iraq's acknowledgment of her choice. But an end was at last put to the Meccan effort in 692, after a six months' siege by the Umayyad army under Hajjaj ibn Yousif al Thaqafi. The Caliph Abdulla died, sword in hand, before the walls. He had already withstood a previous siege, in which the Ka'aba had been destroyed by catapults, until the besiegers, under Al Hussain ibn Numair, had received news of the death of their own Caliph, Yazid, and in dismay had withdrawn, leaving the defenders to repair the damaged Ka'aba. Now, after the capture of Mecca .the Damascene Caliph ordered the rebuilding of the Ka'aba without the improvement made by Abdulla, a gesture of authority over the Meccans and over the Temple and it guardians.

Al Hanafi relates that, the rebuilding by Ibn Zubair having been brought to an end on the 27th of the Muslim month of Rejeb in A.D. 683-4, he and all the inhabitants of Mecca went out to Tanaim and made the lesser pilgrimage called Al Umra, so that ever afterwards it remained a festival. It is no longer importantly observed, but it certainly was so until the year 1201, for then a ruler-to-be, Qitada ibn Idris, took the opportunity of all the inhabitants being outside Mecca for the festival to capture the city unopposed. Al Hanafi, however, may not be correct in supposing this minor pilgrimage to be dated from the days of the Meccan Caliph Ibn Zubair, who may have only revived it, for others say that it was observed, together with a short tribal truce, every year even in pagan times. If there were a tribal truce in Rejeb—that is, at the beginning of the summer—it may have been to allow the tribes to settle in peace on their wells and to visit the marts before the hottest weather, when travelling would be more difficult for them and their beasts. It is possible, therefore, that there was a pagan truce in Rejeb, but that with Islam it had died out, to the inconvenience of Meccans and the tribes, so that Ibn Zubair made use of the natural desire to celebrate the end of the repair and rebuilding of the Ka'aba to re-establish it. In any case, if the work of Ibn Zubair on the Ka'aba Temple was to be petulantly undone by order of the Umayyad Caliph in Damascus, his minor pilgrimage day, in its celebration, was to continue for hundreds of years.

Thus, by the end of the seventh century it had become customary for the Caliphs in Damascus to appoint individuals of their own clan—the Umayyad, who were members of the Qoraish tribe, but not of the Hashimite branch—or, more often, some reliable lieutenant as their Walis, or governing agents, of Mecca, and it must have seemed as if the Hashimites, who held hereditary posts in the administration of the sanctuary and about the Temple, had lost the right to temporal power for ever.

Chapter III

RULERS FROM THE EIGHTH TO THE TWELFTH CENTURY

DURING THE TWO HUNDRED YEARS FOLLOWING THE COMING of Islam the caravan commerce of Mecca had died away, and by the tenth century its rhythm was to be hardly felt any more. The gold-mines of Nejd and the Hijaz border then ceased to work. The dark ages were closing over Europe, the armies of the Muslims having themselves broken down the commercial traditions of centuries when they advanced to occupy the centres with which, in their earlier days, they themselves had traded. The one-time caravaneers had become the conquerors.

But Muhammad had said that Mecca should be visited by every able-bodied Muslim, and so once more the old theme returns, and, taking on the strength which had formerly belonged to the merchants, itself now swells to a long triumphant strain. Islam was no longer, like its pagan predecessor, confined to Arabia, but had adopted people of every race who might apostate in its favour; thus a tribal pagan shrine was replaced by the centre of a world religion. In Syria, Persia, in faraway Spain, in Khorassan, in India, in Africa, the faithful Muslims were to turn for their prayers to face the direction of that nearly waterless valley which the Qoraishi prophet, messenger of God, had turned from a seat of stone symbols into the House of God on earth for millions of men.

Meanwhile the merchants-turned-conquerors, the descendants of Abu Sufyan, were ruling in Damascus and appointing Walis in Mecca, while Ali and the Prophet's descendants had few followers except in Arabia itself and in Persia.

The two strains, the lines of the merchants and of the priests of the Qoraish, join only at Abd-al-Manaf, the son of Qossay,[1]

[1] See pedigree at p. 56.

whose son Abdul Shams was to have descendants who would rule Spain for eight hundred years, who would be masters of Damascus and Egypt, and hold sway over Iraq through armies in Persia and Khorassan. But his son Amr-Hashim's offspring would replace them in Iraq, the Yemen, and Morocco, holding the guardianship of Mecca until the twentieth century.

For centuries the schism was to endure, sometimes rising to an intensity which bred war and civil disturbance, new sects and widespread misery, and for a time, after the Ummayad Caliphial occupation of Mecca, the sectaries of Ali were actually forbidden to enter it or Medina.

The incompatibility of the spirit of the Arabian peninsula with the recognized order of things, whether directed from Syria or Iraq, was to increase and to end in its virtual detachment from the Islamic empire. Even to-day the sectaries of Ali, the followers of anti-Sunni creeds, are, with the exception of Persia, more numerous in their communities and in their proportionate numbers in Arabia than elsewhere; most of the highlanders of the Yemen, the inhabitants of the hinterland from Nejran to Southern Jauf, the tribesmen of Oman with those of part of the Al Hasa, and certain bedouin near Medina are among their number. Behind this defection, this adherence or leaning to Shiahism, was a deep-seated resentment at incapacity to retain control of the Faith and Empire to which Arabia gave birth. Even the Abbassid Caliphate in Baghdad, which in the end overcame the Ummayads in Damascus, was backed by Persian strength and defended from legitimist revolt only by Persian Khorassani forces and bodyguards. The second Abbassid, Al Mansour, coerced the Hijaz to recognize his Caliphate with Persian soldiers, and the great Caliph of Baghdad Haroun al Rashid was compelled to a far more tactful policy of annual state pilgrimages and a vast expenditure, by himself and his wife Zubaida, on the Holy Places, the very year before his accession having seen a serious Alid, or legitimist, rising in Mecca itself.

Mahdi, a predecessor, had visited Mecca in person (in A.D. 776), and, finding the walls of the Ka'aba crumbling with the weight of layer after layer of old coverings,[1] resolved to have it repaired and institute a new system of annual re-

[1] Al Hanafi, Arabic Manuscript No. 845 in the Bibliothèque Nationale, Paris.

covering. The Caliph himself attended the work, and, the repairs to the stonework completed, a ceremonial cleaning was undertaken, the walls being rubbed with civet, musk, and amber. The higher part of the building was drenched with civet; the Ka'aba was then given its first new covering of three coats—of *kibati*, then of *silofel*, and a topmost one of brocade.

Hadi, Mahdi's successor, during his short reign ordered new stone from the quarries at Akhmim, in Egypt, while Haroun exceeded all his predecessors in generosity, both in benefactions to the shrine itself and in the beginning of vast new waterworks, which were continued by his widow. The main scheme was centred round the spring of Hunain, twelve miles east of Mecca, whence a subterranean aqueduct brought the water to Mecca, a number of smaller springs being made to contribute their water, and several reservoirs being arranged at suitable points. Famous among this complex of waterworks was the spring of Zubaida, named after the wife of the Caliph, on the plain below Mount Arafat. The terminal fountain in Mecca was named al Mishash, and now gave the inhabitants water all the year round. The magnitude of the task can be understood only when the nature of the country, the mountains, and the hard rock which had to be cut and mined are seen. But Zubaida, once committed to the task, refused to be deterred, and the feat was accomplished at a cost of one and three-quarter million dinars. It is related that, on the work being ended, the engineers and foremen presented themselves at the palace in Baghdad, with their account books supporting the expenditure for which she had paid, but, receiving the ledgers, she promptly had them cast into the Tigris, announcing regally, if not indeed piously, "We have left the accounting to the Day of Accountings. Let him who has a cash balance keep it, and he who is our creditor, him we will repay." "Then," it is said, "she bestowed upon them robes of honour and dismissed them and they departed full of praise and thanks."[1]

In spite of this Abbassid interest in the welfare of Mecca, Mamoun, the successor of Haroun, saw most of the peninsula rise against him. He it was who in an endeavour to propitiate Alid feeling used green brocade for the covering of the Ka'aba,

---

[1] N. Abbot, *Two Queens of Baghdad.*

green being the Alid colour, instead of the Abbassid black. It is covered in black material, made in Egypt, to this day, having with intervals been given coverings of other colours: white in the time of the Fatimids of Egypt and the Sulaihi dynasty of the Yemen; red being sometimes used in the eleventh century for the coverings sent from Khorassan, and yellow for a covering sent by Sultan Mahmoud Sabaktaqin, of Ghazna, in the tenth century.

The first Abbassid Wali of Mecca was a member of the Abbassid branch of the Qoraish, just as the early Walis under the Umayyads of Damascus had been men appointed from among members of the Umayyad family of the Qoraish. This practice was continued as late as the reign of Haroun al Rashid, when a great-great-grandson of Al Abbas was appointed, one Ahmad ibn Ismail ibn Ali. But in the reign of Mamoun, during his attempt to propitiate the Alids, an Alid, Al Dibaji (the 'silken' or 'beautiful') Muhammad ibn Jaafar al Sadiq (the 'seventh Imam') was given the post. The Umayyad Caliphs of Damascus had faced an earlier and similarly rebellious movement, that of the Kharajites, and now their successors, the Abbassids of Baghdad, were likewise confronted with a rising tide of Shiahism, of legitimism, on which at first they had depended and which they now found more and more difficult to control.

A restlessness was almost everywhere in the Muslim world. By the end of the ninth century there was a serious revolt of the sect called the Qarmatians after their dwarf apostle, Hamdan, or Qarmat. The creed had taken root at Al Kufa, in Iraq, and had later spread abroad to Syria and Bahrain, in the Persian Gulf, directed from Al Hasa, the western province of Arabia, the oasis of Al Hajr becoming the Qarmatian capital. Elsewhere the Abbassid empire was at this time—the beginning of the tenth century of our era and the third of Islam—suffering from the rise of powerful dynasties on its outskirts. In North Africa there was the genesis of the rival Fatimid Caliphate of Kairouan and later of Cairo, related in its tenets to the Qarmatians and the Ismailis; and in the Yemen the Abbassid governor there followed the example of others of his colleagues far from the capital and declared for independence. Now in Western Arabia the Qarmatians rose for a time to power, and

THE DESCENDANTS OF THE PROPHET

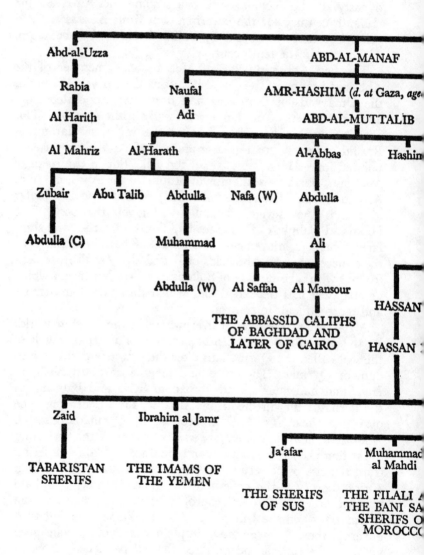

Abd-al-Uzza   ABD-AL-MANAF

Rabia   Naufal   AMR-HASHIM (d. at Gaza, age

Al Harith   Adi   ABD-AL-MUTTALIB

Al Mahriz   Al-Harath   Al-Abbas   Hashim

Zubair   Abu Talib   Abdulla   Nafa (W)   Abdulla

Abdulla (C)   Muhammad   Ali

Abdulla (W)   Al Saffah   Al Mansour

THE ABBASSID CALIPHS
OF BAGHDAD AND
LATER OF CAIRO

HASSAN

HASSAN

Zaid   Ibrahim al Jamr   Ja'afar   Muhammad
al Mahdi

TABARISTAN
SHERIFS

THE IMAMS OF
THE YEMEN

THE SHERIFS
OF SUS

THE FILALI
THE BANI SA
SHERIFS O
MOROCCO

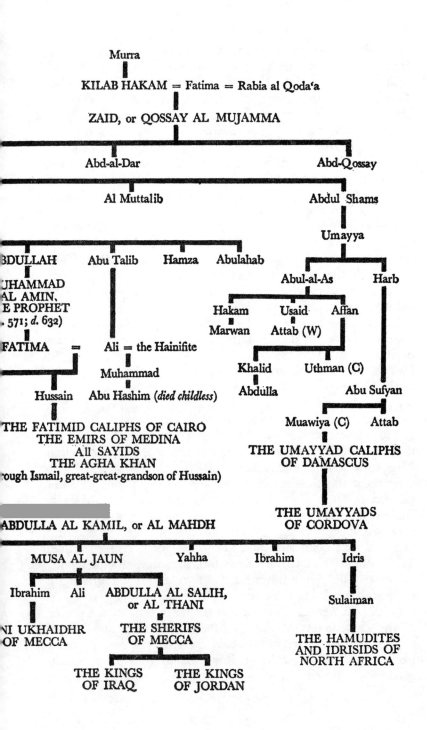

were able to play off the Fatimids of Africa against the Abbassids of Asia. Men were everywhere in expectation, and mused in their hearts whether this pretender or that were the coming Mahdi, the reincarnation of Ali and his line. By 906 the Qarmatians were greatly in the ascendant, particularly in Syria. In Iraq they captured Basra, pretending to do so in the name of the new Fatimid dynasty of the Caliphs of Africa.

Baghdad itself was threatened, and the best generals of the Caliph there seemed unable to overcome the furious fanaticism of the heretics. At last driven off, they retreated into Arabia and turned on Mecca itself.

The Holy City was ravaged in A.D. 929, the bodies of the slain being thrown into the well Zemzem and blood spilt in the inner sanctuary itself. To crown their sacrilege they carried off the Black Stone (January 930) to Al Hajr, their home in Western Arabia, keeping it for twenty years, until induced by Mansour al Alawi, master of Africa, in 950 to return it. Meanwhile the Fatimid dynasty had moved eastward to Cairo and their doctrine had there taken root, to last until supplanted by Saladin. Through the mad Caliph, Al Hakim, and a missionary sent out by him it had brought to birth the religion of the Druses, of the Lebanon and Syria, the Assassins of Persia, and the sectaries of Zanzibar. So, like some strange unkillable plant, this love for the Alids went on, giving off new shoots, and in doing so contrived to bring on the decay of the Abbassid Caliphate, and as it fell into decline Mecca was left more and more to itself.

So great was the degree of insecurity at this period that the pilgrimage from Iraq was altogether stopped, and when it came again the Emirs of the Baghdad and Egyptian pilgrim caravans fought outside Mecca for the privilege of entering first and thus being accepted as the dominant representative. The Fatimids had tried, long before they moved into Egypt, to attain the more powerful position and were gradually successful in gaining the upper hand.

Out of the period of anarchy in the tenth century the power of the descendants of Ali in Mecca and Iraq had grown stronger. It was they who often escorted pilgrims in these troublous times, using their influence to secure temporary agreements to enable the caravans to pass safely. From

Mecca and Medina the members of the Prophet's family, supported by bedouin, had at times defied the Caliph in Baghdad
and now again one of them was to set himself up as a Caliph.
The conquest of Mecca by Ja'afar, the great-grandchild of
one Muhammad al Hassani, who had defied the Abbassid
Caliph al Muqtadir (A.D. 908–32) and raised a bedouin army
in his support, seemed of so little importance that the exact
date was apparently not recorded. Ja'afar's people had frequently held absolute power, whenever the Caliphal influence
weakened, and he had been encouraged and supported in
various ways by the Fatimid as a move against his Abbassid
rival. In any case, the beginning of his rule seems to have been
about 965, for it coincided with the death of Abu-el-Misk Kafur
of Egypt, and its end about 980. The importance of his rule—
the beginning of a new dynasty—lies in the great degree of
independence he attained, marred only by what every successor
was to find: firstly, that the Egyptians held the whip-hand,
because they could starve the Hijaz into submission when the
crops of the Hijaz valleys and of the Yemen were poor or for
some reason were not available to the Meccans, and, secondly,
in the fact that the headship of the Hijaz had lain, since the
days of the first Caliphs after Muhammad, in Medina, and now
it had returned some three hundred and fifty years later to
Mecca.

Ja'afar, the founder of the dynasty, was succeeded by his
son, Isa, who ruled for fourteen years, until 994, during which
time Fatimid troops prevented supplies reaching either Mecca
or Medina until Isa agreed to the reading of the khutba[1] in the
name of their ruler. Isa was succeeded by his younger brother,
Abdul Futuh, who reigned for forty-five years, his rule partly
coinciding with that of the mad Caliph, Al Hakim, of Egypt.
He reached sufficient strength to aim at the headship of Islam
and to seek the fall of the Caliph of Egypt. In this he was
encouraged by the son of the murdered Wezir[1] of the Caliph,
who had fled to Syria and was looking for support and
for a means of revenge for his father's death, and equally by
his own people, outraged by the Egyptian demand to defame
a number of the Prophet's companions and wives, whose names
it had been customary to bless in the khutba prayers. Abdul

[1] See glossary.

Futuh's reluctant attempt to follow Al Hakim's extraordinary and unreasonable instructions had led to immediate disorder in Mecca. Al Hakim's forces had been driven off from the camps of the Syrian bedouin in which the Wezir's son, Abdul Qassim al Maghribi, had taken refuge, and the moment seemed propitious for open revolt. Abdul Qassim and the bedouin chieftains declared their allegiance to Abdul Futuh, ruler of Mecca, who at once travelled to Syria with a personal escort of a thousand Negroes and an army of his Meccan clansmen, taking with him the sword of Ali and the Prophet's wand[1] from Medina. Meanwhile the Caliph Al Hakim had had the wit to send secretly considerable sums of money to each of the bedouin chieftains who had declared for Abdul Futuh, and soon the Meccan ruler noticed that the money of Al Hakim was more effective than his own relics from Mecca and Medina. At the same time came news from the Hijaz that one of his relatives had designs on his rulership and had received backing and money from Al Hakim. Hurrying back to Mecca, he was in time to restore order.

Abdul Futuh was succeeded by his son Muhammad Shukr, a generous man of a poetical turn, nicknamed Aba Abdalla and styled, it is said, Taj al Maali, who, dying without heirs, was succeeded for a time by his slave and then replaced by a member of the Bani Abi Tib clan, Muhammad ibn Abi Fatik. He, in turn, was supplanted by the Yemeni ruler, Ali ibn

---

[1] In the list of relics presented by the Sherif Barakat to Sultan Salim there is no mention of the Prophet's wand. According to Dr Ahmad Ratib in his *History of Turkey*, published in Turkish at Istanbul in A.H. 1326, there are preserved in the Topkapee, at Istanbul, the following: a tooth of the Prophet; clogs of the Prophet; prayer-ring of Abu Bekr; hilt of the Prophet's sword; an arrow; Noah's cooking-vessel; a stone with the mark of a human foot; the Prophet's prayer-ring; the banner of the Prophet, which was ceremoniously inspected once a year by the Sultans and was unfurled at the announcement of a Holy War; two wands of ancient prophets; Abraham's cauldron; David's sword; a golden rainwater spout; a silver cover for the Maqaur Ibrahim from the shrine at Mecca; some water in which the Prophet washed; the turbans of Hassan and Hussain; the swords of Hassan and Hussain; the sword of Ja'afar al Tayyar, the disciple of the Prophet; the sword of Khalid ibn Zaid; the sword of Shuhrabil ibn Hassan; the Prophet's shirt; the key of Mecca; a piece of the door of the Ka'aba, or "door of repentance"; a piece of dried clay; the banners of Hassan and Hussain; the hilts of the swords of the ten chosen companions of the Prophet; the Koran written by the Caliph Uthman, with some spots of his blood which fell upon its vellum when he was killed (this book was in Medina until the First World War, during which it was removed with other treasures when the Turks abandoned the Hijaz. King Hussain claimed it in the war settlement at Versailles, but never received it); a Koran written by Zain al Abidin. None of these objects are exhibited to Christians.

Muhammad al Sulaihi, the first of a short but famous Shiah dynasty of that country, who had come on pilgrimage to Mecca and had stayed as a ruler. He entered Mecca in 1063, but found constant opposition from the former rulers, the Bani Abi Tib, and his men suffered from the humid climate, very different from that of their own mountains, and from an epidemic which greatly reduced their numbers. So that when the Hussainiya family came to him to propose that he appoint a local Viceroy from among them they found him in agreeable mood and ready to accept their nominee, Muhammad ibn Ja'afar, a descendant of Al Hassan, son of Ali, and whose personal style and line was to be known as Abi Hashim.

When the following year the Naqib of the Ashraf, or head of the notables and sayids in Baghdad, Abu Ghanaim, went to make his pilgrimage to Mecca he found that the new Emir was already veering towards the Abbassids in Baghdad, and it was during his visit that the reading of the name of the Abbassid Caliph in the *khutba* prayers was substituted for that of the Egyptian. The Egyptians at once stopped the forwarding of supplies from Egypt to the Hijaz, and thus forced the Emir to raise money for buying supplies at a very high rate, which he did by selling the golden lamps from the sanctuary, the Abbassid Caliph, however, compensating him by a gift of 30,000 dinars.

Meanwhile, in turn, the Bani Abi Tib received secret encouragement and money from the Fatimid Caliph, in Egypt, and, attacking Muhammad, forced him to flee for a time to Yanbu'. From there he organized raids on Mecca and intercepted the supplies to it from Egypt. At the same time the Yemenis stopped caravans from their side, so that the Meccans were forced to yield the city, and the Abi Tib and their Emir, Hamza ibn Abi Wahas, surrendered to Muhammad, who entered the city "riding his famous mare, Dinanir." This is the story, but one wonders if perhaps its origin was not from the *bon mot* of a Meccan wit. Hamza might have good cavalry, but Muhammad's money—the dinars from Baghdad and the Yemen—was the winner? He only once evacuated Mecca, when Seljuk Turks came in such large numbers and with such rude enthusiasm to the pilgrimage, made so many demands upon him, and took so little notice of local customs or of his diplomatic protests, that he and his followers withdrew. Nevertheless the Seljuk Sultan gained his end, becoming named in the *khutba* prayers immediately after the Abbassid Caliph, by then little more than a puppet under him. This indeed was one of the objects which the rough behaviour of the Turks had been intended to secure; for the desire for supplies from Egypt was weakening the Emir in his attachment to Baghdad, in spite of its valuable subsidies. Thus, veering to the strength of Baghdad in 1070, he had turned back to the Fatimids in 1075, when both Sultan Alp Arslan and the Caliph Al Muktadi had died, and once more back to Baghdad after the Suljuk Turks had made their raid-like pilgrimages to Mecca.

When in 1091 these visits were repeated Muhammad took a firmer line and distinguished himself in fighting the savage northerners. It was during this period that the old custom of sending members of Ali's family with the pilgrims, as Emirs of the Caravans, for the sake of their prestige, waned, its being of little use against the Turks. Military men, Turks or Egyptians, or even trusted eunuchs of royal establishments, took their place from then onward. Muhammad was succeeded by his son Qasim, who continued his father's forward policy against the Turks of Baghdad, and adopted a more diplomatic one towards the Egyptians.

At this time the arrival of the annual caravan from Baghdad was always the signal for a general arming in Mecca, and again and again the Turks had to be punished by the Sherif's Negroes and his bedouin. At the very beginning of his reign he had fought the Seljuk commander from Damascus, Usbahid ibn Saratkin, at Al Usfan, fifty miles north of Mecca on the pilgrim road, and defeated him, so that he was forced to turn back to Damascus, giving up his attempt to occupy Mecca. So Qasim ruled until his death in 1124, being succeeded by his son Fulaita, who ruled until his own death in 1132.

He in turn was succeeded by a son, Hashim, who ruled until he died in 1154, and Hashim's son Qasim followed, ruling until 1161, when he fled from Mecca, having been threatened by the Emir of the Iraqi pilgrims. Succeeded by his uncle, Isa ibn Fulaita, he slipped back into Mecca a year later only to be assassinated. Feeling their weakness and fearing repetitions of such interference with their sovereignty, the ruling family began the building of a castle on Jebel Abu Kubais, immediately above the city, into which they could retreat and defend themselves in case of need, and at the same time instituted a more regular payment to the bedouin, some of whom they henceforward kept by them as a standing army. Their decision was none too soon, for in the reign of Isa's successor, his son Daud, and again in that of his second son Mikhthar, the Iraqis constantly threatened them and, in 1176, actually supplanted Mikhthar, after a fight, by the Emir of Medina, Qasim ibn Muhanna al Hussaini. Their plan, however, was quite unsuccessful, the Meccans making it impossible for him to rule for more than a few days, so that he was obliged to withdraw, Daud ibn Isa returning, and finally Mikhthar coming back to the rulership with Daud's agreement. The two brothers were now under frequent pressure of one kind or another from abroad. Taghtakin, brother of Saladin, having stopped for a time in Mecca after his pilgrimage in 1185, and taken over the rulership, the Emirs and their followers went up into the fort on Jebel Abu Kubais, impotently regarding the foreign occupation and daily losing prestige among the people below them in their city. Taghtakin removed the capitation tax on pilgrims imposed by the Emirs, substituting for it an annual subsidy to them and a consignment of grain from Egypt; he kept the Yemeni grain for the use of his troops in that country, of which he was Viceroy for Saladin, thus pleasing the pilgrims and strangling the independence of the Emirs. Worse, from the point of view of their sovereignty and prestige, was Taghtakin's minting of money and distribution of it in Mecca, in the name of Saladin, and his public execution of a number of their chosen young lancemen bodyguards, the chief means of their keeping order. This last act of justice or injustice, for the partisan writers vary according to their patron, was watched by the Emirs from their castle on the Jebel Abu Kubais.

When Taghtakin departed they immediately resumed their former customs, but their people followed them in celebrating Mecca's freedom. The weakened rulers took fees from the pilgrims at a more exorbitant rate, fearing that there was little time left before some new misfortune or interference would come upon them. The proper economic tie of the Hijaz is with the Yemen, and the rulers of Mecca were allied with the Yemeni rulers by descent and sectarian leanings, as descendants of Ali and natural supporters of the Alids. But Mecca, centre of pilgrimage, was continually exposed to outside influences by whoever was or aspired to be the most powerful sovereign in the Islamic world, and so the Meccan rulers or Sherifs were constantly compelled to trim their sails to new political and religious breezes.

The origin of 'Sherif' as a title, which was by now in established use as apart from its employment as a simple honorific, is obscure. The word is not mentioned in the Koran, and as a title it seems to have come into use only about this time during the empire of the Fatimid Caliphs, by whom, according to Al Siouti, it was forbidden as a style except for the descendants of Al Hassan and Al Hussain, the sons of Ali. Various distinguished Arab authors have discussed its exact meaning. Al Hasri, in *Zahar al Adab*, says that it implies descent from the Prophet, courage, a clean pedigree, good manners, and wide-mindedness born of learning. Al Qutaibi, in his *Kitab al Arab*, however, gives only four qualifications: a pedigree going back to the Prophet, a humane character, worthy ancestors, and generosity. Certainly the general meaning is that of inherited 'nobility,' of character, a tolerant, human outlook with a generous feeling of obligation, the very opposite of the rude materialism that sometimes overcomes it. 'Sherif,' and its connected noun of quality 'Sharaf,' has been discussed at length in his book *Mubahath Arabiya* by D. L. Bishr Faris, in his chapter devoted to it called "Tariq Lafdhat al Sharaf," which he published in Cairo in 1939. In any case, by the thirteenth century it was in accepted use as a title for the rulers of Mecca and the leading members of their clan, and has since spread to mean all members of the clan, and is applied in a general way, although not as an individual's title, to all the clans of the Qoraish in the Hijaz. Thus 'Al Ashraf' means all the Qoraish, whether townsmen or still semi-nomad. 'Al Shurafa' means the particularized members of the family, the nobles living in Mecca or those in other capitals who come from the ruling family. 'Al Sharif,' (the singular) unless known to apply to a particular individual, means the Qoraish Ruler of Mecca, or Grand Sherif, in person.

The outlook of a people in such matters produces certain words, and their preserving them confirms their outlook. The Arabians had no titles, in our understanding of the word, other than 'Sherif' and 'Sheikh,' or 'elder,' from the time of Muhammad until our own times, except 'Emir,' a style rather than a title, which could be and was used for any leader of any party, however small, and is not the Arabic for 'prince,' except and until these last few years in the cities. 'Emir' is no more than a 'leader,' and the democracy of the race is seen in the usage of these words and in the lack of formal titles. All the descendants of ancient tribes consider themselves noble, even if they are now ragged bedouin, and their manners betray their pride. Where all, or nearly all, are noble by descent, titles, as in Europe, have never come into genuine employ. So the only families of outstanding nobility in Arabia are those of the Qoraish of Mecca or their cousins here and there in the Arab world.

The chieftainship of Mecca was soon, at the beginning of the thirteenth century, to settle in the hands of one particular branch of the Sherifs, to be held by one clan of the Qoraish, descendants of Amr-Hashim, great-grandfather of the Prophet, through Hassan, grandson of the Prophet, and there remain.

RULERS FROM THE TENTH TO THE TWELFTH CENTURY

	A.D.
Abu Tahir ibn Abul Said al Jaunabi al Karmati (Temporary conquest)	928–

AL HASSANI DYNASTY

Ja'afar ibn Muhammad al Hassani (came to Mecca with the Fatimid pilgrim train from Egypt)	965–980
Isa ibn Ja'afar	975–994
Abdul Futuh ibn Ja'afar (temporarily acclaimed as Caliph in Syria and the Hijaz)	994–1039
Muhammad Shukr ibn Abdul Futuh	1039–1061

AL FATIKI, OR BANI ABI TIB, DYNASTY

Muhammad ibn Abi Fatik (rule taken over by Ali ibn Muhammad al Sulaihi of the Yemen)	1061–1063

ABI HASHIM DYNASTY

Muhammad ibn Ja'afar ibn Muhammad ibn Abdulla ibn Abi Hashim, descended through Musa ibn Abdulla from Al Hassan and Ali (his descent is given in full by Al Fasi)	1063–1091
Qasim ibn Muhammad	1091–1124
Fulaita ibn Qasim	1124–1132
Hashim ibn Fulaita	1132–1154
Qasim ibn Hashim	1154–1161
Isa ibn Fulaita	1161–1174
Daud ibn Isa	1174–1175
Mikhthar ibn Isa, interregnum of Tashatkin, Emir al Hajj from Iraq, who imposed on Mecca Qasim ibn Muhanna al Hussaini, of Medina, who was able to rule for only a few days	1175
Daud restored, who handed over the rulership again to Mikhthar, who ruled until 1200	1175–1200

Sources: Annales de Tabari (Leyden, 1879–1901). French translation of the Persian version by Lotenburg (London, 1867–74), vol. *e*, p. 981, *et seq.*; C. Snouck Hurgronje, *Mekka*, vol. ii, p. 205 *et seq.*; Ibn al Athir, *Al Kamil fi'l Tarikh*, vol. ix, pp. 233–317; Al Fasi, *Shifa al Ghuram bi akhbar al balad al haram*, book iii.

THE RELATION OF THE BANI FULAITA
TO THE BANI QITADA

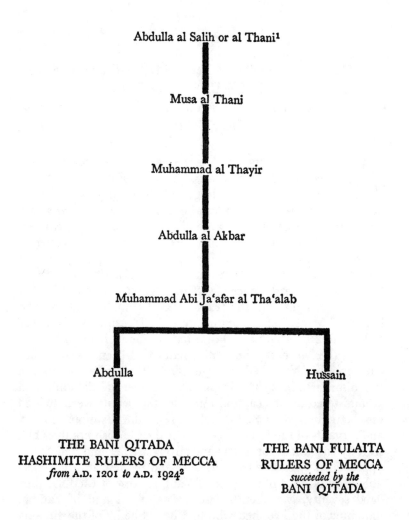

Abdulla al Salih or al Thani[1]

Musa al Thani

Muhammad al Thayir

Abdulla al Akbar

Muhammad Abi Ja'afar al Tha'alab

Abdulla

Hussain

THE BANI QITADA
HASHIMITE RULERS OF MECCA
from A.D. 1201 *to* A.D. 1924[2]

THE BANI FULAITA
RULERS OF MECCA
succeeded by the
BANI QITADA

[1] See pedigree at p. 56 for his descent.
[2] For Qitada's descent from Abdulla see the chronological table at p. 66.

Chapter IV

THE LAST DAYS OF THE EMIR MIKHTHAR
AND THE RULE OF QITADA,
OF HIS SONS AND GRANDSONS
(A.D. 1185–1254)

APART FROM THEIR FAILURE TO FEND OFF FOREIGN INTER-
ference in Meccan affairs, the Bani Fulaita rulers had
been increasingly neglectful of their subjects' interests,
devoting themselves to pleasure-seeking, and increasingly
unsuccessful in maintaining good order. In 1185 nearly a
hundred pilgrims were crushed to death by overcrowding in
the shrine. In 1189 Mikhthar's brother, Daud, had fled with
the silver rim of the Black Stone to Wadi Nakhla. The Ruler
himself had already once fled from Mecca, as a result of a
quarrel and fight with the Iraqi Emir al Hajj, Tashatkin, who
had ruled Mecca before handing over to Al Qasim ibn Muhanna
al Hussaini, of Medina. Qasim having found it impossible to
control the Meccans, the Bani Fulaita had been restored, but
with greatly diminished prestige. For a short time, because of
the disorders, in 1185, Taghtakin, brother of Saladin, had
administered at Mecca, and although the people were divided
into factions, and seemed unable to resist the vexatious soldiery
and servants of the Fulaita, certain of the Qoraish notables had
secretly cast about for a new and stronger ruler and had at last
approached a relative by marriage[1] and by descent, the venerable Qitada, lord of the port of Yanbu', west of Medina, then
aged seventy, a sixteenth descendant of Ali and of Fatima,
daughter of the Prophet, who had been Sheikh of the Juhaina
tribe from the age of twenty-one, and was a distinguished
amateur poet and a doughty warrior. Qitada sent his son
Handala, at the head of his cavalry, to seize Mecca, adroitly
choosing the 27th day of Rejeb for the attack—a day of minor

[1] Authority: Ibn Khaldun.

pilgrimage, when Mikhthar and the notables and soldiers would be outside the walls—so that the city was taken without the loss of a man. It was the 3rd of May 1201. Mikhthar fled to Wadi Nakhla and never entered Mecca again, dying in exile in the Yemen two years later.

The traveller Ibn Jubair, who visited Mecca as a pilgrim in Mikhthar's reign has given glimpses of life there. He wrote:

Salah-al-din [Saladin] exempted the pilgrims from excise, and instead he ordered money and foodstuff to be sent to Mikhthar, the Emir of Mecca. This excise had been applied by the Emir to pilgrims coming by sea. [Saladin had sent 8000 ardabs of wheat and 2000 dinars, according to Ibn Zaini Dahlan.] When arrival of this aid in kind was delayed the Emir again frightened the pilgrims with the threat of the excise. We happened to reach Jedda when there was a hold-up of the pilgrims while the Emir Mikhthar was being consulted. Then he ordered that each pilgrim should be insured by another and only then enter the shrine of God. If the money and the foodstuff allotted to him by Salah-al-din did arrive, well and good; otherwise, he proclaimed, he would not be able to leave his dues with the pilgrims. . . .

Thus we left Jedda only after the pilgrims had insured each other and their names had been registered with the Commander of Jedda, Ali ibn Isa. This man Mikhthar is the descendant of Hassan ibn Ali—God, bless their souls!—but he is not of good deeds. . . .

Ibn Jubair described the scene inside the temple during the pilgrimage season.

When Friday arrives and the time of prayer approaches the preacher enters from the Prophet's door. He wears a black dress embroidered with gold and a black turban embroidered too and a fine green robe. All this was bestowed by the Caliph on the preachers of this country. He comes walking slowly and majestic-ally between two black banners held by two of the men and a third one holding a red stick tied with a long thong, at the end of which is a small tassel. The last man strikes the air with this whip, creating a sharp, high-pitched note which can be heard in and outside the shrine, so heralding their coming. When he reaches the pulpit the preacher stops at the Black Stone and kisses it. Then he walks to the pulpit with the Chief Muezzin in front of him. The latter too wears a black dress, and has a great sword in his hand. When the preacher ascends the first step the Muezzin hands him the sword. He himself strikes the first, second, and third, and the fourth step, then stands facing the Ka'aba, praying silently. He salutes the people ["As Salaam Alaikum"] and the people answer him ["Wa Alaikum as Salaam"]. When the Muezzin has finished his calling to prayer the preacher stands and delivers his sermon. He then sits down and strikes with his sword a fifth stroke. Again he stands praying, mentioning the Prophet and his descendants, especially the four Caliphs, and the uncles of the Prophet, and Hamza, Abbas, and Hassan, and Hussain. Then he prays for the wives of the Prophet, the Abbassid Caliph, Abu-al-Abbas Ahmed al Nasir, and the Emir of Mecca, Mikhthar ibn Isa ibn Fulaita ibn Qassim ibn Muhammad ibn Ha'afar ibn Abi Hashim al Hassani, then he prays for Salah-al-din Abu-al-Mudhaffar Yusif ibn Ayyoub [Saladin], with his brother the heir apparent, Abi-Bakr ibn Ayyoub. At the mention of Salah-al-din all the people present fervently pray for his safety: 'If God, once, loved his servant He bestows on him the love for the people.' They feel that way, because he has done so much for them by abolishing the pilgrim's excise.

We were informed at this moment that Salah-al-din's letter had reached Emir Mikhthar. The most important part of it was his counsel to treat the pilgrims well, to ensure their provisions and well-being, to stop causing harm to them, and that saying that his servants, followers, and others should be instructed to this effect. . . .

During the delivery of the sermon the two black banners are posed on the first step of the pulpit and held by two men. When the preacher finishes his prayer he goes out with the two banners on his right and left sides and the ceremonial whip in front of him, in the same way as when he came in. . . .

The Emir Mikhthar came at sunrise to the holy shrine together with his leaders and readers gathered round him. His Negro guards who preceded him holding upright their shining spears. He was wearing a fine white robe and a white woollen turban on his head. He comes to the Ka'aba at the beginning of each month. . . .

Among the strangest things we ever saw was the howdah of Al Sharifa Jumana, the daughter of Fulaita, the aunt of Emir Mikhthar. The tassels of its curtains were dragging on the ground. Other howdahs there belonged to the women of the Emir and to those of his lieutenants, and there were countless others so that they resembled a vast camp. Fires were lit on both sides of the way, and torchbearers illuminated the camels which were carrying, in howdahs, the more notable ladies of Mecca. . . .

All the women of Mecca attended the Mosque on the 29th day of Rejeb, the men having left the place. It was a stampede. Women were shouting, crying, or praising Almighty God. . . .

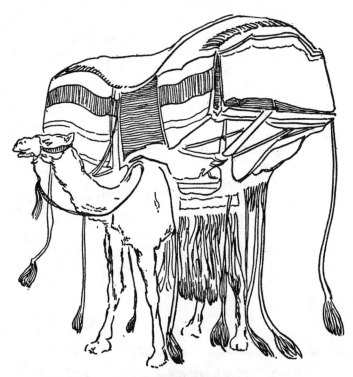

A PILGRIM HOWDAH
Drawn from life by the Author

They spent a greater part of the day going round the place, kissing the Black Stone and touching the corners. This is their most joyful day, because when they come with the men they are deprived of all these things. . . .

The whip is used in Ramadhan in between the prayers and the intoning of the *tarawih*,[1] and it is used three times after the evening call to prayer and three times after the *isha* [dinner] call for prayer. This is the present unusual and especial custom in this sacred mosque. . . .

[1] Special prayers ; see glossary.

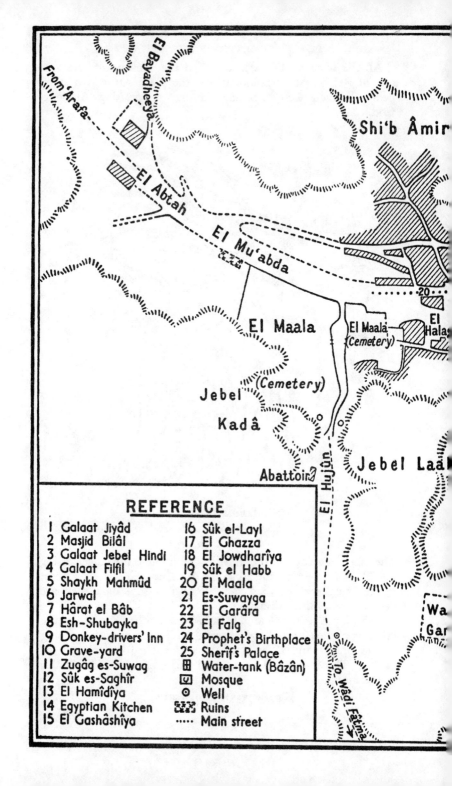

Shi'b Âmir

From 'Arafa

El Bayadheeya

El Abtah

El Mu'abda

El Maala

El Maala (Cemetery)

El Hala

(Cemetery)

Jebel

Kadâ

Abattoir

El Hujûn

Jebel Laa

To Wâdi Fâtima

Wa

Gar

REFERENCE

 1 Galaat Jiyâd
 2 Masjid Bilâl
 3 Galaat Jebel Hindi
 4 Galaat Filfil
 5 Shaykh Mahmûd
 6 Jarwal
 7 Hârat el Bâb
 8 Esh-Shubayka
 9 Donkey-drivers' Inn
10 Grave-yard
11 Zuqâq es-Suwag
12 Sûk es-Saghîr
13 El Hamîdîya
14 Egyptian Kitchen
15 El Gashâshîya

16 Sûk el-Layl
17 El Ghazza
18 El Jowdharîya
19 Sûk el Habb
20 El Maala
21 Es-Suwayga
22 El Garâra
23 El Falg
24 Prophet's Birthplace
25 Sherîf's Palace
⊞ Water-tank (Bâzân)
⬓ Mosque
☉ Well
▨▨ Ruins
····· Main street

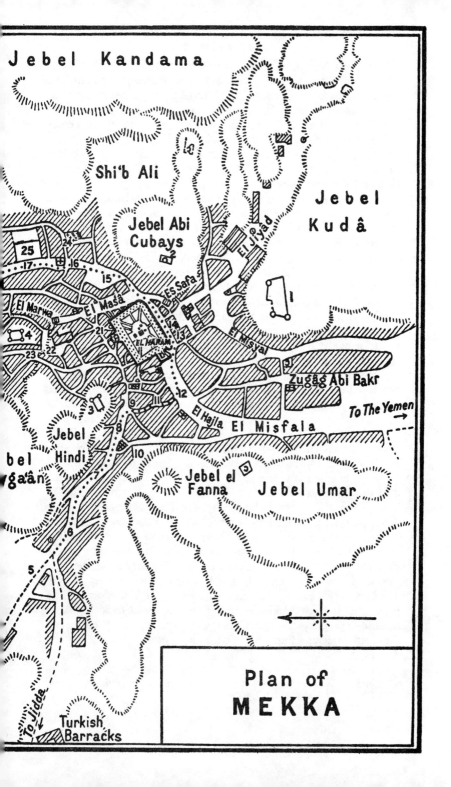

Jebel Kandama

Shi'b Ali

Jebel Abi
Cubays

Jebel
Kudâ

El Jiyad

Es Safa

El Marwa

25

El Masâ

El Misyal

EL HARAM

Zugâg Abi Bakr

To The Yemen

El Hajla El Misfala

Jebel
Hindi

bel
gaân

Jebel el
Fanna

Jebel Umar

To Jidda

Turkish
Barracks

Plan of
MEKKA

The Emir Mikhthar went out to meet Saif-al-Islam Taghtakin bin Ayyoub,[2] the brother of Salah-al-din. Rumours preceded his coming from Egypt for some time, until at last it became certain that he had arrived at Yanbu' and was calling at Medina to visit the Prophet's tomb. It was said that he was going to the Yemen because of a clash of opinion and a sedition which had taken place there among the princes, but the population of Mecca felt uneasy about his arrival. So, the said Emir went out to meet him and pay him homage. . . .

We heard the fanfare on the trumpets of the Emir Mikhthar and the shrill welcoming noise made by the women of Mecca. The Emir left Saif-al-Islam [Taghtakin] after a while. The people were optimistic in view of this event [that is, his leaving him in safety]. Then the forerunners of his soldiers reached the mosque and competed with the Emir Mikhthar in roaming about the holy place. While the people were looking at them they heard a great clamour and saw Saif-al-Islam entering by the doorway of Bani Shaiba. The glittering of so many raised swords prevented a view of the Qadhi, who was walking on his right, or of the leader of the Shaibites, who was on his left. The mosque was crowded with spectators praying for him, and for his brother Saladin. The Chief Muezzin (Al Zamzami) was praying for Saif-al-Islam and praising him. When he reached the great mosque the swords were thrust in their scabbards, the multitude became very quiet and full of humility, but tears were in their hearts. The Qadhi, with the leader of the Shaibites, went around with Saif-al-Islam and the Emir Mikhthar. The latter hurried through this process and went home. When Saif-al-Islam finished his prayer he returned to his camp. On the next day we heard the sound of drums, trumpets, and of thumping. Then there came the Emir Mikhthar wearing a golden dress, with its train trailing behind him. On his head was a new turban interlaced with gold. These had been presented to him by Saif-al-Islam, and he came to show them to the people, and to visit the mosque as a thanksgiving to Almighty God, because previously he had been feeling upset, being most fearful of Saif-al-Islam. On Friday Saif-al-Islam came to the mosque and prayed with Emir Mikhthar under the Abbassid canopy. After finishing the prayer he went back to his camp. On Wednesday, the 10th of Ramadhan, he left for the Yemen with all his soldiers. . . .

[1] Taghtakin was ruler of the Yemen and Arabia from 1181 to 1196. (Authority: S. Lane Poole, *The Mohammadan Dynasties*.)

The Shaibites [the Keepers of the Keys] were early in coming and opening the door of the holy Ka'aba on the first day of the holiday following the pilgrimage. Their leader sat on the threshold, with the rest of the Shaibites inside the Ka'aba, until they knew of the arrival of the Emir Mikhthar. They went out to meet him near the door of the Prophet. He was present in the shrine every day for one whole week while the people were celebrating their holiday. The Muezzin, Al Zamzami, was praying loudly as usual, and praising the Emir, sharing this duty with his brother during the whole week. On the last day of this week the Emir went and sat on the stone bench by the dome of Zemzem, facing the corner containing the Black Stone. His sons sat on his right and left while his attendants were standing, the people looking at them with envy. The Emir brought four of his private poets, who, one after the other, recited their verses in his praise. Then the preacher came with portly pace, between his two black banners, the aforementioned whip continuously cracking in front of him. When he had finished his sermon the people congratulated each other on the holiday by shaking hands and by salutation, and then prayed jubilantly.

On the 28th of the month we saw the dismissed Chief of the Shaibites walking proudly between his sons, with the key of the holy Ka'aba, which had been returned to him, in his hand. We asked those about us how this dismissed Shaibite had resumed his duty after what was attributed to him, and learned that he had borrowed and paid a sum of five hundred dinars as a compensation. We had not been surprised to learn that he had been arrested, because of the acts of vileness committed by him against God's sacred place, which was a common thing, but were astonished that he was released. Corruption has even penetrated to the noblest spot on earth. . . .

On Monday, the 4th or the 5th of this month, there arrived, escaping from Saif-al-Islam, who was advancing on the Yemen, Othman ibn Ali, the ruler of Aden, riding the sea in many boats full of countless valuables, because he had stayed in that province for a long time. When he was gone out a distance in the sea the flame-throwing vessels of the Emir Saif-al-Islam followed him and captured almost all his valuables. So he escaped to the land with only the most precious and lighter belongings and a few of his men. He reached Mecca in a caravan loaded with these supplies and his money, and went to his house which he had had built there. As I understood, he was unscrupulous in his dealings with merchants in his province, taking nearly all their profits to himself, especially from the supplies they imported from India.

So he acquired tremendous and ill-gotten riches. But the events of the time led to his decline. . . .

News arrived that the new moon was seen, but the Qadhi postponed his formal declaration of it until arrival of the messenger who was expected to bring news of the coming of the Iraqi Emir and pilgrim caravan. On Wednesday, the 7th of March, the messenger arrived and confirmed seeing the new moon on Thursday. So the Qadhi, being sure of this, delivered his sermon, telling the pilgrims that to-morrow was their day to go up to Muna. The people got themselves there early and from it to Jebel Arafat. It was a rule that they pass their night there, but they were afraid of the Bani Sha'aba, who used to raid the pilgrims on their way to Arafat. The above-mentioned Emir, Othman, therefore ordered his armed men to stay in the valley to guard the pilgrims. . . .

The Emir established a tent in the valley between the two mountains, and one of his companions ascended Jebel Jaoud on horseback, so reaching its summit. We were astonished how he accomplished such a feat and how his mare reached that unsurmountable altitude. All the pilgrims believed that this Emir shared their blessings and acquired two rewards, one of *jihad*,[1] and the other of pilgrimage, because the safety of God's delegates on such a day is the greatest act of *jihad*. . . .

The Iraqi Emir arrived with an unprecedented multitude, and with him there arrived many Persian princes of Khorassan and notable women, known by the title of 'Khatoon,' and many of them daughters of princes. The quarters of the Iraqi Emir were beautiful and even majestic, with wonderful camps, round umbrella tents, and corridors; the most astonishing we ever saw. He had surrounded them with large marquees of canvas, making of them a wall, and there were gardens and ornamental structures. Inside, the hangings were in black and white, or coloured, like flowers in their beds. The facades of the four corners of these large tents were covered with a pattern of spheroids. The doors of these great tents were high, resembling the doors of real castles, leading into winding corridors, and thence to an open space where the round umbrella tents were installed. The Emir was in fact living in a majestic, mobile city, unequalled by those owned by the monarchs of the West. Inside were all the Emir's chamberlains, servants, and followers. A horseman with his banner could enter the doors without lowering it or bending his head. The large tents were fastened with strong adjustable

[1] See glossary.

canvas ropes fixed by pegs, a peculiar engineering feat. The other Emirs, who had accompanied the Iraqi Emir, had similar camps, but of lesser magnitude. The Emirs' camels were provided with luxurious and attractive litters called *ghishawat*. They resemble coffins in shape, being used by men and women travellers, in the same manner as are the cradles of children, and provided with comfortable bedding. The traveller is so comfortably accommodated in them, as if he is travelling in a soft, wide cradle, balanced by an equal weight on the other side and with a cover sheltering him, that he sleeps tranquilly during the journey, feeling no inconvenience whatever. When the passengers reach their destination they have their large tents to go into, and can enter them while mounted. They then descend on to a stand brought for them, thus leaving the shade of the howdah's cover for the shelter of a house without being affected by the wind or by a ray of sun. . . .

On the second day of Sacrifice the preacher lectured in al Nahif mosque. This holy preacher, known by the name of Taj-al-Din, was sent here and recommended by the Caliph, arriving with the Iraqi Emir, to give religious lectures and administer the law in Mecca. His sermons showed that he was stupid and ignorant and not well versed in Arabic. . . .

The Sudani residents of Mecca and the Iraqi pilgrims clashed, with swords, arrows, and bows. There were many injured, and some of the merchants' properties was looted. Muna, during those three days, had become a great market, where precious gems as well as cheap beads and other goods were sold. The trouble was soon quelled, and the people finished the pilgrimage in peace, thanks to the Almighty, the Master of the Universe. On Saturday, the day of the above-mentioned sacrifice, the new covering for the holy Ka'aba came, driven to Mecca on four camels from the quarters of the Iraqi Emir, preceded by the new Qadhi wearing the Caliph's black robe, with banners over his head and drums beaten behind him.

We went to Wadi al Marr, which was fertile with many palm-trees, a spouting spring irrigating the soil of that vast district, in which are many villages and other springs. Fruits for Mecca— May God protect her!—were brought from this valley. We stayed there on Friday for a peculiar reason; that there was the Queen Khatoon, the daughter of Al Emir Masoud, the King of Al Duroob and of the Armenians beyond the country of the Rumis, one of the three Khatoons who arrived with Emir al Hajj of Iraq, Abu-al-Makarim Tashtakin, the delegate of the Defender of the Faithful, the Caliph, who sent him every year, throughout a period of eight years or more, for this purpose of leading the pilgrims. This Khatoon is the most prominent and highly ranked among the others, because of the vastness of her father's kingdom, in which, we were assured, he had one hundred thousand splendid horsemen. His son-in-law is Nur-al-din, the ruler of Amid and elsewhere. He too commands about twelve thousand cavalry. The second Khatoon is the mother of Muis-al-din, the ruler of Mosul, and the wife of Babik, the brother of Nur-al-din, the ruler of Damascus,[1] may God rest his soul in peace. The third Khatoon is the daughter of Al Daqoos, the ruler of Isbahan, one of the dependencies of Khorassan. . . .

The daughter of Emir Masoud arrived on Thursday, the 6th of Muharram, at the mosque of the Prophet. She was riding in her covered camel-litter, with the litters of her daughters and her servants about her. Fine young men were holding iron rods in their hand, pushing aside the people and making way for her, until she reached the door of the Holy Mosque. There she descended and walked to the small garden between the tomb and the pulpit. The slaves and servants were showering blessings on her. While she prayed under the cover of a shawl, crowds of people came surrounding her, but the iron rods were dispersing them. She prayed in the garden-bed in front of the pulpit, then she walked to the western side and there sat in the spot where, it is said, Gabriel had descended to earth. A screen was thrown around her, beyond which her servants and attendants were standing to execute her orders. She had brought two loads of provisions to be distributed in charity, and remained in that place till night and the arrival of Sadr-al-din al Ispahani, the head of the Shafite sect, who inherited presence of mind and notability. He was late, and the crowds of people were waiting. He arrived with the Emir al Hajj.

Sadr-al-din delivered the most wonderful and affecting speech in both languages. Persians rushed to him declaring their repentance, and offering him their forelocks. He ordered big scissors to be brought to shear one forelock after another, putting his own turban on each of these men, and at once one of his readers or friends put his own turban on the head of the speaker instead of it. He went on with this operation, shearing many forelocks, and then requested the people to do him a great favour. They all responded sobbing. He declared that he wanted them to uncover their heads and stretch out their hands, beseeching the gracious Prophet to have grace on him and to ask God to

[1] Afdhal Nur-al-din Ali, ruler of Damascus, 1186–96. (Authority: S. Lane Poole.)

do the same. Then he started confessing his sins. Men flung off their turbans and stretched their hands out to the Prophet, crying and pleading. The assembly then dispersed, as did the Emir and the Khatoon. . . .

Such was the pilgrimage scene in Mecca at the end of the Emir Mikhthar's rule in the second half of the twelfth century.[1] The new and soldierly old ruler of Mecca, Qitada, who succeeded Mikhthar by force of arms, while still under forty years of age must have marked the rising fortunes of the famous Kurdish soldier of fortune, Nasr Salah-al-din Yusif, or Saladin. Saladin's master, General Nur-al-din Mahmoud ibn Zangi, a general of the Abbassid realm and self-made King of Syria, had set him an example which Saladin had soon followed. When sent by him to Egypt he set about annexing it for himself, becoming monarch in 1169, although the last Shiah Fatimid Caliph did not die until three years later. In 1171 Saladin caused the *khutba* to be read in Cairo in the name of the contemporary Abbassid Caliph, al Muqtadi, instead of that of the Fatimid, Adid Abu Muhammad Abdulla, who lay on his death-bed—the last of a line which had endured for nearly two centuries.

The holy cities of the Hijaz had in a general way, in the eyes of Egyptians, formed part of Egyptian dominions, and in 1173 Saladin had sent his brother, Muazzam Turanshah, to govern Arabia from the Yemen, and by him, two years later, Daud ibn Isa ibn Fulaita, the Emir of Mecca, had been ordered, in the name of the Abbassid Caliph, to renounce his rulership in favour of his brother Mikhthar.

From the north the news of victories and changing rulerships continued to reach the Red Sea. Tripoli of Syria was taken from the Normans in 1172 and all Syria was occupied by Saladin on the death of his former master two years later. He took Mosul, annexed Aleppo, and made the various princes of Mesopotamia his vassals. In 1180 the Christian realm of Jerusalem began its final struggle with the Saracens under Saladin.

A French Knight, Reynaud de Châtillon, who had taken over the rule of the land beyond the Jordan and the castles of Moab and of Montreal-Shaubak, east of the Dead Sea, from

[1] Ibn Jubair was in Mecca in A.D. 1183–84.

where he dominated the pilgrim route to Mecca, had conceived a daring plan. He would attack the heart of Islam itself. The following year, breaking truces with the Saracens, he reached Taima, far down in Arabia, cutting the pilgrim route and robbing rich caravans. Abandoning the attempt by land on the supposed treasure in Muhammad's tomb at Medina, Reynaud determined on pursuing a plan of attack on the Holy Places of Islam from the sea. Saladin countered by building a fortress in northern Sinai as an advance base, but meanwhile Reynaud reconquered Ailat, on the Gulf of Akaba, in a surprise attack. Then, taking vessels from the southern ports of Palestine—Ascalon and other places—he dismantled them and transported them in pieces by camel across the deserts of Idumæa and Wadi Araba, together with those he had had built in parts with wood from a forest near Shaubak. Reconstructing them in the Gulf of Ailat, he mustered five great galleys, each carrying a thousand men, and a number of smaller vessels. While part of this armada under the personal direction of Reynaud laid siege to the Isle of Graye, the rest under one of his commanders plundered the coasts from north to south before Saladin, returning from his campaign on the Euphrates, heard about it. The Christians' galleys, manœuvred by oars, were more mobile than the sailing vessels of the Arabs, and the Crusaders severed the communications of all the smaller ports, seizing the merchant vessels, and destroying Saracen transports. They foundered all the vessels they encountered and took their cargoes during a whole year (1182–83). Farther south, on the west coast, at Ras Benas, they sacked Aidhab, a port on the African shore then of first importance to the pilgrims travelling from the Nile to Mecca. There they burned merchant ships and sank a large vessel carrying pilgrims to Jedda. Their troops, guided by Moslem prisoners, made an expedition northward along the Egyptian coast, and took rich caravans coming from Kosseir. Reynaud's men appeared in all the Red Sea Arabian ports, including Rabigh and Al Hawara, the one at the south, the other to the north of Yanbu', Qitada's fortress. They even appeared in Bab el-Mandeb and as far south as Aden, where they are said to have "captured sheikhs and holy men" while engaged in closing that end of the Red Sea.

Meanwhile—if only just in time—the Arabs of Cairo had organized their counter-attack. El-Malik el-Adil, brother of Saladin and his regent during the Oriental campaigns, had no fleet in the Red Sea, but, emulating Reynaud, he had vessels taken in pieces from the Nile and Alexandria to Qolzoum. In January 1183 this fleet put to sea under the command of Hisam-al-Din Lulu (called Al Hajib, or the Chamberlain), as well known for his piety and charity as for his naval prowess. Less than two months afterwards he had burned three of the Christian galleys laying siege to the Isle of Graye, and enslaved their crews. Before Al Hawara in midsummer he attacked the Crusader fleet. Their ships destroyed, the Christian sailors attempted to rejoin the main column which had already begun its march on Medina. In the desert gorges, five days from the sea and one day from Medina, the three hundred warriors of the West, guided by some Musulman deserters, were attacked on a hilltop on which they had sought to make a stand and were almost annihilated. Of a hundred and seventy who escaped death in the battle and were taken prisoners, some were put to death at the place of sacrifice at Muna, outside Mecca, and at Medina; the rest, with the exception of a handful who escaped and rode overland to the Levant, were taken in humiliating captivity to Egypt, there to be exhibited, before death in public, at the hands of the religious mendicants, students, and fanatical dervishes, on whom that satisfying privilege was bestowed.

Ibn Jubair described the survivors as he saw them there on his way southward to the pilgrimage.

When we entered Alexandria we first saw a great gathering of people who had come to look at the Rumi prisoners entering the city, bound naked on camels, with their faces turned to the tails, surrounded by drummers and trumpeters. When we asked about their story we were told things which were heart-breaking and horrible; that some of the Damascene Christians had gotten together to assemble vessels in the nearest places of the Red Sea, having transported their parts on camels. When they reached the sea-shore they put their ships together and launched them into the sea, and sailed towards the route of the pilgrims—and when they reached the Sea of the Sleepers [the Red Sea] they burned about sixteen vessels, and on reaching Aidhab they took

a great ship bringing pilgrims from Jedda. They also captured
on land a whole caravan which was coming from Kaws to Aidhab,
and they killed every one with it. Then they captured two vessels
carrying on board merchants from the Yemen, and burned foodstuff on that shore which had been destined to supply Mecca and
Medina, glorified by God; and committed horrible crimes, the
like of which had never been heard of by the Moslems, and a
Rumi never reached that spot at all. The most terrible and
horrible event is that they were intending to enter the Prophet's
City to dig him out of the sacred shrine, but the Almighty struck
them down, when they were a day's travel from the city, because
of their venture against Him, meeting their enmity with vessels
constructed in Egypt and Alexandria, carrying the well-known
and glorious Commander Lulu al Hajib, with brave Moorish
seamen. Thus the enemy was followed and overtaken and very
many of them killed, or captured, and distributed among the
Muslim countries, to be killed there, some being sent to Mecca
and Medina.

Saladin resolved to end once for all time this threat on
Mecca, ordered the capture of Reynaud's castle, and the siege
began under his personal orders in the autumn of the same year.
It so happened that the investment was at a time when a
wedding party for Reynaud's stepson was beginning, and the
balls from eight great mangonels bombarding the fortress and
the citadel village fell not only among refugee Christians from
the neighbouring hamlets, but among the jugglers, musicians,
dancers, and lights-of-love brought from Jerusalem for the
pleasure of the wedding guests. But at news of the siege a
sudden last spark of kingship and life entered the dying and
paralysed, blind and leprous king, Baldwin IV, who hastened
with his army to its relief.

Reynaud, however, did not long survive his disastrous campaign in the Red Sea. At the battle of Hattin, near Galilee, in
1187, Saladin defeated the Crusaders and the Kingdom of
Jerusalem fell. The Christian princes and knights were made
prisoners, and Reynaud, the "demon of the West," personal
antagonist of Saladin, invader of the Holy Hijaz, was put to
death without pity on the field in front of Saladin, some say
by him.

Qitada would have been thirty-two years old when Reynaud's force appeared off the Red Sea ports and was destroyed

in the gorges one day short of Medina. He had early acquired fame as a warrior in defeating the Ashraf of the Bani Hirab tribe, from whom he took over Yanbu' and al Safra, the key pass between North and South, and the Bani Ali, Bani Ahmas, and Bani Ibrahim, and it seems probable that part of his military reputation was acquired in the defeat of the Crusaders, who had landed near his home at Yanbu' on their way to Medina.

After the occupation of Mecca by Qitada's son Handhala, Mikhthar's son Muhammad made an abortive counter-attack, and this was followed up by others, supported by Salim ibn Qasim al Hussaini, the Emir of Medina, which city had resisted Qitada and was only reduced to obedience two years after the taking of Mecca by an expedition led by Qitada in person. Qitada returned to Mecca and completed his conquest of the Hijaz by sending a successful punitive expedition against the Thuqaif tribesmen, east of Mecca, and the town of Taif. Ibn al Athir[1] says that a battle took place between him and Salim of Medina at Dhu-al-Halifa, near Medina, in which large numbers were engaged on both sides, so that Qitada failed to defeat Salim, but that Qitada took pains to wean the followers of Salim from him and gradually rendered him too weak to be a menace again.

In 1210, and again in 1212, there were incidents between the people of Mecca and the Iraqi pilgrims. The details of the second affair are given by al Fasi as follows:

> The Emir of the Iraqi pilgrim train was Allah-ad-din Muhammad ibn al Emir Yacout, acting on behalf of his father, a slave of the Caliph, who was Governor of Khuzistan as well as Emir-al-Hajj, and his assistant and guide was Ibn Abi Faras.[2] At the head of the Damascus train was Sumsam Ismail, brother of Sharoukh al Najmi. At the head of the Palestinian train was Al Hajji al Ahuya' Ali ibn Salim, and Rabiha Khatoon, sister of al Adil [Adil Saif-ad Din Abu Bekr, brother of Saladin, known as "Saphadin" to the Crusaders] was one of the pilgrims. At Muna after the ceremonial throwing of stones the Ismailis jumped

---

[1] *Al Kamil fi'l Tarikh*, vol. xii, p. 134.
[2] Al Sibt ibn Jauzi, *Mirat al Zaman*, p. 363. According to Ibn al Athir (*Al Kamil fi'l Tarikh*, vol. xii, pp. 191 and 195), Allah-ad-din was a youth who was "afraid and embarrassed by the incidents," and the following year was replaced as Emir by Ibn Abi Faras ibn Ja'afar ibn Faras al Hilli.

on a Sherif, a cousin of Qitada, who resembled him, and killed him; it was said because they believed him to be Qitada. The man who actually struck the Sherif dead was a Ismaili, one Haroun, nicknamed "Abu Aziz," who it was thought was one of the followers of the mother of Jalal-ad-din. The Negro slaves and the servants of the Sherifs at once broke loose; climbing the hills on either side of Muna they began to catapult and shoot arrows. All next day they looted the pilgrims and there were many casualties on both sides. The elderly Ibn Abi Faris advised Muhammad Ibn Yacout to move the Iraqi caravan from Muna to Al Zahir, the usual Damascus camping ground. . . . When they began to move, Qitada, with his Negroes, believing them to be about to fight, attacked them and looted everything they had. "As I was meant to be killed I will not leave one of them alive," Qitada said. Rabiha Khatoon was then at Al Zahir, having with her Ibn al Satar and the brother of Al Sharoukh and the Damascus pilgrims. The Emir of the Iraqi train took refuge in her tent, and with her was the Khatoon, the mother of Salah-ad-din. Rabiha sent Ibn Satar to ask Qitada, "What is the crime of the people, now that the murderer is known, or is it that you seek any excuse to loot pilgrims, yet knowing who we are?"

He swore that if Qitada did not cease his vengeance he should suffer and that the Caliph would advance from Baghdad, and the Syrians from Damascus, upon him. So Qitada agreed to stop it, but only if the pilgrims paid him in compensation 100,000 dinars. Finally some 30,000 dinars were collected for him from the pilgrims and from the mother of Salah-ad-din. Hundreds of people remained for three days about her tent, for the sake of her protection, being many of them hungry, wounded, naked, and some of them dead or dying.

Qitada was convinced that the assassination had been planned by the Caliph, and so he swore to kill any pilgrim from Baghdad the next year.

Thus the Iraqi pilgrimage returned home in great misery. After a time Qitada sent his son Rajih to Baghdad. He and his men entered the city with swords unsheathed and hilts held out ready for surrender, with shrouds on their shoulders, begging mercy from the Caliph. They were forgiven, and next year a great quantity of gifts and money was sent to Qitada. He was not required to explain his actions and later was asked by the Caliph to visit him in Baghdad.

When, however, Qitada reached the frontier of Iraq, near
Al Kufa, and was met by representatives of the Caliph, one of
them leading a lion on a chain, Qitada, seeing in it an ill
omen, turned back to Mecca, sending his excuses to the Caliph
in verse. His cordial letter began:

> You are my cousin and my friend,
> Truly, here, I am a disposer of men,
> A very dragon among them.
> From a glimpse of my claw they recoil.
> Kings come kissing the back of my hand, while
> The poor find an oasis in its palm.
> Its strength is so great that millstones
> Would not crush it.
>   How foolish of me!
> In truth I am nothing but a delicate flask
> Of musk, whose fragrance would be
> Dispelled, which would break in fragments,
> If I came to you.

The Caliph does not seem to have taken his excuses amiss for
he replied to him in verse.

More than once Qitada said in public that he had a stronger
claim to the Caliphate than the Abbassid Caliph in Baghdad,
and he took a high hand in his relations with the representatives
of Egypt, who had supported the Emir of Medina against him.
C. Snouck Hurgronje[1] points out that he may have been
sustained in his cold, proud attitude by a belief in their desire
to aid his rivals of the Yemen, who had sent envoys far and
wide to ask for help against him when he had pushed his
southern frontier to Hali, on the Red Sea. They obtained,
however, nothing beyond good wishes and money from the
neighbouring Powers, then heavily engaged with the Crusaders,
who had invaded Egypt itself in 1220, and they were doubtless
discouraged by the harshness of the deserts between them and
Arabia, the inaccessibility of which Qitada was to recommend
as their best weapon to his sons when he was ailing in his
old age. "Allah has protected you and your country by its
aridity and remoteness," he said to them.

In any case his foreign relations were always coloured
towards the end by his ambition to rule independently all
Central and Southern Arabia. Any aid for, or even any
friendly correspondence with, a rival in Arabia was to him an

---

[1] *Mekka.*

insupportably hostile act. He is termed "a tall old man, revered, handsome, honourable, and brave, who, simple and devout, often personally called his men to their prayers in the Haram. And who feared none of God's creatures."[1] He treated the turbulent slaves and soldiery of Mecca with strict severity and was feared by them for his firmness and justice.

Towards the end of Qitada's reign, when the old man was failing in health, the Caliph appointed as his Wali or representative in Mecca his favourite, Aq-Bash al Naasiri,[2] a prominent member of the Futuwa, or Youthful Knights. While camping at Mount Arafat he was visited by Rajih, son of Qitada, who asked him to support his candidature as successor to his father. Aq-Bash avoided a direct reply to this request, for he was carrying presents from the Caliph for Hassan, an elder son; but, hearing of the meeting, Hassan supposed that his younger brother had already received Aq-Bash's support, and, returning to Mecca, at once closed the gates and roused his supporters, as in turn did Rajih. When Aq-Bash heard that trouble was already brewing he rode forth from his camp at Shubaika in order to stop it, but the followers of Hassan concluded that he was coming, not to quieten, but to defeat them, although he kept shouting at them that he was not there to fight. His men fled and he was left alone. They hamstrung his mare, which fell with him, and they struck off his head and took it to Hassan on a lance, who ordered it to be displayed at Al Masaa, near the house of Al Abbas. The Meccans under Hassan wished to loot the Hajj al Iraqi, vulnerable and leaderless after Aq-Bash's death, but the Emir of the Damascus pilgrims warned them that his brothers, the King of Damascus, Al Muadhdham Sharaf-ad-Din Isa, and Al Kamil, King of Egypt, would march against them.[3]

Aq-Bash had been bought by the Caliph Nasr li-din-Illah when fifteen years of age for five thousand dinars, one of the largest sums ever paid for a slave. He was said to be the

---

[1] Al Sibt ibn Jauzi, *Mirat al Zaman*: the events of the year A.H. 617.

[2] His full name and titles were Nur-al-din Aq-bash al Naasiri ibn Abdulla al Duwayidar al Munadhiri—*see* Al Sibt ibn Jauzi, *ibid.*

[3] Al Fasi, *Shifa al Ghuram bi akhbar al balad al haram.* Ibn al Athir has an almost similar account (*Al Kamil fi'l Tarikh*, vol. xii, p. 361). Al Sibt ibn Jauzi's account was supported by that of Ibn Kuthir al Dimishqi in *Al Badiya wa al Nahiya* (A.H. 617), who relates that Aq-Bash had been one of the envoys to Sultan Adil from the Caliph, when the former was besieging Sinjar.

handsomest youth in Iraq, and being also wise had become the constant companion of the Caliph, who had given him the coveted honour of leading the Iraqi pilgrim caravans, already conducted by him for three successive years before that in which he was killed. The Caliph's grief was so great on hearing of his death that there was no welcome to the returning caravan, and no drums were beaten or banners unfurled, on its entering Baghdad.

Qitada, bedridden and dying, was even less inclined to express a wish to his clan that Hassan now should succeed him, and was quite deterred from it when Hassan removed by murder an uncle who was a likely successor. The woeful dirge of wailing women sounded once more in Mecca; but, ruthless and furious, on hearing that his father might now arrest him for murder Hassan hurried to Mecca and after a violent scene smothered him with his bedclothes.[1] The old man was ninety years of age by the year of his death, 1220. Another brother at Yanbu' was sent for by Hassan, and, being a possible rival, was murdered. All other males of the family fled the country. Thus a dynasty which was to last seven and a half centuries began in tragedy.

According to the Sayid al Samarqandi, quoted by the author of *Tandhid al Uqud*,[2] Hassan next killed the Emir of an Iraqi pilgrim caravan and hung up his head from a waterspout in the shrine. The only reason for the punishment was his suspicion that the Iraqi had come to support his brother Rajih.

The following year (1221) the Viceroy of the Yemen, Al Aqsis ibn al Malik al Kamil, alias Al Masoud Yousif, son of the King of Egypt and the last of his line, entered Mecca and attacked Hassan at Batn al Masaa inside the city, so that he fled, and Al Masoud's soldiers occupied and looted it. Al Fasi says that

Al Masoud caused trouble at two pilgrimages by challenging the Iraqi right to put up their flag on Mount Arafat instead of the Yemeni. Moreover he killed doves at the well of Zemzem with a catapult and with his sword hit people on the tendons of their heels saying, "Walk slowly, slowly, the Sultan is sleeping, drunk

[1] Ibn Khaldun's account says that "it is alleged" that he had him poisoned with the aid of a slave serving-girl.
[2] Al Hussaini.

in his palace." You could see the people running from him in crowds but he stopped all the thieving, robbery and mischief with fear of this madness of his.[1]

The lieutenants of the mad Viceroy of the Yemen remained in Mecca for seven years; Salim al Yacout, Al Masoud's freed slave, ruling there for a time, and when al Masoud died, of paralysis,[2] in Mecca in 1228, his lieutenant-governor, Nur-ad-din Umr ibn Ali ibn Rasoul, established his own authority, both in the Yemen and its Arabian dependencies, and succeeded as overlord in his stead.

Hassan had mustered reluctant troops from Yanbu' to attack the Yemeni force in Mecca, but was defeated and went to Iraq to seek the Caliph's support, and after wandering for a time in that country died in Baghdad, being buried in Al Kadhimain, without ever returning to Mecca.

His brother Rajih now made a new bid for the city. Defeated in his first attempt, in 1229, he returned with Rasoul's Yemeni troops and remained at the head of the Government until Egyptian soldiers arrived at the following pilgrimage to reverse the position once more.

In 1232 Al Malik Mansur Umr ibn Ali of the Yemen provided Rajih with a really large force with which to turn out the Egyptians, but he was again obliged to flee before Egyptian forces, which included six hundred horsemen under command of the Emir Jafril, at the time of the next pilgrimage. It was not until 1237, when Nur-ad-din Ali ibn Rasoul, of the Yemen, arrived in person with a thousand horsemen, that their joint attack was finally successful.

Within the year al Malik al Kamil, ruler of Egypt and Syria, died, and the *khutba* was read henceforth in the name of Al Mansur, of the Yemen. Rajih remained in Mecca, ruling as Wali for Al Mansur, until Salah Najm-ad-din al Ayyub, the successor to power in Egypt and Syria, arrived in person with superior forces, in 1240, bringing Shiha ibn Qasim al Hussaini, of Medina, to be installed as his puppet instead of Rajih, who fled once more. The Yemeni troops, however, as now was become customary, returned when the Egyptians retired after the pilgrimage. Nur-ad-din spent the month of

---

[1] *Shifa al Ghuram bi Akhbar al balad al haram.*
[2] Ibn al Fuwti, *Talkhis Majma' al Adab fi al Alqab* (A.D. 1228), under his "news of the year 626."

Ramadhan with his men in Mecca, and at the end of it sent for the courageous Abu Sa'ad al Hassan ibn Ali ibn Qitada, who ruled as his Wali from 1241 for four years, until he was killed by Jammaz ibn Hassan ibn Qitada on his arrival from Damascus with a large force. The troops had been given to the latter on the understanding that he would have the *khutba* read in the name of the Sultan Nasr Salah-ad-din Yusif.

Changes were now even more rapid. Jammaz had not ruled more than two months when his uncle Rajih, by then a very old man, once more arrived in Mecca, and he in turn fled. In 1254 Ghanim ibn Rajih supplanted his father, who had by now been ruler of Mecca no fewer than eight times, until he himself was driven out a few months later by Idris ibn Qitada, who was supported by his nephew, Muhammad Abu Nomay ibn Abi Sa'ad. The latter was to rule, with some short intervals, for nearly fifty years.

Meccans, looking back on the half-century since the death of Qitada, must have ardently regretted his firm and comparatively tranquil rule and deplored the continual change and fights over them since his death.

The turning of Qitada's sons for support to Egypt, the Yemen, or Syria, contrary to his advice, as nationalism had not acquired currency in everyday thought, was no more than an error in an expediency that was customary. Christian Crusaders had joined Mongols or Muslims, against Muslims, or fought among themselves. The Ayyubids, the descendants of Saladin, and the Rasoulis of the Yemen, to whom they had appealed, like the Abbassids of Baghdad, were at least all Muslims.

THE NEAR DESCENDANTS OF QITADA

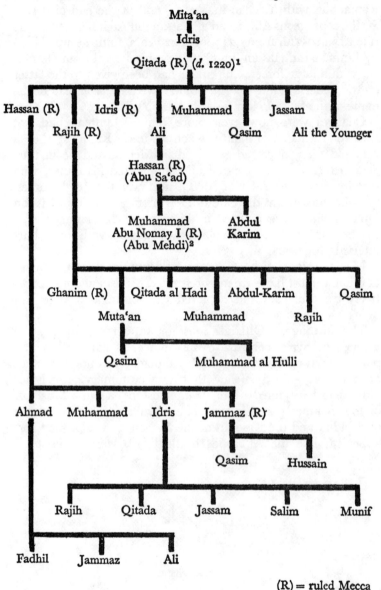

(R) = ruled Mecca

[1] For descent see chronological table at p. 66.
[2] See pedigree at p. 105 and each successive pedigree for continuation to the present day.

Chapter V

MUHAMMAD ABU NOMAY I
AND HIS SONS AND GRANDCHILDREN
(A.D. 1255–1455)

Q ITADA'S ANCESTRAL CASTLE AT YANBU' WAS LONG RE-
tained by his descendants, although they ruled Mecca.
There they retired if affairs went badly for them, while
a brother or some other member of the family would in turn
take over their office of Sherif of Mecca. About 1245 it was
nominally bought from them by the representative of the
Yemen so that "no more Egyptian landings would take place
there." At the same time Abu Sa'ad was appointed Deputy
Commander and adjutant of the Yemeni forces in Mecca,
coming from Yanbu' to take up this office. His mother was an
Abyssinian concubine, and evidently a woman of good humour,
for she is related[1] to have said to him, when he was setting off
for his first fight, "Behave yourself well, my boy. If you prove
to be courageous people will say, 'Look at this descendant of
the Prophet.' If you are not brave they will say that it is
because his mother is a slave."

As a boy of seventeen Muhammad Abu Nomay, who had
been brought up in the same spirit, was in Yanbu' when he
received news that Rajih was mustering a force of the Bani
Hussain of Medina, intending to ride against his father, Abu
Sa'ad, in Mecca. Seven hundred Medinese horsemen, he
heard, had set out under Isa al Haroun, called the Knight of
Knights. So Abu Nomay mounted forty men, all he could
raise, and rode off in haste to warn his father. On the way he
overtook Rajih and Isa with their force, and, catching them
unaware, his attack was completely successful. The Knight
of Knights fled, his turban, becoming unwound, tripped his
horse, and he was forced to turn and was nearly captured.

[1] Quoted by C. Snouck Hurgronje, *Mekka*, vol. i, p. 80.

The author of *Tandhid al Uqud* quotes as his authority for this anecdote Sayid Ja'afar al Hassani, giving some verses of his on it. Abu Sa'ad at once rewarded his youthful but courageous son with the co-rulership.

A few years later Jammaz ibn Hassan ibn Qitada, first cousin of Abu Sa'ad, as told in the preceding chapter, marched on Mecca from Damascus with a large force provided by the Sultan of that city and of Aleppo, one Nasr Salah-ad-din Yusif, great-grandson of Saladin, in whose name he had promised henceforth to read the *khutba*. Having successfully forced his way into Mecca he killed Abu Sa'ad, whose son, Abu Nomay, took refuge in Yanbu', and did not return from there to Mecca until he entered it with his uncle Idris ibn Qitada. He was then at once restored to the co-rulership of Mecca. By 1255 Idris and Abu Nomay were strong enough to rid themselves of the Yemeni Wali, Ibn Birtas. Surrounded, after a fight with them, the Wali bought off himself and his men, and left for the Yemen.

In 1258 news reached Mecca of the fall of Baghdad to Hulagu the Mongol. The Caliph and his sons had been killed and the Mongols were in occupation of the capital. The Persian caravans had already been stopped for eleven seasons, and now, for nine years more, no pilgrims came from Iraq.[1]

In 1269 the remarkable Mameluke King of Egypt, Al Dhahir Rukn-al-Din Baybars Bundukdari, made the pilgrimage with an immense following in great state. It is said that his camp was supplied with fresh vegetables every day by a continuous series of posting camel-riders, and that letters, and even flowers, from Egypt were brought to him daily for most of the journey. He left behind in Mecca a Wali who presented a *kiswa* for the Ka'aba on which was embroidered his master's name.

Baybars, whose prestige was now immense, had been brought from Kiptchak as a boy, and was originally sold at Damascus

[1] Henceforth the *kiswa* (see glossary) for the Ka'aba usually came from Egypt, where later the income of a whole village was especially allotted to it, under a law made by the Sultan Al Nasr Muhammad ibn Kalaoun; they came, however, at least twice from Aleppo, in 1385 and 1394, and are sometimes recorded as coming from elsewhere—for example, in 1403 from Damascus, and in 1404 from Baghdad. See Al Hussaini (*Kitab Tandhid al Uqud al Saniya bi Tamhid al Dawla al Hassaniya*) and Ibn Zaini Dahlan (*Khulasat al Kalam fi Bayan Umara al balad al haram*) under events of the years concerned.

for eight hundred silver pieces, but returned because of a filmy defect in one of his blue eyes. Dusky in complexion, he was tall and of a commanding voice, brave and energetic and ever on the move. Fond of travel, it was said of him, "A day in Egypt, a day in the Hijaz; here in Syria, now in Aleppo." At this time he was approaching the zenith of his career, and, being an exemplary Muslim who had re-established in Egypt the fallen Abbassid Caliphate of Baghdad, he had found time between campaigns to make his pilgrimage. For two hundred years slaves were to rule Egypt, and he was the first of their sovereigns to visit the Hijaz and of that singular line to influence directly the Holy Places of Islam. Sir William Muir says in his *The Mameluke or Slave Dynasty of Egypt*:

> We search in vain for a parallel in the history of the world. Slaves have risen on their masters and become for a moment dominant. But for a community of purchased bondsmen, maintained and multiplied by a continuous stream of slaves bought, like themselves and by themselves, from Asiatic salesmen; such a community ruling at will over a rich country with outlying lands —the slave of to-day the sovereign of to-morrow, the entire governing body of the same slavish race; that such a state of affairs should hold good for two centuries and a half, might at first seem incredible, but it is the simple truth of the Mameluke dynasty during the fourteenth and fifteenth centuries.

Baybars had done his best while in Mecca to patch up an understanding between Idris and his nephew, who had recently been fighting, and gave his Wali similar instructions.

A year later, however, after Baybars' Wali had left for Egypt, Idris and Abu Nomay again quarelled openly, and, each raising forces, met at Khalais, where Idris was wounded and unseated by Abu Nomay, who in person cut off his head and re-entered Mecca in triumph.

According to Al Fuwti, in his book *Talkhis Majma' al Adab fi al Alqab*, a Meccan Sherif, whose name is given variously as Zaid and Abdulla ibn Abi Nomay, fled to Iraq where he was welcomed by Ghazan Mahmud, the ruler (A.D. 1295–1304), and given the village of Al Muhajariya, at Hillah al Sifiyah, the remainder of the library of the famous Mustansariya School, founded by the Abbassids, and other gifts. He stayed there until some quarrels among, and with, the local tribes induced him to return to Mecca, carrying, perhaps, some of the Mustansariya books with him in his camel-bags.

In 1291 came good news for the Muslims. The castle of Akka, or Acre, on the Syrian shore, last stronghold of the Crusaders had fallen. From now onward, as Gibbon has said, "a mournful and solitary silence prevailed along the coast which had so long resounded with the World's Debate." The two-centuries-old menace was at an end, and for another five hundred years no Western armies were to march there.

Abu Nomay ruled, with some short intervals—in 1271, when Jammaz ibn Shiha, of Medina, and Ghanim ibn Idris took over; and in 1288, when again and later they alternated for a time—until he died on October 9, 1301. His son Humaidha used to say of him that he had five good qualities: honour, generosity, patience, courage, and poetry. Piety, it will be remarked, is not mentioned, and the impression received in reading the Arab historians, and in spite of his honorific title of the "Star of Religion," is that he was more soldierly than religious. He was a heavy man, "tactful and solemn,"[1] dark-complexioned, more at home in the desert camps than in a mosque. He ruled the last thirty years alone and independently; a reign, which began turbulently, ended peacefully and to his honour. He had by one account thirty sons, and by another fourteen and twelve daughters.[2] Just before his death at the age of seventy he had abdicated in favour of two of his sons, Humaidha and Rumaitha, and this procedure of abdication in favour of sons was subsequently often followed by his descendants, when their health failed in old age, to ensure the succession they desired. His burial at Al Ma'ala was carried out in a fashion that had already become traditional for the Grand Sherif, the body being carried round the Ka'aba seven times in the way prescribed for living pilgrims. A cupola was built over his tomb in the cemetery, which was to become the burial-place in Mecca of the Sherifs.

In the same year, 1301, Bibrus Jashankir, ruler of Kerak, came to Mecca for the pilgrimage, and Abu Ghaith, another

---

[1] Al Hussaini, *Kitab Tandhid al Uqud al Saniya bi Tamhid al Dawla al Hassaniya*.
[2] Ibn Saud of Arabia has well over thirty sons. The number is not unusual up to this day for Arabian rulers and sheikhs.

son of Abu Nomay, complained to him of his brother's rule. He supported Abu Ghaith and Ataifa, another of Abi Nomay's sons, persuading the Rulers, Humaidha and Rumaitha, with a show of force, to leave Mecca with him. They soon, however, managed to escape, returning to Mecca in 1303.[1] The four brothers constantly quarrelled both with each other and with their own co-ruler. The clearest accounts of the frequent and confusing changes in the rulership in the next decade are given by Al Fasi and Ibn Khaldun.

Humaidha quarrelled with Rumaitha, the stronger-willed of the two brothers, and fled to Iraq to take refuge with the Mongol ruler and seek his aid in return for a promise to have his name read at the *khutba* prayers.

Already, in 1314, in one of the quarrels between the brothers, Humaidha had killed Abu Ghaith.[2] Ibn Zaini Dahlan[3] says that he was murdered by Humaidha, who concealed the body, taking it to his house, and then invited his brothers to a meal. When they arrived a slave with drawn sword came to stand behind each of them, while their brother, Abu Ghaith, was carried in, cooked whole. Humaidha had intended to frighten them, and he was so successful that from that day onward they planned his death. Reactions from that meal, if it is a true story, seem a likely reason for his flight to the Mongols in Iraq, which therefore may have closely followed it.

About 1318 Humaidha returned from Iraq with Shiah and Mongol support, and removed Rumaitha. Humaidha at once, as promised, changed the name in the reading of the *khutba* from that of Al Nasr of Egypt to Abu Said Khurbandr, the Mongol, of Baghdad. Al Nasr, outraged, dispatched a force to arrest Humaidha, who, forewarned, escaped from it, but was killed three years later, in 1320, at Wadi Nakhla, by a Turkish slave in the pay of the Egyptian ruler, with whom he hoped to curry favour. Meanwhile Ataifa, who had been in Egypt, took over the rulership, and with him Rumaitha once more became co-ruler.

It was at this time that Abu Said, the Mongol, in his effort to demonstrate his paramountcy at Mecca sent a golden *mahmal*

---

[1] Ibn Zaini Dahlan, *Al Jadawil al Mardhiya.*

[2] Ibn Khaldun, however, says that he was killed in a fight at Wadi al Marr (*Kitab al 'ibar wa diwan al mubtada wa al khabar fi ayyam al Arab wa al barbar*, vol. iv).

[3] In his *Al Jadawil al Mardhiya.*

at a cost of no less than 250,000 dinars, but Al Nasr of Egypt regained his own popularity in the holy places on supplying the people of Mecca and Medina with corn during famine.

In Rumaitha's reign the Negro Emperor Mansa Musa, of Mandingo, reached Mecca for the pilgrimage with a great train, said to number 15,000, and with many sacks of gold. His pilgrimage was long remembered by those who witnessed it.

In 1325 the Negro Emperor reached Mecca for his pilgrimage. The splendid and spectacular scale on which it was conducted caused such a sensation that the name of the Emperor quickly became familiar throughout the civilized world. He had set out across the desert in 1324, the seventeenth year of his reign, accompanied by thousands of followers. He rode on horseback, preceded by five hundred powerful slaves, each carrying a staff of gold weighing 500 mithkals, or about six pounds. In his baggage train of camels were a hundred loads of gold, each weighing three kantars, or about 300 pounds. The magnificent caravan passed through Walata and Tuat and thence to Cairo, bound for Mecca. Musa's piety and open-handed generosity and the fine clothes and good behaviour of his black followers quickly made a favourable impression. His own pale complexion, usually described as red or yellow, gave the Negro monarch a distinctive appearance, which contributed to the sensation he caused. The sole object of his journey was the performance of a religious duty and, in spite of the pomp with which it was carried out, it seems to have been free of political motives. Only with the greatest difficulty was he persuaded to interrupt his spiritual exercises in order to pay a formal visit to the Sultan of Egypt. When the time came to continue the journey to Mecca, the Sultan made elaborate arrangements to ensure the utmost comfort for the Negro potentate.

Al Umari, who was in Cairo twelve years after Mansa Musa had left it on his homeward journey, found the inhabitants still loud in their praises. His popularity was largely owing to a lavish distribution of gold and because the masses had benefited from the highly profitable trade which they had done with his followers, simple folk who would readily pay five dinars for a garment worth only one. Fine clothes and slaves . . . appealed to the Negroes most, and these commodities formed the bulk of their purchases. In consequence of Mansa Musa's visit so much gold came into circulation that its value in Egypt fell considerably and even in Al Umari's time the price had not recovered.

Mansa Musa did not confine to Cairo this prodigal display of wealth. In the Holy Cities of Hijaz he was even more generous. It is not astonishing to learn that by the time he had returned to Cairo he had come nearly to an end of his immediate resources.

On his homeward journey he was accompanied by a poet of Granada, generally known as Al Sahali, to whom he had become attached in Mecca. While he was still in the desert Mansa Musa heard of the capture of Gao, the Songhai capital of the Middle Niger, by Sagmandia, one of his generals. The news of this enormous gain of territory caused Mansa Musa to visit Gao on his way home, making an impressive entry into that city and receiving in person the submission of the Songhai king.[1]

So ended the pilgrimage to Mecca of the pious, pale-faced, and wealthy Emperor of Middle Africa.

Another distinguished visitor at this time was the observant and widely travelled Ibn Batouta. His account[2] of Mecca is as follows:

The title of Emir of Mecca was held by two brother Sherifs at the time of my arrival there, "Asad-ad-Din," or the "lion" of religion, Rumaitha, and "Saif-ad-Din," or the "sword" of religion, Ataifa, who were sons of Abu Nomay, ibn Abi Sa'ad ibn Ali ibn Qitada, the Hassanite. Rumaitha was the elder, but he insisted on Ataifa being named first in the prayers because of his widespread reputation for justice. The residence of Ataifa is to the right of Marwa and that of Rumaitha in the convent of Al Sharabi, near the Gate of the Bani Shayba. Drums are lengthily beaten every morning at the doors of the two Emirs.

The charity of the Meccans, their generosity and good manners are distinguished. They give the poor to eat before they begin a feast, inviting them politely and serving them themselves. Meccans often give half or a third of their bread away.

They are particularly cleanly dressed, usually in white. The men make a very great use of heavy perfumes, of collyrium darkening round the eyes and toothpicks of a local green wood.[3]

---

[1] E. W. Bovill, *Caravans of the Old Sahara, an Introduction to the History of the Western Sudan*, p. 71 *et seq.*

[2] C. Defremery and B. A. Sanguinette, *Voyages d'ibn Batoutah.*

[3] These toothpicks are still in use and favour. King Ibn Saud himself employs them and offers them to his favoured guests. The bedouin and soldiers use collyrium, 'kohl.' Amber, the basis of their scents, is found in the Persian Gulf.

The women are beautiful. They also use greatly scents and unguents, to a point when some of them go without food in order to be able to afford them. They go round the mosque on Thursday nights, when their perfumes fill the sanctuary and remain long after they have passed.

There was in Mecca one Hassan the "Barbaresque," the mad. Formerly sane, he was the servant of Najm-al-Din of Isfahan, but he had been bewitched by a fakir. He drank, ate, and was clothed at the expense of the people, who regarded him as a great benediction. The Emir Saif-al-din al-Mulki took him away with him to Egypt.

At the Friday sermon when the preacher enters he is dressed entirely in black, with a turban and a *thailasan* [a muslin veil hanging from the turban or shoulders down the back] which is also black, furnished by the Malik al Nasr of Egypt. He walks slowly, with dignity, between two black flags carried by two muezzins. He is preceded by one of the chamberlains of the shrine holding the *farka'ah*, a stick having at the end of it a thin lanyard, which he cracks with a high, thin note, as a sign, heard by those in and outside the shrine, that the preacher is entering. He goes to kiss the Black Stone. Near him is the muezzin of Zemzem, who is the senior muezzin. He too is dressed in black, carrying a sword on his shoulder. The two standards are placed on either side of the pulpit, and as he is about to mount the steps the muezzin gives him the sword, with which he strikes the first step. He thus draws the attention of the congregation, and he does the same with the other steps. He strikes a fourth time at the top. He makes a prayer in a low voice, facing the Ka'aba, and then turns to the public, bowing to his right and to his left, and the congregation returns him his salute. He then sits and all the muezzins give the call to prayer, at the same time, from the dome of Zemzem.

Then he prays for Muhammad the Prophet of God many times, for his family, for the Prophet's uncles Hamza and Abbas, his grandsons Hassan and Hussain, their mother and for Khadija, the prophet's wife, for Al Malik al Nasr of Egypt, for the Sultan, the champion of Islam, Nur-al-din Ali, son of the Sultan Yusif ibn Ali ibn Rasoul and for the two lords, the Sherifs, descendants of Hassan, Emirs of Mecca, and for the Sultan of Iraq, but not for the latter recently. He prays again after his sermon and then returns whence he came; and the order of his going is as before, but reversed.

On the first day of the month the Emir of Mecca goes out ceremoniously, surrounded by his officers. He is dressed in white, with a turban and a large sword. He exhibits great calm and dignity. He goes to the shrine where he makes a prayer and two genuflexions, kisses the Black Stone, and does the seven circuits. As soon as he finishes the chief muezzin, of Zemzem, prays for him and congratulates him in a loud voice on the beginning of the new month. After which he recites a poem in praise of him and of his ancestors. The Emir then again makes his genuflexions and returns. He does the same thing every time before he travels, or when he returns from travel.

At the beginning of the month of Rejeb, the Emir orders the beating of drums and loud sounding of trumpets. The first day he goes out, mounted magnificently, accompanied by the people, horsed or on foot and all armed. The cavaliers ride in circles and the footmen attack each other throwing their javelins in the air. They go out to a place of tourney, and then return to the shrine. Every one is dressed in their best clothes for the holiday, the Emir being accompanied by his family, his officers, and his Negro halberdiers. The whole month is consecrated to good works, especially the first day, the 15th, and the 27th.

As the neighbouring highland tribes, including the Zahran and Ghamid, came into Mecca for the celebrations and brought them many provisions, prices, I noticed, fell during Rejeb.

Ibn Batouta's description thus confirms that of Ibn Jubair. In his second account, written during another visit, Ibn Batouta said:

In that year [A.D. 1328–29] there was a civil disturbance in Mecca, between the Emir Ataifa and Aidamour, commander of the Sultan of Egypt's guards.

A certain Yemeni merchant was robbed and complained to Aidamour, who said to Mubarak, son of the Emir, "Get rid of these robbers." He answered, "I know of none. How can I be rid of them? In any case the Yemenis are under us and you have no right over them. If something has been stolen from an Egyptian or a Syrian let me know and make your claim." Aidamour was furious and replied in heat, striking Mubarak, so that he fell down. Fighting began at once. Among those killed by the Turks was a woman said to be inciting the Meccans to fight. The judge, the prelates, and others carrying their Korans before them gradually restored peace. Malik al Nasr, hearing of this, was sad, and sent some of his troops to Mecca. So Ataifa and his son fled and, Rumaitha and his sons went to Wadi Nakhla. When the troops arrived Rumaitha sent an envoy to

ask for a safe conduct, which was granted him. He was honoured
and the troops returned to Egypt, for Malik al Nasr was a sweet
and humane man.

Incidentally Ibn Batouta complains that the heat in Mecca
was so great that the stones in the courtyard of the Temple
burnt his feet.

In the following year the Iraqi pilgrims from Baghdad
brought with them an elephant sent by Abu Said Khurbandr,
the "Tartar King." They took him with them wherever they
went, even making him do the pilgrimage and kneel, taking
him up to the Ka'aba and to Medina. None knew the intention
of the Tartar in sending this elephant on the pilgrimage. From
Iraq up to his death in the gateway of Medina his expenses
were 30,000 dirhems.[1]

Egyptian influence was now increasing in the Hijaz. There
were quarrels among the two surviving brothers who ruled
Mecca, arrests by the Egyptians, and releases, with hardly an
interruption. At one moment both Ataifa and Rumaitha were
ordered to visit Malik al Nasr in Egypt, where he detained
Ataifa, who died in prison there in 1343, allowing Rumaitha
to return to rule, assisted for a time by his son Ahmad. The
Egyptian ruler, tired of the quarrels in Mecca and of the
attempts to increase Yemeni influence there in order to
counter his own power, at this time contemplated the
complete effacement of the Sherifs, but was dissuaded by the
Ulama in Egypt from such a drastic step, likely, such was
the prestige of the Sherifian family as descendants of the
Prophet, to cause serious disturbances among the Muslim
faithful, his subjects.

At this time Ahmad was sent by his father, Rumaitha, on an
expedition across Nejd, occupying Hilla, in Iraq, where the
Ilkhan Mongol rule was dissolving. On his departure he was
warned by his father against ogres in that country, and when
he was killed there Rumaitha said at once that he had known
that he would come to harm in Iraq.[2] The Iraqi pilgrims, fearing Rumaitha's vengeance, and because of the disorders in
Mesopotamia and lack of security in the Iraqi desert consequent
on the collapse of the Mongol rule, ceased to come for eleven years,

---

[1] Al Fasi, *Shifa al Ghuram bi akhbar al balad al haram.*
[2] Al Hussaini, the author of *Tandhid al Uqud*, who quotes as his source "Umdat
al Talib."

until the reign of Rumaitha's son Ajlan, to whom in 1344, two years before his death, he had handed over his authority.

The new ruler, styled the "Glory of Religion," and nick-named the "Swift," who was thirty-seven when he succeeded, lived to be seventy, ruling, with intervals, for some twenty-five years. During his reign the influence of the rulers of Iraq was in abeyance and that of the Yemen had come to an end, so that the Egyptian Mamelukes were alone and increasingly dominant.

Rumaitha, his father, had already found it politic to make Thaqaba, another of his sons, co-ruler with Ajlan, but almost at once, in 1346, the Sultan of Egypt imposed upon them Sanad, one more son of Rumaitha, as a third partner.

In 1350 the Egyptians and the followers of the Ruler of Mecca joined in an attack upon the King of the Yemen, Mujahid Ali, while he was at Muna making his pilgrimage. His camp was completely looted and he himself arrested and taken to Egypt. He was later sent back under escort to the Yemen, but on reaching Yanbu' was rearrested for out-spokenness about his treatment by the Egyptians, and taken to Kerak for further imprisonment, whence eventually he was sent, after a visit to Jerusalem, via Aidhab (the port opposite Jedda) to the Yemen.

In 1358 the ruler of Egypt sent with the pilgrims a force under Al Emir Jarkatmur of Mardin, who brought with him Muhammad ibn Ataifa as the new Sherif. On arrival in Mecca he sent for Sanad, who was with his brothers in the Yemen, to be a co-ruler with Muhammad, and Sanad brought with him his brother Mughaimis, Ajlan being instructed to visit Egypt, where he was detained. A few months later the people of Mecca rose and attacked Sanad and the Egyptian soldiers. Muhammad had remained neutral, but when the Egyptian force left with the returning pilgrimage he found it expedient to follow it.

Ajlan now came back to rule once more, and Sanad fled to the Yemen, Mughaimis being killed in a fight between the Sherifs, in which the Egyptians were involved, in 1359. Thaqaba, who had lived a retired life outside Mecca for some years, now returned and restored order, obtaining a promise from the Egyptian soldiers that they would all leave Mecca and follow up the pilgrims to Yanbu'.

In 1360 Ahmad joined his father, Ajlan, in the rulership, being given a quarter of the revenues and ruling for twenty-five years. In the last fifteen years of his reign Ajlan undertook the building of several forts, water-cisterns, almshouses, and schools. He brought to an end the taxing of the pilgrims by the slaves of Mecca, compensating the latter from his own treasury. It is related that he owned a particularly large number of Negroes, horses, and sets of armour. From 1359 up to 1369 he allowed the name of the Mongol Sultan to be read in the *khutba* prayers, the Sultan sending him an annual subsidy until that year. On the other hand, probably instigated by the Egyptians, he persecuted the Zaidite Yemenis in Mecca. A muezzin who favoured them was flogged until he died, and their leading men were tied up to posts and whipped with leather thongs. The Sherifs themselves had quietly, almost secretly, subscribed to the Shafite rite of Islam, from the political point of view the then dominating rite in the Moslem countries. Ajlan died at Judaida, in the Wadi al Marr, in 1375, and was buried at Al Ma'ala after the established form of ceremonial burial.

Ahmad, the "Meteor of Religion," successfully following his father's lead, giving Mecca a peaceful reign, soon became so powerful that Egypt began to fear him. Several times he was asked to visit that country, but each time made excuses. Towards the end of his reign, fearing perhaps his relatives or the Egyptians, he habitually wore chain-mail, and for that reason—pilgrims being obliged to strip and wear only the 'Ihram' loincloth—he did not make the pilgrimage. His fears were justified, as he was poisoned in 1386,[1] and his son Muhammad was stabbed a hundred days later by an unknown man who escaped through the crowd of pilgrims at Muna.[2] The boy was only twenty. It was generally believed that his death was plotted by the Emir of the Egyptian pilgrims at the instigation of his cousin, a nephew of Ajlan, Anan ibn

---

[1] Ibn Khaldun says that he died in bed (*Kitab al 'ibar wa diwan al mubtada wa al Khabar fi ayyam al Arab wa al barbar*, vol. v, p. 480, *et seq.*).
[2] Ibn Khaldun says that he was stabbed from behind as he leant forward to kiss the *mahmal* on its arrival from Egypt, and was left writhing where he fell.

Mughaimis. In any case he was immediately succeeded by Anan, who had come with the Egyptian pilgrims, his appointment having been approved while he was in Egypt by the ruler, Barquq, the first of the new Burji Mameluke dynasty. He was made to accept as co-rulers Ahmad ibn Thaqaba and Aqil ibn Mubarak ibn Rumaitha. Meanwhile Kubaish collected supporters from the tribes and attacked him, but was himself killed in one of the fights with Anan's followers. The following year, in 1387, Barquq approved the deposition of Anan and the succession of Ali, still a boy, another of Ajlan's sons; so Anan, a failure, returned to Egypt, where he died in 1401.

Ali[1] ruled for seven years, when he was killed by some of his officers, being replaced, for one year, by Muhammad ibn Ajlan, acting on behalf of Hassan ibn Ajlan, who was away in Egypt. In that year Timurlane began his invasion of the West, entering Baghdad in 1394; so that the pilgrimage from Iraq again failed to come for several years.

As soon as Hassan ibn Ajlan arrived in Mecca from Egypt he appointed his son Barakat to be his co-ruler. Two years later he recommended his son Ahmad to the Egyptian Sultan, who approved his co-rulership and ordered that Hassan himself should be styled "Deputy of the Sultan" for the whole of the Hijaz, and that his two sons be the rulers of Mecca. He built almshouses for men and women, and was widely praised for his clement rule.

In 1415, for a reason that is unexplained, but probably owing to the intrigues of his relatives or of the Hussainite of Medina at the Egyptian Court, Hassan and his sons were supplanted by Rumaitha ibn Muhammad, for a year, at the end of which they were reinstalled, Hassan having sent his son Barakat to plead with the Sultan of Egypt for his renewed support. In 1423 the same thing occurred. There was an interval of a year, when they were replaced by Ali ibn Anan ibn Mughaimis, but again reinstalled. Hassan died in Egypt, while visiting the Sultan, Ashraf Saif-el-Din Barsbay, in 1425, at the age of fifty-four and was succeeded by his son Barakat. Hassan had seen his father ruling in complete independence, in the time of the Bahri Mameluke Dynasty, but himself had

---

[1] Ali was still in office when Ibn Khaldun wrote.

felt the weight of Egypt's influence increase under the new Burji Mameluke dynasty, and had been forced to yield to it. He had ruled for sixteen years, during which time he had built up a great fortune and had acquired a much admired reputation for piety and literary ability.

THE NEAR DESCENDANTS OF ABU NOMAY I

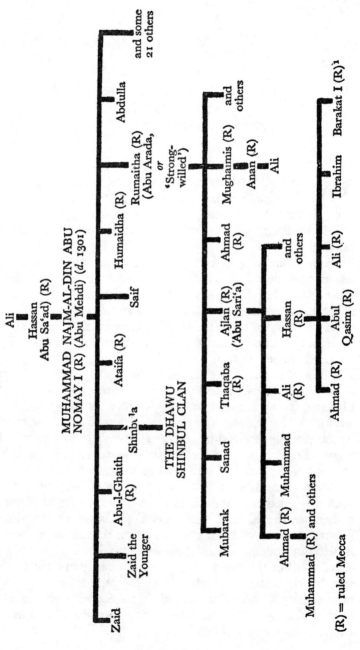

(R) = ruled Mecca

[1] See pedigree at p. 112.

Chapter VI

BARAKAT I,
HIS BROTHERS, AND HIS SON
(A.D. 1425–98)

WITH SOME SHORT INTERVALS WHEN HIS BROTHERS ACTED for him, Barakat ibn Hassan ruled from the death of his father in 1425 until his death in 1455. Like his father, he was famous for his literary knowledge and poetical prowess, and when he was in Egypt, in 1447, the Sultan, Zahir Saif-al-Din Jukmuk, personally invited the nobles and most of the distinguished literary men in Cairo to meet him. His fame soon became so high that numerous students came daily to learn from him. During his reign he repaired the water-point of Ain Hunain and the mosque there, and numerous almshouses in Mecca itself were built or repaired, some of them being so well built, according to Al Hussaini, that they were still in use in the eighteenth century.

So Barakat was generally and widely revered, not only for his integrity and intellectual ability, but for piety and good works. An early, if not the first, mention of a *khila'*, or robe of honour, being received by the Sherif from Egypt occurs in his reign. From this time onward it began to signify a public warrant of deputed authority, without which the Sherif would hardly be considered as fully competent. A *kiswa* or *khila'* in itself is a gift denoting nothing more than a desire to please or to honour, the Ka'aba itself receiving a *kiswa*, or covering of honour, and a ruling Sherif could affirm that he might receive it without having thereby placed himself in a position of vassalage; but the fact that it was customarily and for so long sent by the ruler in Baghdad, in Egypt, or Constantinople immediately on accession, and always accepted, came to mean in time that without this investiture something of a Sherif of Mecca's authority was lacking.

Barakat's attitude towards the rulers of Egypt is described as having been "artfully tactful." It was, however, in his reign, under pretence of its being an escort for engineers engaged on repairs to the Holy Place, that a regular garrison of fifty cavalrymen was sent from Egypt to Mecca, and their commanders, while executing the Sherif's orders, in reality achieved an especial and independent position owing to the presence of their picked squadron and because of their ability to report independently to Egypt on the situation in Mecca. Their commander was sometimes called "Emir of the Turks in Mecca" or even "Inspector of the Holy Places," and when later the Ottomans succeeded to this system he was known as the Sanjak of Mecca and was accorded high rank at the Sultan's court. In 1455 Barakat used the Egyptian political representative at Jedda as a channel of communication in reporting his choice of a successor to himself, and so the Egyptian agents gradually acquired a position somewhat similar, although more complicated and variable, to that of the British agents at the mediatized Indian Courts in the nineteenth and early twentieth centuries. It was thus under Barakat that the presence of the Walis, or agents, became regularly accepted, if not always approved, by the Sherifs. During the rule of his father, Hassan, the revenue system had become more or less stabilized, and he inherited and continued various customs that endured for many centuries.

It was established, for example, by his reign that one-quarter of the value of wrecked ships went to the ruling Sherif, and likewise a quarter of all gifts sent or brought from abroad "for the people of Mecca" and one-tenth of all imported goods, including a tenth of the cargo of all Indian ships destined for Jedda.

From the middle of the fifteenth century a proportion of the revenue of the Jedda custom was allotted to the Egyptian, or, later, Ottoman, Pasha of that place. The amount varied from time to time between a quarter and a half of the whole. If a foreigner died in Mecca without heirs his fortune went to the Sherif. The zakka, or poll-tax, collected from the bedouin, if they were not too poor, also went to the Sherif. Of all his total income from these public sources a half was usually allotted by him for distribution to other leading members of the Sherifian families.

In time various other taxes were imposed on pilgrims, either on landing at Jedda or on the road into Mecca. Furthermore, persons wishing to embellish the Temple had to obtain a permit, first from the Caliph and then from the Sherif, and it was customary to give the Sherif at the time an amount sometimes as much as the cost of the work, and always considerable.

As his Chief Secretary, or Wezir, charged in particular with financial matters, the Sherif usually chose a foreigner. The customs officers, too, were usually either foreigners or members of the Sherif's family. Governors of the small towns and the districts were often bedouin chiefs or sherifs. The 'lance-men,' or bodyguard, were generally freed-men, who themselves had slaves trained as soldiers. The Sherif had a corps of Negroes and in addition he had a body of mercenaries, or professional soldiers—mostly from South Arabia, but some of them non-Arab—and he could call upon the bedouin tribes, whom he subsidized annually for this purpose. It is recorded that whenever, at this time, news was brought by a *mubashshir*, or herald of good news, he went from house to house of the Sherifs and at each received a robe of honour and all the Sherifs hoisted flags on their houses. In general the mode of living of the Sherifs was still modest. A great turban was the only sign of a difference between the ruling Sherif and his people, except on occasions of ceremony, when he wore the wide-sleeved, gold-embroidered coat-of-honour. In spite of his position the Ruler was always addressed in simple and direct fashion by his people, and in particular by the bedouin, a custom they have maintained until this day.

When the Sherif Barakat died, at Wadi al Abar, being buried at Al Ma'ala in Mecca his son Muhammad was away in the Yemen, looking after his father's estates, but he at once returned to take over the rule, having the recommendation and support of Jani Beg, representative in the Hijaz of the Egyptian Sultan. In 1447,[1] a few years before Barakat's death, a Grand Wezir of the Ottoman Sultan Murad II, had made the pilgrimage in great splendour, without the significance of the display being gauged as a portent in Mecca, but as Barakat was dying the astonishing news of the fall of Constantinople

[1] C. Snouck Hurgronje, *Mekka*, vol. i, p. 99.

to the Turks was received[1]; the great Christian capital, which had resisted the spirited onslaught of the early Muslim troops and the weightiest attacks of the Abbassids, had at last fallen to the more earthy and lusty Ottomans.

Muhammad ibn Barakat, like his father, continued the repair of buildings in and about the shrine and near Mecca. He rebuilt the little mosque of Maimuna, near Mecca, where the twelfth wife of the Prophet was married and had sentimentally asked to be buried, placing a domed roof, supported by four pillars, over her grave, which remained standing until destroyed by the Wahhābi Puritans in the nineteenth century.

In 1467 Sultan Kaitbey of Egypt, who was to be a constant benefactor of Mecca, abolished the excise duties, compensating the town by a subsidy, and ordering that an inscription to that effect be carved on a pillar in the Temple. Repairs were made to the quarters reserved for the Egyptian pilgrims, to their mosque and its minarets, and a new house built for the Emir of the Egyptian pilgrims. The Muzdalifa mosque was newly lime-washed, the well at Aarfat cleaned, and the water-channels from Jebel Rahma to Wadi Na'aman, which had not run for 160 years, were reopened. Every year some similar work was undertaken, ordered from Egypt. The interior of the Ka'aba was roofed with marble by order of Kaitbey in 1476 and the following year four schools, one for each of the main rites of Islam, and a new almshouse were ordered.

Meanwhile, in 1472, the Iraqi pilgrims had been refused permission to make their pilgrimage by the Emir of the Egyptian pilgrims. Their Emir was arrested and the pilgrims forcibly prevented from entering Mecca, while the *mahmal* from Iraq, in spite of offers of great sums to Meccan charity, was refused in 1476.

The following year for an unexplained reason the Sherif raided Jizan, on the Red Sea coast on the borders of the Yemen, burnt it, and destroyed the fort. For long Jizan was a contested frontier town, usually under the Sherif; its revenue from the salt-mine of Zuhara being considerable. In the early nineteenth century the Sherif's revenue from Jizan was

---

[1] Constantinople fell on May 29, 1453. From this point in this book the Turkish name Istanbul has been used for old Byzantium.

15,000 thalers from its customs and 10,000 from the salt-mine.[1] It is now within the Hijaz province of Saudi Arabia.
In 1479 Kaitbey came in person as a pilgrim. Kaitbey, a Circassian, had been freed by Sultan Jukmuk, who had bought him as a boy for fifty dinars. An accomplished spearman and unusually intelligent, he had been his favourite, and from that position, in his turn, risen to the rulership. He was accompanied to Mecca by a prodigious number of slaves and almost his whole court, which is said to have been characterized by "a rude and versatile barbarity."[3]

Saying that he had dreamed that he would wash the interior of the Ka'aba himself, he did so ceremonially, with all the Ulama and the Keeper of the Keys, the Sheikh Umr ibn Rajib al Shaybi, in attendance. On leaving the Hijaz Kaitbey remitted to the Sherif one-tenth of the dues from the Yemeni pilgrims—that is, surrendered to him his own half-share of a tenth. The relations of the two men were such that the Sherif Muhammad named one of his sons after him. Kaitbey continued his benefaction of the Holy Cities in the Hijaz, and the following year, on hearing that the Prophet's mosque at Medina had been struck by lightning and burnt to the ground, he wept and ordered its rebuilding at his personal expense.

At this time, towards the end of Muhammad's reign, came news of the rising power of Shah Ismail Safawi, the Persian, who was to contend with the Ottoman Empire and add to the political problems of the Sherifs.

The Sherif Muhammad, who died in 1495, had sixteen surviving sons and was succeeded by one of them, Barakat, who had as a child studied in Egypt, so that his reputation for learning and piety, like that of his father and grandfather, was already high before he succeeded.[3]

If the reigns of Barakat ibn Hassan and his son were marked by ever stronger political influence from Egypt, they nevertheless enhanced the spiritual prestige of the Sherif and brought peace to Mecca. In them, and in their successor Barakat ibn Muhammad, or Barakat II, the prestige and almost sacrosant position of the Sherifs as Emirs of Mecca was fully established.

[1] C. Didier, *Séjour chez le grand-chérif de la Mecque*, p. 106, *et seq.*
[2] Sir William Muir, *The Mameluke or Slave Dynasty of Egypt*.
[3] Al Hussaini gives details, quoting as his authority *Ghayat al Maram bi akhbar balad al haram*, by Abdul Aziz ibn Fahad al Hashimi.

If for momentary political reasons individual Sherifs were
sometimes ill-treated by the neighbouring emperor of the day
or by their own relatives the family continued to rule, respected
and revered by the Muslim world.

THE NEAR DESCENDANTS OF BARAKAT I

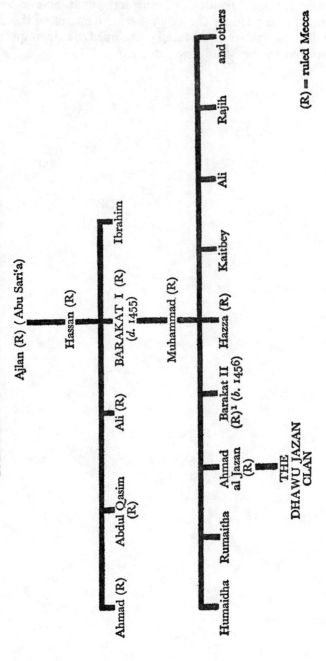

Ajlan (R) (Abu Sari'a)
|
Hassan (R)
|
Ahmad (R) — Abdul Qasim (R) — Ali (R) — BARAKAT I (R) (d. 1455) — Ibrahim
|
Muhammad (R)
|
Humaidha — Rumaitha — Ahmad al Jazan (R) — Barakat II (R)[1] (b. 1456) — Hazza (R) — Kaitbey — Ali — Rajih — and others
|
THE DHAWU JAZAN CLAN

(R) = ruled Mecca

[1] See pedigree at p. 127.

Chapter VII

BARAKAT II

(A.D. 1495–1524)

A S A CHILD BARAKAT IBN MUHAMMAD IBN BARAKAT, KNOWN
as Barakat II, had been sent to school to Egypt, accompanied by the judge Ibrahim al Dhuwhairi. In the list
of forty religious teachers whom he frequented, given by Al
Hussaini, are the names of several women, from which it
would seem that female teachers were then common in Egypt.
He made exceptional progress in his theological studies, and
was early accepted as an Alim.[1]

When his father died the Sultan of Egypt, Muhammad ibn
Kaitbey, approved his accession, but he soon found himself
in difficulty with his brothers Hazza and Ahmad al Jazan.
His reign began in some uncertainty, but ended peacefully,
his character being much affected, it would seem, by a late
but fortunate marriage.

Although he at once strove to make peace with his unruly
brothers, they finally succeeded in deposing him, looting his
horses to prevent a counter-attack. The mild and religious
Barakat placidly waited in Jedda until the next pilgrimage
season, when he returned to Mecca with the Egyptian pilgrim
escort. Hazza was then sent to live in exile at Yanbu'; but, in
spite of promises of good behaviour, raised a force and advanced
on Mecca again, defeating Barakat at Al Mu'ashar, whence
the Sherif fled to Lith, living there until he heard of Hazza's
death. Hazza's brother, Ahmad al Jazan, then tried to forestall his return, but Barakat entered Mecca just in time and
received a *khila'* and a letter of sympathy from the Sultan
of Egypt.

He accompanied the returning pilgrimage to Yanbu', because Ahmad al Jazan had looted the Damascus pilgrims, and

[1] See glossary.

a punitive expedition against Ahmad was planned; but both his own and the Emir of the pilgrims' forces were defeated before they were ready to take the field in strength, the Sherif's son Ibrahim being captured. Ahmad al Jazan, thus encouraged, raised an even larger force with which to take Mecca itself, and Barakat, ill and outnumbered, retired before him to the Yemen, where, in turn collecting a force, he once more tried to take Mecca, but was hotly pursued by Al Jazan, whom however, he managed to mislead. Moving swiftly and finally eluding him altogether, he quickly doubled back and entered Mecca, where the whole city welcomed him. Thus, when Al Jazan reached the outskirts of the city he found the Meccans to a man prepared to resist him, and he was easily driven off. Camping at Bir Shama, he sent to Yanbu' and elsewhere for reinforcements, and for the sixth time advanced on Mecca and, although Barakat's men were entrenched, succeeded in forcing an entry. So once more Barakat fled to the Yemen until, Egyptian soldiers arriving at Jedda, Al Jazan hurriedly vacated the city.

Barakat's rule now seemed to be at long last established, but when he returned and hastened to meet the commander of the welcome Egyptian troops, Al Maqarr al Ashraf Titub, he was arrested by him and taken to Egypt via Yanbu' in chains; for at Yanbu' Titub had reached an agreement with Al Jazan, for a very large sum of money, to support his own rule in Mecca. The mild and pious Barakat arriving in Cairo in chains, both the Sultan, Al Ghouri, and his people were astonished and extremely displeased, and he was at once released and a handsome compensation given to him. It was Titub, the corrupt Egyptian commander, who now found himself in difficulties and dangerously unpopular with the court and people, while Barakat was everywhere welcomed in the houses of the notables and Ulama[1] of Cairo. He stayed there until 1503, when, hearing of the assassination of Al Jazan in Mecca, he took French leave and once more set out for the Hijaz. On the way he met a messenger, Sayid Batfa al Hussaini, coming from his brother Humaidha to the Sultan, and at once, with belated decisiveness, had him killed, confiscating his presents for the Sultan.

---

[1] Plural of Alim.

Unknown to the Government in Egypt, the Egyptian soldiers in Mecca, after assassinating Al Jazan, during the encirclement of the Ka'aba had proclaimed Humaidha, who was now, on the approach of Barakat, preparing to flee.[1] Meanwhile Barakat, wishing to visit Medina and to raise the Zubaid tribes en route for Mecca, struck eastward from Yanbu', and on his way spent a night with one Humaidan ibn Shaman al Hussaini. It so happened that at the time one of the Hussaini family had asked for the hand of Humaidan's daughter Ghubaiya, and the marriage preparations were already under way. Barakat, however, asked for the girl and the father and bridegroom agreed. It was by her that Barakat had his son Abu Nomay, who was born on May 3, 1505. Barakat used to pat his hand on the boy's head and say, "You are my lucky star. I was always unlucky until you were born." He was fifty-three when his child was born, and his fortunes and his character, it seems, began to change. On his arrival in Mecca Barakat took over the government of the whole Hijaz, and his brother Kaitbey became Wali of Mecca itself with Barakat's son Ali as his co-ruler.

It was at this period that Ludovico Varthema, of Bologna in Italy, visited Mecca. He wrote:[2]

At length we arrived at Mecca, and there was a very great war, one brother with another, for there are four brothers, and they fought to be Lords of Mecca. . . .

Under "The Chapter showing how Mecca is constructed, and why the Moors go to Mecca," he writes:

We will now speak of the very noble city of Mecca, what it is, its state, and who governs it. The city is most beautiful, and is very well inhabited, and contains about 6000 families. The houses are extremely good, like our own, and there are houses worth three or four thousand ducats each. This city is not surrounded by walls, for the walls of the said city are mountains, and it has four entrances. A quarter of a mile distant from the city we found a hillside where there was a road cut by human labour. And then we descended into the valley. The governor

---

[1] Ibn Zaini Dahlan says that Al Jazan was killed by some "Rumiin" (Byzantinians or Europeans) in 1502, but Al Dhuhairi says that he was killed by "Circassian Turks"; so "Egyptian soldiers" is more likely to be accurate.

[2] *Travels in Egypt, Syria, Arabia Deserta and Arabia Felix, Persia, etc., A.D. 1503 to 1508*, pp. 31-49.

of this city is a Sultan, that is, one of the four brothers, and is of the race of Mahomet, and is subject to the Grand Sultan of Cairo. His three brothers are always at war with him. On the 18th of May we had entered into the said city of Mecca from the north. On the side towards the south there are two mountains which almost touch each other, where is the pass to go to the gate of Mecca. On the other side, where the sun rises, there is another mountain pass, like a valley, through which is the road to the mountain where they celebrate the sacrifice of Abraham and Isaac, which mountain is distant from the said city about eight or ten miles. The height of this mountain is two or three casts of a stone by hand, and it is of some kind of stone, not marble, but of another colour. On the top of this said mountain there is a mosque according to their custom, which has three doors. At the foot of the said mountain there are two very beautiful reservoirs of water. One is for the caravan from Damascus; which water is collected there from the rain and comes from a great distance. Now, let us return to the city. At the proper time we will speak of the sacrifice which they make at the foot of the said mountain. When we entered into the said city we found the caravan from Cairo, which had arrived eight days before us, because they had not travelled by the same route as ourselves. In the said caravan there were sixty-four thousand camels and one hundred Mamelukes. You must know that, in my opinion, the curse of God has been laid upon the said city, for the country produces neither grass nor trees, nor any one thing. And they suffer from so great a dearth of water, that if every one were to drink as much as he might wish, four *quattrini* worth of water daily would not suffice them. I will tell you in what manner they live. A great part of their provisions comes from Cairo, that is, from the Red Sea. There is a port called Zida [Jedda], which is distant from the said city forty miles. A great quantity of food also comes there from Arabia Felix, and also a great part comes from Ethiopia. We found a great number of pilgrims, of whom some came from Ethiopia, some from India Major, some from India Minor, some from Persia, and some from Syria. Truly I never saw so many people collected in one spot as during the twenty days I remained there. Of these people some had come for the purposes of trade, and some on pilgrimage for their pardon, in which pardon you shall understand what they do,

The Chapter concerning the Merchandise in Mecca

First we will speak of the merchandise, which comes from many parts. From India Major there come a great many jewels and all sorts of spices, and part comes from Ethiopia; and there also comes from India Major, from a city called Bangchella, a very large quantity of stuffs of cotton and of silk, so that in this city there is carried on a very extensive traffic of merchandise, that is, of jewels, spices of every kind in abundance, cotton in large quantities, wax and odoriferous substances in the greatest abundance.

The Chapter concerning the Pardoning in Mecca

Now let us turn to the pardoning of the said pilgrims. In the midst of the said city there is a very beautiful temple, similar to the Colosseum of Rome, but not made of such large stones, but of burnt bricks, and it is round in the same manner; it has ninety or one hundred doors around it, and is arched, and has many of these doors. On entering the said temple you descend ten or twelve steps of marble, and here and there about the said entrance there stand men who sell jewels, and nothing else. And when you have descended the said steps you find the said temple all around, and everything, that is, the walls, covered with gold. And under the said arches there stand about 4000 or 5000 persons, men and women, which persons sell all kinds of odoriferous things; the greater part are powders for preserving human bodies, because pagans come there from all parts of the world. Truly, it would not be possible to describe the sweetness and the odours which are smelt within this temple. It appears like a spicery full of musk, and of other most delicious odours. On the 23rd of May the said pardon commences in the above-mentioned temple. The pardon is this: within the said temple, and uncovered, and in the centre, there is a tower, the size of which is about five or six paces on every side, around which tower there is a cloth of black silk. And there is a door all of silver, of the height of a man, by which you enter into the said tower. On each side of the door there is a jar, which they say is full of balsam, and which is shown on the day of Pentecost. And they say that that balsam is part of the treasures of the Sultan. On the side of the said tower there is a large ring in the corner. On the 24th of May all the people begin, before day, to go seven times around the said tower, always touching and kissing the corner. And at about ten or twelve paces distant from the said tower there is another tower, like one of your chapels, with three or four doors.

In the centre of the said tower there is a very beautiful well, which is seventy fathoms deep, and the water is brackish. At this well there stand six or seven men appointed to draw water for the people. And when the said people have gone seven times around the first tower, they go to this well, and place themselves with their backs towards the brink of the well, saying, "Bizmilei erachman erachin stoforla aladin," which means, "In the name of God, God pardon me my sins." And those who draw the water throw three bucketsful over each person, from the crown of their heads to their feet, and all bathe, even though their dress be made of silk. And they say in this wise, that all their sins remain there after this washing. And they say that the first tower which they walked round was the first house that Abraham built. And all having thus bathed, they go by way of the valley to the said mountain of which we have before spoken, and remain there two days and one night. And when they are all at the foot of the said mountain, they make the sacrifice there.

The Chapter concerning the Manner of the Sacrifices in Mecca

Every generous mind is the most readily delighted and incited to great deeds by novel events. Wherefore, in order to satisfy many of this disposition, I will add concisely the custom which is observed in their sacrifices. Every man and woman kills at least two or three, and some four and some six sheep; so that I really believe that on the first day more than 30,000 sheep are killed by cutting their throats, facing the east. Each person gives them to the poor for the love of God, for there were about 30,000 poor people there, who made a very large hole in the earth, and then put in it camels' dung, and thus they made a little fire, and warmed the flesh a little, and then ate it. And truly, it is my opinion, that these poor men came more on account of their hunger than for the sake of the pardon; and as a proof that it was so, we had a great number of cucumbers, which came from Arabia Felix, and we ate them all but the rind, which we afterwards threw away outside our tent. And about forty or fifty of the said poor people stood before our tent, and made a great scrambling among themselves, in order to pick up the said rinds, which were full of sand. By this it appeared to us that they came rather to satisfy hunger than to wash away their sins. On the second day a cadi of their faith, like one of our preachers, ascended to the top of the said mountain and made a discourse to all the people, which discourse lasted for about an hour, and he made in their language a sort of lamentation, and besought the people that they should weep for their sins. And he said to them in a loud voice, "Oh, Abraham, well-wished for and well-loved of God!" And then he said, "Oh, Isaac, chosen of God, friend of God, beseech God for the people of Naby!" and then were heard very great lamentations. And when he had finished his sermon, the whole caravan rushed back into Mecca with the greatest haste, for at the distance of six miles there were more than 20,000 Arabs, who wanted to rob the caravan, and we arrived for the defence of Mecca. But when we had gone half way, that is, between Mecca and the mountain where the sacrifice is made, we found a certain little wall four fathoms high, and at the foot of the said wall a very great quantity of small stones, which stones are thrown there by all the people when they pass that way, for the objects which you shall hear. They say that when God commanded Abraham that he should go and sacrifice his son, he went before him, and he said to his son that he must follow after him, because it was necessary to fulfil the commandments of God. The son answered him, "I am well pleased to fulfil the commandments of God." And when Isaac arrived at the above-mentioned little wall, they say that the devil appeared to him in the form of one of his friends and said to him, "My friend Isaac, where art thou going?" He answered him, "I am going to my father, who is waiting for me in such a place." The devil answered him: "Do not go, my son, for thy father will sacrifice thee to God and will put thee to death." And Isaac replied, "Let it be so; if such be the will of God, so let it be." The devil then disappeared, and a little further on he appeared in the form of another dear friend of Isaac, and said to him the above-mentioned words. They relate that Isaac answered with anger, "Let it be so," and took a stone and threw it in the devil's face: and for this reason, when the people arrive at the said place, each one throws a stone at the said wall, and then they go to the city. We found in the street of the said city 15,000 or 20,000 doves, which they say are of the stock of that dove which spoke to Mahomet in the form of the Holy Spirit, which doves fly about the whole district at their pleasure, that is, in the shops where they sell grain, millet, rice, and other vegetable productions. And the owners of the said articles are not at liberty to kill them or catch them. And if anyone were to strike any of those doves, they would fear that the country would be ruined. And you must know that they cause very great expense within the temple.

The Chapter concerning the Unicorns in the Temple of Mecca,
not very Common in other Places

In another part of the said temple is an enclosed space in which there are two live unicorns, and these are shown as very remarkable objects, which they certainly are. I will tell you how they are made. The elder is formed like a colt of thirty months old, and he has a horn in the forehead, which horn is about three *braccia* in length. The other unicorn is like a colt of one year old, and he has a horn of about four *palmi* long. The colour of the said animal resembles that of a dark bay horse,[1] and his head resembles that of a stag; his neck is not very long, and he has some thin and short hair which hangs on one side; his legs are slender and lean like those of a goat; the foot is a little cloven in the fore part, and long and goat-like, and there are some hairs on the hind part of the said legs. Truly this monster must be a very fierce and solitary animal. These two animals were presented to the Sultan of Mecca as the finest things that could be found in the world at the present day, and as the richest treasure ever sent by a king of Ethiopia, that is, by a Moorish king. He made this present in order to secure an alliance with the said Sultan of Mecca.

Sultan Qansouh al Ghouri's wives and his son Nasr Muhammad visited Mecca in 1514, and the Sherif Barakat returned with them to Egypt, making his third visit there and being richly rewarded by the Sultan. Barakat, from now onward, ruled in amity with his brother Kaitbey and his sons Ali and Abu Nomay until his death in 1524.

It is related by Al Hussaini of Barakat's son Abu Nomay that when he was eight years old he was sent for his education to Egypt, accompanied by Sayid ibn Ajil and the Shafite and Maliki judges. The Sultan, Qansouh al Ghouri, who was about to dispatch a military expedition, welcomed him and taking him between his knees asked him what he had to say. The boy replied with the verse from the Koran, "Verily I have opened the way for victory to you." The delighted Sultan at once gave orders for his recognition on his return to the Hijaz as co-ruler of Mecca, in replacement of the late Kaitbey, his uncle.

---

[1] The earlier translation by Richard Eden says 'weasel'-coloured. From his description the unicorn may be an oryx.

The success of the Spaniards against the Moors at this time was followed by a Portuguese threat to India and South Arabia, and soon Jedda was to become a base for wars. The Sultan Al Ghouri fitted out a fleet of fifty sail under the command of Mir Hussain al Mishrif al Kurdi, a prominent member of his court and a well-known glutton, and dispatched it to the Red Sea to counter the maritime advances of the Portuguese from the Indian Ocean. Hussain's ships were manned by Arab sailors, his marines being fifteen hundred Christians and slaves. Returning to Jedda, he proclaimed his decision to build a wall round it, in order, as he announced, to protect the townspeople from the neighbouring tribesmen, but he was in evident great haste, calling upon every able-bodied male to join in the work. Many of the houses were demolished to furnish material for the work or because they were in the line of the fortification,[1] and the immense task was finished within a year.[2] Meanwhile the Sultan of Egypt had received renewed appeals for help from the kings of Gujarat and the Yemen.

Al Hanafi gives an account of those days in his *Burg al Yamani*, or "Downfall of the Yemen":

It was in the early years of the century that to the misfortune of the Muslims the Portuguese for the first time penetrated to India. . . .

Encouraged by their success, they left nothing undone in order to come by knowledge of that sea, and they were instructed which routes to use by a clever Arab pilot and sailor, Ahmad ibn Majid. The commander of the Portuguese . . . invited him to eat with him and made him drunk. Affected by the wine, he told the Portuguese that he ought to keep away from the coast in certain parts and sail far out at sea, and that later they could safely approach it, and so they reached India safely . . . finally they made themselves masters of Hormuz . . . great reinforcements reached them . . . the Muslims did not dare risk sailing for fear of seeing their ships captured by the Portuguese, who were everywhere on the coasts. These attacks determined the King of Gujarat to appeal for aid to Qansouh al Ghouri, Sultan of Egypt. He sent ambassadors to him, asking especially for instruments of war and for cannon with which to repel the Franks. . . . Amr, Sultan of the Yemen, likewise implored his

[1] Al Hussaini, *Kitab Tandhid al Uqud.*
[2] The walls of Jedda were recently (1949) demolished to make room for houses and a road.

aid because of the ills brought upon the Muslims on the seas and up to the ports of the Yemen.

Qansouh readily agreed . . . and gave the command of the relief expedition to Hussain al Kurdi . . . with a large force of marines under Salman al Rais, styling Hussain "Governor of Jedda" from the time when he arrived there, in 1511.[1]

In building the wall Hussain had used great violence and when progress was slow ordered one unfortunate to be walled up in the masonry. Only after much persuasion by the notables and large payments was he induced to rescind his barbarous order. Duarte Barbosa says:

> A short time ago, Mirocem [Mir Hussain] the Moorish Captain of the Soldan's ships, whom the Portuguese had defeated in India, ordered that a fort should be built at Juda, for after his defeat he had not the courage to return to his country without doing some service to his king, and so he determined to ask the King of Cambaya, who is called Soldao Mahomet (1458–1511) . . . for a great sum of money to build the said fort . . . pointing out that it would be no great wonder if the Franks should enter this port and destroy the House of Mafoma.[2]

Barbosa relates that a distinguished Yemeni Arab merchant adventurer arriving at Jedda from Gujarat, with a cargo of spices, was asked by Mir Hussain for news of the Portuguese, and, receiving a reply that they were well established and building a fort, asked him, "Why hast thou then the boldness to come to Mecca, being a friend of the Portuguese?" The trader, named Calipha, tartly answered, "I am a merchant, and am powerless, but thou wast a captain of the great Soldao and hadst it in thy hands to turn them out of India. Why didst thou leave them there, and why art thou building a fort here?" Mir Hussain furiously ordered Calipha, as he stood, in his fine clothes, and all his crew to set to work on the walls, carrying lime and stone. All of which Calipha related on his return to Calicut. In point of fact, the strong fortifications of Jedda did deter the Portuguese, who never attacked, turning back without entering its roadstead.

As soon as the wall was completed Mir Hussain set sail for the Indies, but the Franks were by now equally strongly

---

[1] That is, after his first abortive cruise.
[2] *The Book of Duarte Barbosa* (Hakluyt Society, 1918–21), vol. i, p. 47.

installed, and soon after seeing Sultan Mudhaffar, the Shah of Gujarat (1511-25), he was obliged to leave again without having taken any effective action, returning defeated to the Island of Kamaran, in the Red Sea. From there he sent representatives to the Sultan Amr of the Yemen, giving them rich presents for the Sultan and asking for supplies for his men. Amr, listening to his Wezir's advice, refused to provide the supplies, supposing that to do so once would be to invite an annual levy. His reply infuriated Hussain, who decided to attack him and remove the rulership from him. His men were delighted, and he was strengthened in his intention by an offer of support from the Zaidis of the mountains, who leapt at the opportunity of ranging themselves against Amr, by whom they had been ill-treated. They tactfully offered not only to pay Hussain's soldiers, but supply them with victuals and furnish them with horses.

The Sherif Izzat-al-Din, son of Ahmad, Lord of Jizan, in spite of his close relationship with Amr, also offered his services. Likewise the Lord of Loyaya, the Fakih Abu Bekr, who promised to open a road for the intended invasion, and to guide it and also provide supplies.

The inhabitants of the Yemen at that time had never taken into use guns or cannons, so that Hussain's men slaughtered them in hundreds at every encounter.

They were so frightened by the noise of the artillery, its smoke, and their losses that they fled to Zebid, their capital, and shut themselves up there, taking with them some of the balls which had caused them so many losses. After a few more similarly pathetic battles the Emir was master of Zebid, entering it on June 20, 1516, at the head of his Turks, Moroccans, Egyptians, and Syrians, and of his auxiliaries of the Zaidis and the force of the Sherif of Jizan. Amr, with his brother and son, had already fled to Taiz, so that the victorious army at once began its ravaging and looting of the capital. Hussain had in his suite an infamous tax-gatherer called Tougan, who quickly made a roll of the inhabitants and their houses and extorted large sums from them. For seventeen days Mir Hussain was entirely occupied with Tougan in collecting 'taxes.'

He then set off for the coast and Aden a far richer and

happier man, taking with him Salman al Rais, but leaving
Barsbey, another lieutenant, and the Sherif of Jizan to reduce
the neighbouring provinces. As he sailed down the coast the
lords of the coastal towns one after another hastened to offer
their surrender, each accompanied by payments of great sums
of money to him. The tales of his successes and his cruelty
terrified the people of Jedda, who knew that they might expect
him on his return voyage.

He then razed the citadel of Aden, but, his siege otherwise
proving abortive, sailed for Jedda with his enormous spoils
in the autumn of 1516—to let loose on that port all the
ingenuities of his fiendish mind. He set up special racks,
furnaces, and torture chambers with appropriate instruments,
for his inventiveness in vice, torture, gluttony, and extortion is
said to have been unequalled anywhere.

Meanwhile the power of the Mamelukes was failing, and
Salim, the Ottoman, conqueror of the Sultan Al Ghouri and
of Tuman Beg, his successor and last of the Mameluke dynasty,
proclaimed the Hijaz part of his empire.

The elderly and pious Barakat at once sent his son, aged
thirteen, the Sherif Abu Nomay, to the court of Salim, who
was well pleased to receive the homage of the Sherif of Mecca,
descendant of the Prophet and guardian of the Temple. He
acknowledged his position and confirmed his independence in
the district of Mecca, and it is by virtue of that act, according
to Al Hanafi, that the Sherifs since enjoyed their privileges as
rulers. At the same time, after hearing his account of affairs
in the Hijaz from the thirteen-year-old Sherif Abu Nomay,
Salim gave him a warrant for the killing of Hussain al Kurdi,
so that his return to Mecca was at once made the occasion
for a public holiday. Barakat received, too, by his hand, the
Sultan's formal acknowledgment of his sovereignty over Mecca
and Medina, of the whole of the Hijaz, and over Jedda, on the
sole condition of recognizing the supremacy of the Sublime
Porte. He had the firman read out to the people and publicly
put on the cloaks of honour sent to him by Salim, being congratulated by all his people. Next day he ceremoniously
ordered the reading of the *khutba* in the name of the Ottoman
Sultan and then sent for the Mameluke commander, Mir
Hussain al Kurdi, telling him that the Sultan had demanded

his presence in Cairo. The licentious admiral was given into the ready hands of some simple Negro slaves, who took him with vengeful relish, to Jedda, where they embarked him on one of his ships and, taking it into deep water, trussed him up with chains, attached bags of stones, and threw him overboard, to gurgle and drown. His followers quickly dispersed, and all those who were caught came to ends suited to them, good or bad, as might be their deserts.

Some who succeeded in reaching Zebid, in the Yemen, joined Barsbey, to whom Hussain al Kurdi had confided the command there on his departure for Jedda. Barsbey, encouraged by these reinforcements, planned a new campaign of conquest in the Yemen, and the Sultan Amr, hearing of his preparations, made ready for resistance, but Barsbey's force arriving in front of Taiz in 1517, which he took easily, Amr abandoned it to be sacked by the enemy. Barsbey, pursuing his victories, was exposed to an attack by Amr, whose force marched against him only to be utterly defeated; so Amr and his brother were killed, his dynasty thus ending in May 1517.

Barsbey enjoyed only two short months at Sana; then collecting his own immense booty on 8000 camels, apart from the loot carried for his men, he marched via Najara towards Zebid, but near there was attacked by the Arabs of the Bani Hawbaish and some other tribes, he and his principal officers being killed and his men dispersed, all their booty falling into the hands of the tribes. Most of the survivors who reached Zebid agreed to the leadership of Iskander, a Circassian, who received the Sultan's authority to be his Governor, while others who attached themselves to Ramadhan, the "Byzantine," put on Turkish dresses and declared that they too acknowledged the authority of the Sultan.

Thus, when the Sultan's new representative, or Sanjak, in Jedda, Hussain al Rumi, arrived there he found that there was still a large number of well-armed ships brought and left behind by Mir Hussain al Kurdi and also a well-stocked arsenal. He therefore obtained promises of support from the Sherif of Mecca and the Pasha of Cairo's agreement to his marching into the Yemen, but on arriving near the frontier, hearing of the death of Sultan Salim, and at the same time that Iskander was preparing to resist him, he returned to Mecca without accomplishing anything.

Following troubles in Cairo, however, when Ahmad Pasha revolted, Salman al Rais, who had commanded the marines for Hussain al Kurdi, hurriedly left Cairo and went for asylum to Mecca. On his arrival he encouraged the Sanjak Hussain to renew his attempt on the Yemen, and himself began by attacking the Portuguese established on Kamaran Island, which they were using as a base for their raids on the Red Sea ports. He killed many, took and sold a large number of prisoners, and then summoned Iskander Beg al Karmani of the Yemen to surrender. Enlisting in his cause the Sherif Izzat-al-Din of Jizan, he marched on Zebid, where the inhabitants insisted on surrender of their garrison. Iskander, however, fell into the hands of the Sherif of Jizan, who spared him his life, but immediately became, in consequence, the enemy of Salman. Thus they came to blows, and the Sherif of Jizan was killed, Salman losing some two hundred of his bodyguard. Hearing of the re-establishment of order in Egypt under the Grand Wezir Ibrahim Pasha, Salman hurried off to join him there, leaving Hussain in the Yemen to restore order, and in the same year, 1524, the Sherif Barakat died in Mecca.

THE NEAR DESCENDENTS OF BARAKAT II

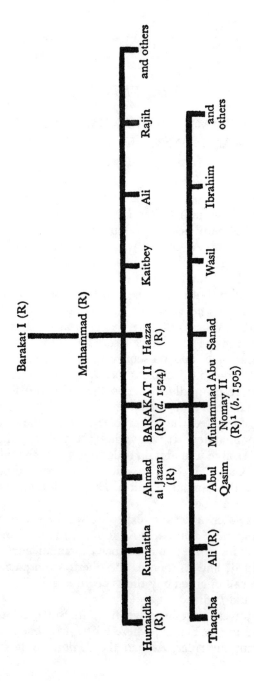

1 See pedigree at pp. 136–137.

(R) = ruled Mecca

Chapter VIII

MUHAMMAD ABU NOMAY II,
HIS SONS, GRANDSONS, AND GREAT-GRANDSONS
(A.D. 1524–1632)

MUHAMMAD ABU NOMAY, KNOWN AS ABU NOMAY II, succeeded his father, Barakat, at the age of nineteen. He had already been to Egypt twice, once as a child of seven, when Sultan Al Ghouri was still reigning, and again, four years later, to welcome on behalf of his father the new ruler of Egypt, the Ottoman conqueror Sultan Salim the Grim, and the First. With both rulers he had had a striking success.

Hardly was he in the saddle as ruler than a Turkish force arrived at Jedda on its way to the Yemen and the Indies in a new attempt to repulse the Portuguese. The ships entered the harbour in June 1526, and no sooner were the troops landed than they began to rob the citizens, behaving in a most lawless fashion. Prices rose rapidly owing to their demand for large supplies, so that this time, being evil, was long afterwards remembered and called the "year of Salman," the name of the Turkish commander. It was with great difficulty that the young Sherif was able to maintain order until after the pilgrimage, when the 'Capudan' Salman, and the Governor-designate of the Yemen, the famous Khair-al-Din, and their soldiers embarked for the Yemen.

A few years later a second expedition under one of the Sultan Salim's slaves, Sulaiman al Khadim, until then Governor of Cairo, sailed from Suez, but neither Sulaiman nor any of his people landed; and as soon as the Sherif's representatives had paid their call of ceremony the expedition sailed again for South Arabia and India.

In 1539, however, after his adventures in India, related by Al Hanafi, and in the Yemen, where on his way back he had killed in his tent the ruler, Ahmad the "Pilot," Sulaiman al

Khadim was again reported to be approaching the Sherif's domains. At Jizan, which Abu Nomay had taken over the previous year, he put in a governor of his own with a garrison, turning out the Sherif of Mecca's representatives. In April 1539 he arrived at Jedda, and, staying for the pilgrimage, he and his men committed many excesses and delighted in cruelty, showing little respect for the Holy Places. Nevertheless, when he left the Sherif took the opportunity to send his son Ahmad with him to the Sultan Sulaiman I, at Istanbul, both he and Ahmad being particularly well received. This was the greatest year in the reign of the greatest Ottoman Sultan, whose territory extended from the confines of India almost to Gibraltar, from Budapest to the Euphrates, and the Sultan may well have been in a generous mood. Unfortunately plague was abroad in Istanbul. Several of Ahmad's party died, including Qadhi Arar, one of the three judges who were with him, and he himself fell ill. When at last he returned to the Hijaz, safe and well rewarded, his father and all the notables of Mecca gave him a ceremonious reception at Wadi al Marr, with much reading of complimentary poems. But he never completely recovered from his illness in Istanbul, dying some six years later, to his father's very great grief.

From then onward Abu Nomay devoted himself increasingly to good works, lavishly helped by the Sultan Sulaiman's bounty, and much assisted by his right to half the customs dues of Jedda, a right in which he had been confirmed by the Sultan after chasing away some Portuguese ships which had appeared off Jedda in 1541.

The ceiling of the Ka'aba was rebuilt in 1551 to the order of the Sultan, and at the same time further sums were sent to the Sherif for charity. A regular pilgrimage caravan was now established from the Yemen, and in 1555 a *mahmal* was sent by Mustafa Pasha, the Sultan's Viceroy in the Yemen, in addition to that from Syria and Egypt.

In 1557 the water at Arafat, coming from Jebal Kurra, had ceased to run and to provide Mecca, so a request for help in repair of the channels was sent to the Sultan, whose sister asked to be allowed to pay for the work ¿ t an estimated cost of 35,000 dinars. The Egyptian Daftardar, or treasurer, Ibrahim Bey, was made secretary and organizer of the scheme, and she at once sent him 50,000 dinars. He arrived with four hundred Mamelukes and engineers from Damascus, Aleppo, and elsewhere. The chief engineer at once gave orders for the digging of a canal as far as Bir Zubaida, but the workmen came upon rock, which he endeavoured to dissolve by burning a great quantity of fuel, until the firewood of the entire neighbourhood was finished and the people were utterly exhausted and disheartened. A number of his servants and slaves had died by now, and, being himself worn out, he had his own tomb dug and died, ten years after the beginning of the works. In spite of the Sherif's recommendation that the scheme should in future be directed by the Governor of Jedda and the Chief Justice of Mecca, the Sultan again ordered that the new Daftardar of Egypt, Muhammad Bey Akmal Zadi, take over. He in turn failed and died. At last Qasim Bey, the Governor of Jedda, and Hussain, the Maliki judge, were appointed. In 1571 Qasim died, and the water had still not reached Mecca, but one month after his death the judge brought the water to Mecca, and a party of rejoicing was held for him in his garden at Al Batha. The money spent had amounted in all to 5 lakhs 700 dinars, and over and above it the Sultan's sister lavishly rewarded the judge. Immediately following this success orders were sent by the Sultan for the repair of the temple, which took four years. The Sultan thereupon ordered the following words to be written in gold between Bab Ali and Bab Abbas, two of the gates of the Shrine: "Allah, Muhammad, Abu Bekr, Omar, Uthman, Ali."

In 1565 the Sultan's Viceroy in the Yemen, Mahmoud Pasha, visited Mecca on his way to Egypt, having handed over charge to Radhwan ibn Mustapha, and impressed all who saw him, including Al Hanafi, by the magnificence and luxury of his suite and everything appertaining to it.

In July of the same year there came as a pilgrim a humble Portuguese slave. His account of Mecca, accurate in every particular though brief, was recently rediscovered by Signor G. L. della Vida written in code in the margin of an Arabic book (No. 217) in the Vatican library.[1] He left Rabigh on the last day of June bound for Mecca and with "here people go

---

[1] *The Moslem World*, vol. xxxii, No. 4, October 1942 (Hartford Seminary Foundation).

naked until Mecca" he begins his story of the actual pilgrimage, without however describing the Sherifs. His name and
history is unknown. A German, Hans Wild, taken prisoner
by the Turks in Hungary was taken to Mecca about the same
time, returning to Germany in 1611, and a few years later a
Venetian boy, Marco de Lombardo, captured crossing the
Mediterranean with his uncle, a sea-captain, was sent to
Mecca from Egypt as escort to his owner's son, his story being
published later by Eugène Roger, a missionary.

In 1569 Sinan Pasha arrived at Mecca en route to take over
charge in the Yemen, his army behaving well and causing no
trouble either then or on his return journey to Egypt.

The Sherif's reputation for sanctity and good work grew and
his style became the "Star of Religion," or Najm-al-Din. He
devised the *qanum*, or law of succession rules of the Hashimites,
eliminating the other descendants of his forbears from the
succession. From him descend the Dhawu Zaid, the Abādila,
including the Dhawu Aun, and the Al Barakat ruling clans.

In 1575, owing to sudden heavy rain and because the moat
outside the temple had been long neglected and had been
allowed to fill up, spates came into the city and flooded the
mosque up to the level of the Black Stone in the Ka'aba. For
thirty-six hours it was impossible to use the Shrine, and every
Meccan aided in the work of cleaning and repair, and the
digging out of the torrent bed to ten feet deep, so that the
water would not in future enter the Shrine, but be carried by
the new cut into a second channel some way short of the
mosque.

Under the Sultan Salim II the entire rebuilding of the temple
was undertaken at a cost of 110,000 new gold pieces from the
Sultan's treasury, without counting the cost of wood from
Egypt or the iron for instruments used in the work, or of the
bars, pents, and gilded copper crescents made in Egypt and
sent to Mecca for it. The work, about which full details are
given by Al Hanafi, was not finished until the reign of the
following Sultan, Murad III, near the end of Abu Nomay's
own rule.

Owing to the great wealth and success of Ottoman arms,
Mecca had been strikingly embellished and had otherwise
prospered under Abu Nomay, whose devotion to the interests of

Mecca and of his religion had enhanced the reputation of the Sherifs of Mecca. The history of this time is largely a tale of new works in Mecca, the building of almshouses, and of pilgrim khans, of schools and courts built or repaired, of great works inside the temple itself and on water channels between the hills and Mecca. The city was probably never so happy as it was under the Sherif Abu Nomay II, who ruled until he was eighty years of age, having joined his father in the co-rulership at the age of ten, and then ruled alone, except for the help of his son Hassan, after Ahmad's death, from the age of nineteen. He died in Nejd, ten days' march from Mecca, in 1584, and the procession with his body, mourned with sustained and loud cries by the women of Mecca, entered the city as his successor, Hassan, who had posted from the Yemen, entered it from the other side.

Hassan was already fifty-nine years old. He hoped that his son Masoud would be his co-partner, but he was soon thwarted by his brother Thaqaba. Both Thaqaba and Masoud, however, died soon afterwards. It is from the former that the Bani Thaqaba of the Qoraish, some of whom are still in the desert as bedouin, descend.

In his dealings with the nomad peoples Hassan was severe and despotic, and it was said that in his time the bedouin would swear falsely by anyone or anything except the name of the Sherif Hassan. Poets flourished in his reign and were greatly encouraged by him. He built the palace known as the "House of Happiness," and his rule was long looked back on as a golden age, just as, at the same period, the Turks looked on the Sultan Murad III and the Moroccans on Mawlay Ahmad, as the last of their able and good rulers and their times as relatively prosperous and kindly. By the unanimous choice of the sherifs he was succeeded by his son Idris, known as Abu Aun, who took his brother Fuhaid as his co-partner, the latter selecting Muhsin ibn Hussain ibn Hassan, his nephew, as his own partner; but later himself withdrawing in 1610 to Turkey, where he died. In 1624 Idris died, leaving the rule to Muhsin, and four years later disaster overtook the Sherif and the Meccans.

The arrival of one Ahmad Pasha, Governor-Designate of the Yemen, had been heralded at Jedda. Unfortunately for the Sherif and for Mecca, one of the Pasha's ships with his personal luggage in it was wrecked on a reef near Jedda and sank in comparatively deep water. He had sent messages to Mecca asking the Sherif for two divers to retrieve his baggage, and the consequences are related by Al Hussaini, in *Tandhid al Uqud*. After many days of diving, nothing having been found, the Turks came to believe that the Sherif Muhsin, who had not himself come to Jedda, must have instructed his divers not to try to succeed in their work. A poor and scheming sherif, Ahmad ibn Talib al Hassan, a cousin of the Ruler, who had arrived in Jedda at the time, was thought to have poisoned the Pasha's mind, by this suggestion, against the him. In any case the Pasha arrested and executed both the Governor of Jedda and the messenger between himself and the Sherif of Mecca, and giving money and troops to the impoverished sherif Ahmad ibn Talib, instructed him to supplant the Ruler in Mecca. At this moment the Turkish Pasha died suddenly, possibly poisoned by relatives of the men he had had executed. Jedda was already in turmoil when the Sherif Ahmad left it, taking all the available Turkish troops to Mecca, encountering Muhsin and the Meccan forces—mostly sherifs—at Tannim on his way. The pious sherifs wishing to avoid bloodshed, the Ruler Muhsin was obliged to quit the field, the Turkish troops following the sherifs into Mecca. There Sherif Ahmad arrested and executed the Mufti of Mecca, Abdul Rahman al Murshidi, attempting to justify the murder on several irrelevant grounds. He said that the Mufti had unreasonably prevented his (Ahmad's) marriage to one Sultana bint Ali Shihab and, more-over, during the ceremony of her marriage to another had referred to Ahmad as a devil; further, that when Ahmad's brother had died the Mufti came to give his condolences dressed in white; lastly, that Ahmad had found beneath a cushion on his predecessor's couch a *fatwa* against him by the Mufti. In any case, the Sherif Muhsin was obliged to flee to the Yemen, where he died in despair, in exile, in 1629.

In 1630 a new Governor of the Yemen, Qunsowa Pasha, being on his way to the Yemen with a large army, was ordered to take the opportunity to punish the Sherif Ahmad, of Mecca, for the murder of the Mufti. Hearing of his arrival, a member of the Sherif's family, Masoud ibn Idris ibn al Hassan, who had come to fear that Ahmad was turning against him as he had already turned against others, secretly left Mecca and went to meet the Pasha at Yanbu'.

The ruling Sherif himself went out to meet Qunsowa Pasha on his arrival near Mecca, was courteously welcomed by him, and reassuringly invited to inspect the soldiers and the *luwand*,

TYPES OF JANIZARIES
After " Taskilat wa qiyafat askariya," by Mahmoud Shawkat

or marines, who were drawn up on the plain in front of their tents. As soon as the Sherif arrived the drums were beaten and the trumpets blown, the barbaric music continuing throughout his tour of the ranks with the Pasha and the Sanjaks. The glitter of the arms and the tulip-red uniforms, the fierce appearance of the superior officers, surmounted by large Roman cockades above their towering headdresses, gave a frightening impression of warlike ability, only here and there belied by the youth of those in the ranks.

This proud array, the Moslems of them fortified by the pilgrimage to God's house, was to leave in the following week for the tedious desert march on which many would inevitably die.

Three days later Ahmad, with three sherifs—his wezir, the Treasurer, and the Chief of his Bodyguard—went to say goodbye to the Pasha. At Qunsowa's camp-quarters they were, as

SOLDIER'S   JANIZARY   OFFICER'S
HEAD-DRESS   EMBLEM   HEAD-DRESS

After " Taskilat wa qiyafat askariya," by Mahmoud Shawkat

hitherto, made welcome, invited to enter and to play chess. As the sun set the game ended. Men of the *luwand* entered the tent and the Sherif Ahmad was throttled. The other three were told to return with their news to Mecca, where they found that Masoud ibn Idris al Hassan had already taken over the rule.

During Masoud's short reign the entire Ka'aba fell down, owing to floods again entering the Haram.[1] Some five hundred people lost their lives in and round Mecca, drowned in the spates following upon the cloudburst and the storms which had

[1] See glossary.

THE NEAR DESCENDANTS OF ABU NOMAY II

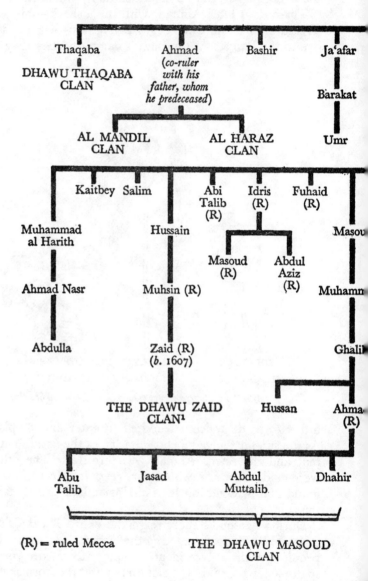

(R) = ruled Mecca   THE DHAWU MASOUD
                                      CLAN

[1] See pedigree at p. 17

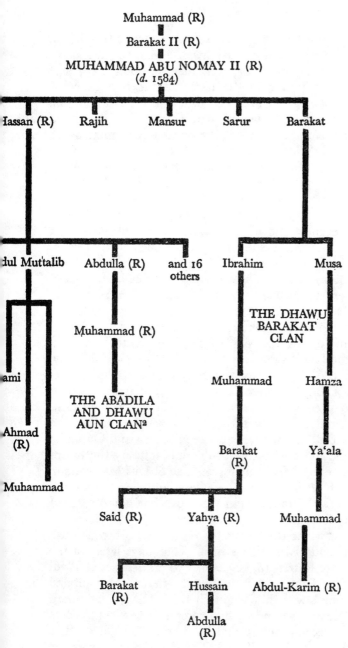

Muhammad (R)

Barakat II (R)

MUHAMMAD ABU NOMAY II (R)
(*d.* 1584)

Iassan (R)   Rajih   Mansur   Sarur   Barakat

dul Muttalib   Abdulla (R)   and 16 others   Ibrahim   Musa

ami   Muhammad (R)   THE DHAWU BARAKAT CLAN

Ahmad (R)   THE ABĀDILA AND DHAWU AUN CLAN[2]   Muhammad   Hamza

Muhammad   Barakat (R)   Ya'ala

Said (R)   Yahya (R)   Muhammad

Barakat (R)   Hussain   Abdul-Karim (R)

Abdulla (R)

[2] See pedigree at p. 164.

swept the hills north of the city. In consequence the Sultan
Murad IV sent an architect, Ridhwan Agha, a eunuch, to
repair the Haram. While he was there Masoud died, and
Ridhwan, seizing power in the name of the Sultan, ruled
Mecca until, having received his orders from Istanbul, he
asked the sherifs to select one of themselves. They appointed
the eldest of them, Abdulla ibn Hassan ibn Muhammed ibn
Abi Nomay, who, however, abdicated after nine months in
favour of his son Muhammad, sending for Zaid ibn Muhsin,
from the Yemen, to be his son's partner, himself dying in the
year 1631.

The disturbances, political and natural, which the people of
Mecca had recently known were little compared with what
now befell. Qunsowa Pasha's army had failed in its task in
the Yemen, owing to the brutality of his methods and the
indiscipline of his men, looting and rapine having been ordered
whenever it entered a town. As it was now rumoured that he
had sailed for Egypt and that his infamous army was on its
way home, the people of Mecca were in great fear.

From Qunfidha, on the coast south of Jedda, there came a
message to the Sherif signed by two of the Aghas of the army,
Mahmoud and Ali Bey, saying that they were marching homeward to Egypt, but that they would prefer to spend a few days
in Mecca to prepare themselves for the long road onward.
The Sherifs, reflecting the fears of their people, refused to
receive them, ordering the wells between Mecca and Qunfidha
to be filled in, and on hearing of this inhospitality the troops
determined to enter Mecca by force. The Sherifs Muhammad
and Zaid, with their clansmen, soldiers, and slaves, took the
field, camping at Birkat Ma'ajin when the Turks had reached
Saadiya, only forty miles south of Mecca.

To the support of the Sherifs came hurrying the Turkish
Sanjak from Jedda with all his men. Four days later, in the
early morning of March 18, 1631, the two armies met at Wadi
al Abar. The fighting was unusually fierce, Muhammad
being killed, and with him eight sherifs. The young Sherif
Hazza was gravely wounded, and later lost his hand, while
five hundred Meccan soldiers and spectators were killed. The
loyal Turkish Sanjak himself died of exhaustion soon after the
battle. Zaid, alone of the leading nobles, managed to escape

to reach Medina in safety, and Mecca itself was left open to the victorious rebel army.

The soldiers seized the food supplies and killed and ate camels and looted where and what they fancied; and, according to Al Hussaini, between them raped every virgin and every

A JANIZARY OF ARABIA FELIX

After "Türk askeri kiyafertleri," by Muharram Fayzi (Istanbul, 1933)

boy in the city, those of gentle birth being the first to be seized by the lustier soldiers of lower grades. For a week they continued forcibly to make the young of both sexes drunk, so with greater facility to indulge their wantonness. Meanwhile the nomads took the opportunity to revolt, looting caravans on the way to Mecca with impunity. Jedda, which had refused to submit, was then invaded and suffered like Mecca, the richer merchants being tortured to make them reveal their hoards.

From Medina the Sherif Zaid had been sending messenger after messenger to Egypt, imploring help. The Sultan dispatched at once seven Sanjaks, representing a considerable force, and a *khila'* for Zaid, which was put up on him in the Prophet's mosque at Medina before he began his return march on Mecca. The soldiers had meanwhile installed the Sherif Nami ibn Abdul Muttalib al Hassan as their puppet ruler, and, news reaching them of the advance of the army from Egypt under the Sherif Zaid, supported by his own Meccan and Medinese troops, they left hurriedly for Taraba, in the interior, taking with them Nami and his brothers, the sherifs Said ibn Abdul Muttalib and Abdul Aziz ibn Idris. It was the time of the afternoon prayer when they passed the Bab el Nabi, now called the Bab al Haririn, and the muezzin was calling to prayer. At that moment the banner fell out of the hands of their standard bearer, an ill omen for their future, as they thought, and so it was.

In the darkness of the night the Sherif Abdul Aziz, who had taken care to be splendidly mounted, rode away from their camp at Jebal Harra for Yanbu'. The next morning, finding a sherif missing, the rebellious troops put Nami and Said under guard, and continued their flight. Meanwhile in Mecca a sherif, Ahmad ibn Qitada ibn Thaqaba, proclaimed Mecca God's country once more and that the prayers were to be read in the name of Sultan Murad. The following day Zaid entered the city.

Chapter IX

ZAID IBN MUHSIN,
FOUNDER OF THE DHAWU ZAID CLAN,
AND OTHERS, AND HIS GRANDSON
(A.D. 1632–1716)

ZAID, BORN IN THE SOUTH, IN THE WADI BISHA, WHILE HIS father was in voluntary exile, was twenty-five years old when he was given the *khila'* in Medina, and entered Mecca as its ruler. The date of his birth has been preserved by Al Usami, who is quoted by Al Hussaini. A fortune-teller, using sand, he says, came to the *mejlis*[1] of Zaid and announced, "When your mother conceived you it was Ramadhan 1015 [January, A.D. 1607.]" The Sherif was astonished, and embarrassed too, for sexual intercourse is incorrect in the fasting month of Ramadhan; but, asking his mother, he heard that it was indeed so, for, his father, as she explained, returning happy after successful raiding, the first thing he had done was to pleasure her.

On entering Mecca the young ruler was sufficiently politic to insist upon completing the pilgrimage rites before pursuing Nami and the rebellious Turks. Some of their laggards meanwhile surrendered through the mediation of the Emir of the Damascus pilgrimage, one Ibrahim Pasha. Zaid next held a council of war at which he assembled all the Sherifian family and the senior Turkish officers, or Sanjaks, and the Ulama of Mecca. The Meccan forces carrying firearms, then new weapons for Arabian fighting, came up with the main body of the rebels at Taraba, on the edge of the Nejd plateau, and there defeated them so that they retreated into the castle of Kabil, from where Ali Bey sent a messenger to the Sherif, offering to surrender if his own and Mahmoud's lives were spared. This was at first accepted, but in the face of public

[1] See glossary.

feeling in Mecca the Sherif had to give way in the case of Mahmoud Bey, who was beaten and tortured, then paraded naked, strapped on a camel, face upward, head to the tail for greater indignity, through the streets of Mecca.

Having crucified him, they made cuts in his arms and shoulders and put pieces of cloth soaked in oil in the cuts and set fire to them, and next they took him down and put his right hand and left foot on one hook on a post erected in Al Ma'ala cemetery, and left him thus suspended, above his grave . . . until he died. And . . . he was cursing, abusing, storming until he died; then he was lowered from the post and buried. As for Ali Bey he came to no harm, since he had arrested Mahmoud for them; moreover when he was in Mecca, during its rape, he had. taken care of Zaid's women, and daily sent to ask them what they needed. The conduct of this handsome man was good, so he was spared.[1]

Nami, who had ruled for a hundred days, and his brother Said were tried by the Ulama and the Sanjaks in session, and when the Ulama were asked for their verdict they replied, "The Judgment of God"; whereupon the accused were at once taken aside by a batch of soldiers and executed with swords, their heads being exposed to the people on the roof of the retreat of the followers of Sheikh Abdul Qadir al Qilani.

Zaid's early life in the south had given him knowledge and confidence beyond his years and unusual among his clansmen of Mecca, while his friendship with the people of the tribes and of the oases of the little-known country about Bisha was a support to him when faced with increasing Turkish interference. When Sultan Murad, however, conquered Baghdad in 1638 he requested Zaid to expel the Persians from Mecca, a demand which he and the people of Mecca resented, but, unwilling to be labelled as heretically inclined, felt compelled to accept, to their pecuniary loss. When the Sherif had asked for troops from Egypt, to rid Mecca of the mutineers, he had also asked for remission of part of the customs control at Jedda by the Egyptians, but now he found that the Turkish official sent to Jedda for this purpose in 1642 was nominated an Inspector of the Holy Places, and was bent on increasing, rather than reducing, Egyptian and Turkish control. Zaid,

[1] Al Hussaini, *Kitab Tandhid al Uqud.*

now much incensed, and determined to maintain his authority, appointed Ibrahim, a son of his former co-ruler Muhammad, as his regent in Mecca, and, having given secret orders to a tribal sheikh to manage the death of the Turkish Inspector, set about preparing for an expedition of prestige through the tribes.

The arrival of the Sultan's favourite black eunuch, Bashir Agha, the Abyssinian, was now announced. Travelling as a special representative of the Sultan, he had been given extra-ordinary powers and was respectfully received in Egypt. Zaid disliked the thought of deference to him, but felt constrained to send a deputation to welcome him at Yanbu' and at the same time to report to him by quick messenger upon the size of the force with the Agha.[1] His agents not only reported the size of this force, but that the Agha had just received a letter from Istanbul that the Sultan, Murad IV, had died, a fact he was concealing. Zaid immediately altered his whole reception programme and even removed some of the furnishings of the guest quarters prepared for the mission. Nevertheless, as it approached Mecca, the Sherif went out to meet the eunuch. As they rode back into Mecca he kept spurring his horse, in order to be always a little in advance of him, and on coming near the Palace said over his shoulder, "May the Sultan rest in peace," so that Bashir understood that the Sherif also knew that his mission had been made insignificant by the Sultan's death.

A few days later the Sherif set out on his expedition among the tribes. The blackamoor emissary about the same time started for Taif, in the mountains, in order to meet Mustafa Beg, the Turkish inspector of Jedda, being anxious to obtain the alliance and support of a colleague in the Turkish service. Mustafa Beg, however, was already on his way back, and, while travelling, his escort being strung out ahead and behind him in a narrow valley, and riding alone except for his horse-holder, an Arab ran up and stabbed him with a dagger, so that he died within three hours. The Sherif was far away in Nejd, at Al Kharj, when the news reached him that his wish had been fulfilled. He had already determined upon a visit in force to Medina, but hardly had he arrived there, being still

[1] Al Hussaini, *Kitab Tandhid al Uqud*, and C. Snouck Hurgronje, *Mekka*, vol. i.

camped outside the walls, when the Turkish Qadhi of Medina was murdered on his way to late prayers.

He had been riding past the Daftardar's, or Accountant-General's, office after dark with three followers, when a man rushed out, to run him through with a sword, and escaped. The dying Qadhi fell forward over the neck of his horse, which went on with him into the mosque and up to the praying niche of Othman, the Fourth Caliph, where the assembled faithful in consternation lowered him. He kept calling out, "O Messenger, O Prophet of God," until he died there.[1]

The Turkish soldiers now ran to arms and the gates of the city were hastily manned, while guns were trained upon the lights in Zaid's camp. Many of the people on the walls were shouting towards the camp, "Go away from us," and the confusion was increasing. Zaid sent some Egyptian officers, bearing written disclaimers, but, unable to persuade the sentries to open, they were obliged to push their papers under the doors. Only after their perusal were the gates opened to admit the emissaries and the soldiers returned to their quarters. An inquiry was begun next day and many persons were detained, but all released, one by one, for lack of evidence.

At the same time Ghitas Beg, the Turkish successor in Jedda, nominated Abdul Aziz ibn Idris as Sherif of Mecca, so that Zaid was forced to return and fight them. At their encounter Ghitas and Abdul Aziz were defeated and begged for mercy through Mubarak ibn Bashir. With an escort of fifty, Ghitas was sent back to Jedda, from where, an order for his dismissal being received from Constantinople, he shortly left for Yanbu' and Egypt, being joined by his protégé, Abdul Aziz, who soon afterwards died of cholera. In 1600 Ghitas was made Emir of the Egyptian pilgrims, and Zaid was so astonished and upset on his arrival that he only shook hands with him, and ever since that day the ancient custom of the Sherif's embracing the Emir-al-Hajj on the arrival of the pilgrim train in Mecca has ceased.

Owing to locusts in the Yemen and the Hijaz, there was famine in Mecca in 1659. Prices in the bazaar were pegged, but it was not until the crier was told to announce the abandonment of that order that cereals began to come in from neigh-

[1] Al Hussaini, *Kitab Tandhid al Uqud.*

bouring countries and the shortage came to an end. There followed good years with plenty of rain, notably in 1662 and in 1665, so much so that in the former year spates flooded Mecca, and Zaid in person took charge of the clearing up of the damage caused by the floods, in which six of the inhabitants were drowned. Owing to the exceptional rains the harvests were rich and "In these years an *ardab* of wheat sank as low in price as three *harouns* and a *mann* of cheese was only two *halaqis*."[1]

In this time of plenty, in 1666, Zaid died. Founder of the line of the Bani Zaid, he had staved off the Turkish attempts to interfere in the affairs of Mecca and the Hijaz, largely through his influence with the tribes acquired by having spent his boyhood among them.

His son Sa'ad succeeded him, but not without difficulty. His most popular rival was Hamud ibn Abdulla. Imad Effendi, the Turkish representative from Jedda, was in Mecca, and he at once decided in favour of Sa'ad, adding reservations when he found that opposition parties were forming. Others had come to him and pressed the claims of Muhammad Yahya, another son of Zaid, assuring him that Zaid had formerly obtained the Sultan's sanction for his succession to him. Nevertheless he sent his men to Sa'ad with the *khila'*, but with it a message that he had had no authority to recognize him as more than an acting Kaimakam.[2] The party happened to be met by rivals of Sa'ad going into Imad Effendi's house, who quickly carried back this latest news to their supporters. Zulficar, a faithful old Turkish slave of his father, who was perhaps in touch with Imad Effendi, mustered Sa'ad's men, while Hamud's men were still only talking about the possibilities of fighting. After three days the struggle began. Each side, barricaded into their houses, fired at the other from a distance that was often quite safe. After three days of house-to-house fighting and skirmishes in the market peace was declared, and Mecca gave itself over to celebrations for the same number of days.

Sa'ad at once sent to Egypt another trusted slave of his father, an Abyssinian named Bilal like the first muezzin of Islam, with an account of the events in Mecca, and to ask for

---

[1] Al Hussaini, *Kitab Tandhid al Uqud*.　　　[2] See glossary.

confirmation of his appointment. The request was transferred
to Istanbul, and meanwhile Hamud and Muhammad Yahya,
his rivals, had separately sent their own messengers. Hamud's
messenger was found killed in Cairo two days after his arrival,
with his letter still on him. Muhammad Yahya, on the other
hand, had relied upon a following in Medina, where many of
the notables had signed a petition in his favour and sent it,
supported by an offer of forty thousand dinars, to the Governor
of Egypt.

Sa'ad, however, it was who in the end received the Sultan's
approval, and Hamud in consequence at once left Mecca for
Wadi al Marr. From there he began a campaign of terrorizing
Mecca, sending men in at night to rob and frighten the inhabitants by ingenious tricks; so, he hoped, to create disorder and
dissatisfaction with Sa'ad's rule.

At the same time he claimed that Sa'ad had promised him
a large sum of money should he become Sherif, and non-pay-
ment of this he turned into a complaint of ill-treatment, which
he laid before the Emir of the Egyptian pilgrimage on his way
into Mecca, warning him that he could not permit his pilgrim
caravan to proceed until he had paid the sum owed him,
100,000 ashrafi. The Emir, Uzbek Bey, promised that he
would make Sa'ad pay 50,000, upon which the pilgrims were
allowed to pass, and Sa'ad did in fact give the sum promised
by Uzbek. The Emir of the Damascus pilgrimage next
attempted to make peace between Sa'ad and Hamud, who
was given leave to appear to plead his case in Mecca. While
found guilty of causing disturbances in Mecca and of robbery,
no one dared pronounce sentence either in his favour or in
Sa'ad's.

Hamud thereupon determined upon raising his case before
the Sultan, sending representatives for this purpose, with
gifts, to Umr Pasha, Governor of Egypt; but half-way they met
messengers from Ibrahim Pasha, who had replaced Umr
Pasha, carrying letters to the Sherif which recommended him
to reach a peaceful settlement. Hamud's men nevertheless
went on to Egypt and were well received, until, the Egyptian
messenger not returning from the Hijaz, they became at first
unpopular, suspected, and later under grave suspicion. The
Pasha of Egypt now raised a force to attack Hamud, who was

believed to have killed the missing messenger, and Hamud in turn raised the Juhaina tribe from near Yanbu'. The Egyptians had had instructions from Cairo to march straight on Mecca and there to join the Sherif before giving battle, and this their commander, Yusif Beg, obstinately did by the most direct route, in spite of earnest warnings from some merchants who had sought the protection of his army for their merchandise. His force was destroyed and he himself was captured, together with his women, and he soon afterwards died in prison. When this news reached Cairo all the Sherifian messengers and followers there were killed, but the Ulama of Cairo refused to sanction the execution of the four sherifs themselves, who remained in prison until the Governor, Ibrahim Pasha, was some time later supplanted.

Hamud thus was able to continue his career as a kind of Arabian Robin Hood, successfully fighting as far afield as the deserts frequented by the Anaiza, Awazim, Mutair, and Dhafir tribes of Al Nejd, far over in the east of the peninsula. It was not until 1670, after the battle of Al Nasar, that at last Hamud came to Taif to swear eternal friendship with Sa'ad on the tomb of Sayid Abdulla ibn Abbas.

Meanwhile, in 1667, Mecca had suffered the worst famine of its history. Even cats and dogs, bats and rats, were eaten. Some people were obliged to sell all their possessions for food. The poor attacked the houses of the rich, and men fell dead in the streets from weakness, or sitting themselves down never again rose up. The conditions in Jedda were the same or even worse. The people of Mecca went in a body to the Sherif, demanding punishment of the Nadhir, or City Governor, and the Muntasab, or Mayor, and both were dismissed and punished by beating. The people ground chick-peas and broad-beans to make bread, until finally nothing was left. The bedouin—in particular, the Ataiba tribe on the plateau of Nejd, the Hudhail, and the Lihyan from near Mecca—became savage, looting wherever they had some hope of finding food or valuable goods. They came riding pillion on their camels in hundreds to raid the settlements, and the Sherif pursued them whenever he could; until at last, just before the pilgrimage, ten shiploads of supplies came to Jedda from Egypt, and the famine was ended.

In June 1668 a comet was seen clearly in Mecca, and it was on that very day that Sheikh Muhammad ibn Sulaiman al Maghribi, or the Moor, had erected a sundial in the courtyard of the mosque, so that ignorant people attributed what had been seen in the sky to what the Sheikh had done on earth. The case was referred to the Sherif, who in conjunction with the Qadhi ordered its removal, but after an appeal to the Shaikh-al-Islam, the head of the Ulama in Istanbul, the stone was ordered to be re-erected, "so long as it is for the benefit of the Moslems."[1]

In the same year, at the time of the pilgrimage, there came two *khila'* for Sherif Sa'ad, one from Sultan Muhammad II himself and the other from his Governor of Egypt, but the number of pilgrims was unusually small because of fear of a fight between the soldiers and Sherif Hamud. After the pilgrimage the Sherif and the Egyptian force decided on a campaign against him and they went together to Yanbu', whence, however, Hamud fled without trace.

In the following year occurred the disturbing arrival of one Hassan Pasha, travelling with the Damascus Hajj. It was said in Medina when he arrived that he was carrying an order from the Sultan to take over the rule of the Hijaz and to depose the Sherifs of Mecca. From notables of Medina, to whom this news was not unwelcome, the tale quickly reached Mecca. In consequence, all the sherifs decided not to leave Mecca, even for the sacrifice on Mount Arafat. They refused to pay him deference, the shopkeepers closed their stalls, and no one would serve his men.

Hassan Pasha asked that a council might be held, at which he sought to dispel suspicion, and, their immediate fear once being removed, the Meccans treated him better. For a day or two the arrival of the Shah of Persia's caravan and a vast

---

[1] Al Hussaini describes the heavenly phenomena seen at this time: "On 23 Ramadhan 1078 A.H. [February 23, 1668] there was a great blaze in the west and in length it became so long that it covered a third of the sky. It vanished gradually and disappeared finally on the 8th Shawwal—that is, fifteen days later. On 11 Moharram 1079 [June 21, 1668] two hours after sunrise a strong beam of light was seen coming from the sun or from close to it. It extended westward and it was too bright to regard without being temporarily blinded. The colours of the beam were blue, yellow, and red. Both edges later disappeared and the centre became greater and larger until it burst with a noise like thunder, so that the people thought that it was a gun going off. After the burst the remainder of the light turned into smoke and then disappeared." (*Kitab Tandhid al Uqud.*)

treasure for the Temple and the people of Mecca made them forget Hassan Pasha. The pilgrimage was moving tranquilly to its close when, during the throwing of stones, there was a disturbance in the Temple area. Hassan Pasha, who was mounted, rode to the Temple to restore order, and received three bullet wounds. He was placed in a litter and carried slowly back to his quarters, his men, with sullen diligence, killing every one they met on the way. The civilian inhabitants fled to Muna and the valleys, while the Sherif, heavily escorted, returned to Mecca, reaching it at dusk.

He at once gave orders to be ready for war. Vivid and near-by lightning, which a few days earlier had killed a man near the Shrine, alone lighted up the darkened and nearly empty city. The Sherifs and the remaining notables hastened to councils of war, or of peace, according to their tempers, Sa'ad in the end ranging himself with those in favour of peace. Opening his treasury in generous, but calculated, munificence, he handed over large sums, much of it lately received from the Shah, for distribution to his family, and to their Negro officers, and left the city for Yanbu', in order to save Mecca by his withdrawal.

From Mecca the wounded Hassan Pasha supported a regency by Ahmad al Harith, a cousin of the Sherif, and in turn left the city for Syria, dying of his wounds near Gaza.

Sa'ad returned to Mecca before the next pilgrimage season, but was alarmed to hear of unusually large Turkish forces, under one Hussain Pasha, accompanying the pilgrims.

Cheleby Evliya, the well-known Turkish traveller, who made the pilgrimage in 1671, gives an account[1] of these days and says:

> Hussain Pasha went to the pilgrimage to Mecca at the head of a formidable escorting force. He showed a remarkable liberality towards the pilgrims from different parts of the Moslem world. News of his open-handedness impressing Sherif Sa'ad favourably, he presented Hussain Pasha with two pure-bred horses, six young Abyssinian slaves, precious stones, different clothes, soda-ash (kalay), aloes-wood, amber, ornamental glasses and crystal drinking-cups, and fifty camel-loads of foodstuffs and sherbets. These were brought to him by the kithuda, or agent, of the Sherif,

[1] Seyhatnamesi.

who kissed Hussain Pasha's hands and remained standing till he
was permitted by the Pasha to sit. The Pasha was camped at
Wadi Fah, two stages from Mecca, and here he slaughtered
forty sheep and camels as thanksgiving for safe arrival. All the
Ulama, men of piety, leading clergy, and sherifs had come to
meet the Pasha, and each, according to merit and in the order
of their precedence, were presented to him to make him their
compliments. Next the Egyptian Emir-al-Hajj, Uzbek Bey, the
Governor of Jedda, Bakliji Muhammad Bey, and seven Aghas
commanding Egyptian companies, their adjutants, sergeants,
head-cooks, and chamber-attendants came forward in turn with
their detachments and presented themselves to the Pasha and
were offered sherbet and incense. The agent was asked by the
Pasha why the Sherif had not come in person, and expressed a
hope that he was quite well. The agent gave some diplomatic
excuse for the Sherif's absence. The Pasha then quoted the
proverb, "When the mountain can not move to meet the man,
man should go to it." He accepted the gifts sent by the Sherif
Sa'ad with thanks and asked the attendant to return his greetings
to the Sherif. The Pasha then ordered his entourage to move on,
and, on arriving at Mecca, performed the prescribed preliminaries
of the pilgrimage, and made a surprise call on Sherif Sa'ad, who
became quite embarrassed by the Pasha having behaved so gently
in appeasing him. He invited Sa'ad to honour him with a visit
early next morning because His Majesty the Sultan had sent him
a *khila'* with a Royal Firman. From there they would, if the
Sherif pleased, together enter Mecca with the pilgrims and the
Muslim army. By these honeyed words, Sherif Sa'ad was set at
his ease. He offered the Pasha's entourage sherbet, and burned
for them incense, and sent him ten parcels of amber, three necklaces of pearls, a box full of precious stones, ten bags of robes,
and three Abyssinian slaves. In return, the Pasha pulled out a
bejewelled dagger from his own belt and thrust it into the belt
of the Sherif. Sherif Sa'ad was a man of medium height, brown
in complexion, with a thin moustache, and like Hatim Tai in his
lavish generosity. The Pasha returned to his quarters and
ordered all the sergeants of companies to warn their troops to
be on guard that night and await further orders.

Chelebi Evliya explains why Hussain Pasha had been dis-
patched to the holy land at the head of three thousand
Egyptian troops, supplied by Ibrahim Pasha, Governor of
Egypt, three thousand more sent by the Governor of Syria,

and two thousand picked by Istanbul, the latter as the Pasha's own bodyguard, making eight thousand troops in all. He says that one year before his own, Chelebi Evliya's, pilgrimage, Ankabut Ahmad Pasha had instructed his agent, Hasan Pasha, the Governor of Jedda, to undertake the task of having the Holy Shrine repaired and reorganized. He had instructions to make all the Sherifs and notables pay for the expenses to meet the cost of the repairs. It was, however, obvious at once that the Sherifs would not tolerate this levy or any interference, and while thousands of pilgrims and Hasan Pasha's troops were in the Shrine about to perform the ritual of the pilgrimage the gates of the Shrine were closed and they were besieged inside. Thereupon, Hasan Pasha's ten detachments passing through the Omar Gate gained the roofs of the Shrine with the hope of defending themselves and the pilgrims.

The attendants of the Sherif had by this time climbed Jebel Qubais, while Sherif Sa'ad had occupied the seven minarets of Mecca and manned their stories with his marksmen, who started to fire on the beleaguered pilgrims and troops from them and from adjoining seminaries, wounding seven hundred and killing two hundred persons in the precincts of the Shrine. Nothing like this bloody massacre at the Shrine itself had ever occurred before, even in the days of Zubair, of the tyrant and sadist Yusif al Hajjaj. The fighting lasted one day and one night, in spite of the Holy Koran's verse, "Let there be no adultery and no fighting during the pilgrimage." The courtyard of the Shrine was heaped with corpses, Hasan Pasha himself was hit by bullets, and the property of the pilgrims and troops looted. As the Egyptian troops were retreating on Egypt, they were overtaken in Wadi an Nar, or the Valley of Fire, by mercenaries of Sherif Hamud, and many of them put to the sword and spear. Thus when this ghastly news reached Asitana [Istanbul], the Sultan ordered that eight thousand troops from Egypt and Syria be placed under the command of Hussain Pasha, as already stated. ... So that by the time this army had arrived at Al Abtah valley and the Ma'ala mountain track, whence Mecca can be descried, scores of thousands of pilgrims and inhabitants had assembled and stood in rows to greet the dazzling array of Hussain Pasha's army, shouting, "May God preserve you, O Wezir," and, "May God grant you victory, O troops of the Sultan." It was only thus that in this year, 1671, we arrived safely at Mecca, on 10th Dhul Hijja.

Evliya, continuing his story, says:

Hussain Pasha established his camp in the valley of Ma'ala
with all the troops and the pilgrims about him. There he ordered
that a hundred sheep be slaughtered and distributed to the poor.
After that the armies of Egypt met the Syrian and Meccan
troops and the notables and the attendants of the Pasha assembled
at the Royal Diwan. Only Sherif Sa'ad did not attend. Each
one of those present received a *khila'*, and all joined hands and
escorted the Pasha to Ma'ala Shrine. While there the representatives from the four religious rites of Islam gave a *fatwa* that the
armed forces could join the religious ceremonies accoutred, provided that they wore their coats and trousers inside out, and so
in this fashion they performed the ceremonial tour. After this
the leaders gathered for consultation, in compliance with the
Pasha's wish, to consider the question of the Sherif, who was in
addition one of the Sultan's honorary Ministers. They all agreed
that Sherif Sa'ad and the people of Mecca were in, or, at least,
planning, revolt. Hence they considered that Sherif Sa'ad should
be dismissed from office, and that Sherif Ahmad should be
appointed in his place to take the oath of loyalty to the Sultan.
When this was decided they all went up to Mount Arafat, joining
in the pilgrimage procession. The Pasha, when told of this
decision, sent to them asking: "Have you any formal letter or
decree from the Sultan to this effect? And even if you have such
a royal letter, should we implement it at this time of the pilgrimage? What will happen to these two hundred thousand pilgrims,
who are altogether helpless? If this your choice were to be
carried out, all these God's creatures will be destroyed by the
Arabs." On hearing this, all the leaders of Egypt and Syria
said, "Let it be according to the will of the Pasha." Thereupon,
the Pasha took a Royal *khila'*, a stone-marten fur-coat and the
Royal Firman, and went, at the head of seventy-eighty horsemen,
to Sherif Sa'ad's residence, where he invited all the nobility to
come and in their presence had read out to them the Royal
Decree and the letter of the Grand Wezir, which Sherif Sa'ad
took and kissed. With his own hand Hussain Pasha helped
Sherif Sa'ad to put on the fur-coat, the Royal present. Then
the Pasha took the oath of allegiance and was followed by all
the other notables and dignitaries of Mecca. The Pasha then
turned to Sherif Sa'ad and said, "May it be pleasing to God;
you are invited to the Muna market-place." The Pasha's words
were interpreted to the Sherif who accepted the invitation by
saying, "With all my heart I accept the invitation," and going

forth at the head of his entourage he went to the appointed place, where he offered the Pasha coffee, rose-water, sherbet, and incense. The Sherif then presented the Pasha with precious stones in leather bags, two pedigree mares of great beauty and two pure-bred riding-camels, and with each gift went also the Abyssinian slave who brought them. Thereafter, they all went to Muna and Arafat with much pomp, accompanied by camels with howdahs, and litters for men and women, while drums, tambourines, and pipes were played. They rejoiced for four days, and since Sherif Sa'ad was confirmed in his office, the whole city of Mecca went out to Arafat with unusual relief and particular jubilation. The elders of the tribes round Mecca declared that they had never in all their lives seen such a host of decorated nobility assembled to celebrate such a feast.

On the second day of the feast of the pilgrimage, however, Hussain Pasha sent five hundred Egyptian armed troops and another detachment of a thousand horsemen to Arafat and occupied the head of the water-supply. He also sent seven platoons to hold the road to Mecca and to Muna, which was done without opposition. He thereupon ordered the pilgrims to move to Mecca and only an armed force to remain. Later, all the Diwan officials, notables, army chiefs, leaders of the Hashimites, and others gathered at Hussain Pasha's headquarters. At that moment Hassan Agha, who had been sent to invite Sherif Sa'ad, came back with the news for Hussain Pasha that the Sherif Sa'ad had fled, leaving everything behind.

The Pasha then issued orders that forces be sent to occupy and seal all the Government offices in Mecca and Muna. As regards Sherif Sa'ad, when he saw that the huge force under the Pasha had occupied the heads of the water-supply he sensed the trouble awaiting him, and after a skirmish, in which some forty persons were wounded, and most of their horses killed, he, at the head of a group of his attendants and family, escaped to Taif.

Hussain Pasha first presented the man who had brought him the news with twenty gold liras. Then he turned to the nobility and chiefs and explained to them his reasons for turning down their former advice about the deposition of Sherif Sa'ad, when they were consulted at Al Ma'ala. Had he accepted it then, the pilgrimage would not have been performed peacefully. Having explained this, he asked their opinion as to whom he should appoint to succeed Sherif Sa'ad. Again they advised him to invest Sherif Ahmad, but the Pasha pointed out that Sherif Ahmad belonged to Sherif Sa'ad's party, and, if he were to be appointed, revolts and disturbances would never cease at Mecca.

As that clan had murdered Hassan Pasha, so they would do the same with others. The perspicacious Pasha consequently proposed that Sherif Barakat be appointed to the rulership.

The assembly approved his proposal, and Barakat became the Sherif of Mecca. A Royal Decree was read and Hussain Pasha personally dressed the new Sherif in a stone-marten fur-coat and presented him with a specially fine or Royal *khila'*, and he, before everybody else, took the oath of loyalty. This was followed by the reading of the opening chapter of the Koran and the kissing of the Sherif's hand by the Sheikh al Islam, Busrawi Muhammad Effendi; and by his brothers; by the Mulla of Mecca; and the representative of the Mawlawi Anatolian sect; Hafiz Effendi, the Mulla of Medina; the Syrian Emir-al-Hajj, Harmush Pasha; the Egyptian Emir-al-Hajj, Uzbek Bey; Ibn Abi Shawarib [the "Mustachioed"], the Commandant of Jedda; Brigadier Muhammad Bey; Baklaji Muhammad Bey; Burunsiz [the "Noseless"] Ahmad Agha; the Kethuda, or Agent, Ibrahim Pasha; the Treasurer, Mahmud Agha; Ajem-zada; Siyawush Agha; and Khoja Baykush-Zada Hasan, and all the chiefs of the seven army detachments and the nobles of Mecca, all of whom congratulated and kissed the new Sherif's hands. This was followed by many salvoes of rifle- and gun-shots. Then the Pasha and the Sherif Barakat rode side by side at the head of the leaders and notables, while the Syrian and Egyptian armed forces saluted them, to the Arafat mosque, and there worshipped, and once again, having received the Sherif's blessing, took the oath of loyalty. Hussain Pasha and Sherif Barakat on their way passed by the Jebel Nur, and from there the Pasha's aide-de-camp, Heykalzada Agha, approached the Sherif and led him with a great following and in pomp to his own residence at Mecca. On arrival another salvo of guns and rifles was fired. As soon as the Sherif reached the Shrine he performed the religious ritual. As to the Pasha, he returned at the head of his army to his residence at Ma'ala, and only later came back at the head of his seventy or eighty personal bodyguardsmen to the Ka'aba.

When Sherif Barakat, on becoming Sherif, entered Mecca with a great procession he went to the Shrine and sat three stairs below the Prophet's pulpit, where all the notables, the religious sheikhs, imams, scribes, learned men, dignitaries, and a multitude of people gathered and took the oath of allegiance before him. It was then announced that as the Peace of God and of the Ottomans was now reigning three days and three nights might be observed as a period of merriment, and that everybody should decorate his house and beautify his shop, according to his ambition and ability, while all the main roads of Mecca be especially cleansed for the occasion. Thus Mecca was again a happy town, and if any of its inhabitants had any worry or grief he could enter the house of God, and all his worries and sadness would pass away after Sherif Barakat was installed, and that is why the inhabitants rejoiced for three days.

On his accession Barakat exiled all the late Sherif Sa'ad's clan, the Bani Zaid, and sent a detachment in pursuit of Sherif Sa'ad, who escaped from Taif through Taraba and Bisha, and thence, via the Harb tribe, to Turkey. In 1676 Sa'ad visited the Sultan, Muhammad IV, who was at Adrianople, and returned to Istanbul with him, being made several offers of sinecure appointments in Turkey and given presents, including three hundred mule-loads of food supplies annually. Through his friendship with the Chief Eunuch he met the Sultan's mother, who well rewarded him and promised him his wishes, although in the event he was sent for the time being to live in exile at Wiza, in the Balkans.

The appointment of Barakat was in part, or largely, owing to his support by the traveller Muhammad ibn Sulaiman, the Moor, an astute astronomer whose sundial had caused trouble in Mecca. He had returned to Mecca with Hussain Pasha, and, as a friend of the brother of the Grand Wezir of Turkey, a man of unusual influence, to whom he had given lessons in astronomy during his stay in Mecca for the pilgrimage, and with whom he had afterwards visited the Sultan. He had been well received by the Sultan, and, obtaining his confidence, had asked him for several reforms at Mecca, which the Sultan approved. Among them were the giving of money bequeathed by Sultan Jukmuk to the poor in the form of pottage and bread, as formerly, the income having, he alleged, been recently misappropriated to their own use by the notables, also the stopping of drum-beating and dancing in the seminaries of the dervish orders, the stopping of women going out on the night of the Prophet's birthday, an end of evening processions on certain saints' days, which had come to be orgiastic, and the use of a proper accounting system in the religious bequests office.

Barakat's first expeditions were against the Harb tribe, which had so often attacked the pilgrim trains from the North and had for centuries blackmailed the Emirs of the pilgrim caravans. He was successful, and order was soon restored throughout the Hijaz. The only untoward incident in Mecca during his reign was an alleged defilement of the Ka'aba by a Persian. The people of Mecca—doubtless to the pleasure of the Ottomans—were in consequence much excited against all Persians, and it was only by great firmness, and through proclamations calculated to allay excitement, that more violent disturbance was avoided.

In Medina some of the Turkish garrison attacked and killed Barakat's agent on the grounds that he had abused the Sultan, but the Sherif refused to be roused into direct action, wrote to the Sultan asking for redress, and sought peace.

The next year thirty-five of the sherifs, under one Ahmad ibn Ghalib, who was long to be a trouble-maker, left for Damascus, with a view to visiting Istanbul and complaining against Barakat, but they were stopped there by the Governor and were made to write out their complaints. These were sent on by hand of only two of their number. Their chief request was for a subsidy and the withdrawal of Muhammad ibn Sulaiman, the Moorish astronomer.

In the same year, 1682, Barakat died and was succeeded by his son Said. The Sultan sent him a *khila'* and a firman at the same time, ordering the exile of Muhammad the Moor to Jerusalem, and directing that the income of the country be divided into four equal parts, one part to go to the Sherif, and the other three to the remaining members of the family.

Said for a time sought to delay the execution of this order by the Sultan, which had originally been a suggestion made some years earlier by his father, when himself out of office in Istanbul, and probably prompted by Muhammad the Moor, but the arrival and contents of the letter becoming known in the Meccan diwans, he was forced to implement it.

No sooner had he done so than Ahmad ibn Ghalib and his supporters used their portions to enlist unusually large numbers of bodyguardsmen, so that the Sherif, pursuing his father's clement policy, complained to the Sultan's representative, and, sending for his revenue collectors, asked them to provide funds for extra guards and night-watchmen for himself and the people. The Turkish Pashas and the Ottoman notables in consequence sought to stage a meeting in the Sherif's house,

sending for Ahmad that he might defend himself. He refused
to come, but agreed that he would meet them in the Sanctuary,
and replied that, as for his having a bodyguard, this was an
ancient and a well-known custom of Meccan nobles. Meanwhile his supporters put on their armour, saddled their horses,
and ordered their men to be ready to fight. The leading Pasha,
Salah, Emir of the Pilgrims, sent a message to Ahmad that
peace would be imposed by force if he would not accept it
peacefully, the drums of the janizaries beat to quarters, and
the citizens hurried to their homes. Ahmad's reply to the Pasha
was simply, "The sword is ours and not to farm-hands from
Damascus." The Ottomans, who were not yet ready to fight,
sent another letter to Ahmad, and two days later, no reply
having come, Salah Pasha, ready and wishing to depart,
changed his tactics, visited him, and, kissing his hand, begged
his forgiveness.

In reply to his deferential letter to the Ottoman Sultan's
representative in Egypt, complaining against the members of
his family, the Sherif received only a *khila'* and a polite answer,
to which he in turn replied, pressing for troops since disorder
was increasing. Shops were often broken up and looted or
people killed for their purses in the streets, vice of all kinds led
by the slaves and military followers of the sherifs was the
fashion, and there were even cases of women being raped before
their men could interfere.

At the end of the pilgrimage of 1683 the Sherif Said, overwhelmed by disorders that he could not bring to an end,
appointed Ahmad ibn Ghalib to act for him, and rode off to
catch up the Damascus pilgrim caravan.

Ahmad ibn Ghalib collected his people and proposed the
succession of Masoud ibn Sa'ad, but meanwhile Said's reports
on the state of disorder in Mecca and the misrule of the Negroes
there had reached the Sultan, who, much disturbed, had sent
at once for Ahmad ibn Zaid, then in exile at Qirq Kanisa, in
Asiatic Turkey, requesting him to accept the rulership of the
Hijaz.

Ahmad caught up the down-going pilgrim train at Al Ala,
in the Northern Hijaz, and put on the *khila'* in Medina, entering
Mecca in 1684. Sa'ad's Wezir, a Yemeni and a popular man,
was reappointed as Ahmad's Wezir, and the famous patriarch

Sheikh Salama ibn Murshid ibn Suwait, of the Dhafir tribe of Iraq, was welcomed at Mecca and made an arbitrator and peacemaker between the members of the Sherifian family.

As soon as order was restored in Mecca, Sherif Ahmad set out to punish the Anaiza tribe of Nejd, who had taken the opportunity of disorders in the Hijaz to become mutinous, defeating them decisively.

In the autumn of 1686 the Sultan sent a message to the Sherif to tell him that he had won a great victory over infidels, the Muslims having taken over 70,000 prisoners and recovered all the territories in Europe formerly lost. This was, in fact, the year in which Hungary was lost by Turkey, Vienna having already been lost after a series of defeats beginning in 1664 and ending in the Treaty of Passarowitz, in 1718. I suppose his message to have been an attempt to maintain confidence in Ottoman strength, and to counter rumours of the truth.

Ahmad ibn Zaid died in 1687 and an attempt to succeed him was at once made by Ahmad ibn Ghalib, who had formerly been the cause of the disorders in Mecca and promoter of the misrule of the slaves. The Sultan's Governor of Egypt had meanwhile promised Said ibn Sa'ad ibn Zaid the insignia of the rulership. Said, thus emboldened, ordered the setting up of barricades in the streets of Mecca, and prepared to resist the force of Ahmad ibn Ghalib, then assembling in the Wadi al Marr, at the same time sending his representatives to ask Ahmad to show them any royal decree of his authority.

The Turkish commanders were much annoyed by this trouble-brewing, and advanced on Mecca, which Said evacuated, remaining in Taif for two months, until the Ottomans sent him his father's khila', with a letter of authority from his father to act for him and deported Ahmad ibn Ghalib to the Yemen. There, telling the Imam's son, Al Nasr li-din illahi Muhammad, later ruler of the Yemen, whom he found at al Arish, that the Hijaz and even Egypt and Syria were now easy to conquer, Ahmad received from him an army of four thousand men, a very considerable sum of money, and the aid, as his commanders, of three of the ruling family, Qassim ibn al Muayyad, Hassan ibn al Mutawakkil, and Ali ibn Ahmad. This was the signal, not for an advance on the Ottoman Empire, but for a series of local fights, an attempt on Sana itself, and a disagreement between the son of the Imam and Ahmad on the one hand and between the Imam and his other sons. In the end Ahmad established himself at Jizan, on the Red Sea, until later on he went to Damascus by a roundabout route, via the sandy deserts of the Dahana, in Central Arabia, where he died in or after 1693.

Meanwhile, in Mecca, Muhsin ibn Hussain ibn Zaid had succeeded Ahmad ibn Ghalib, if only for a short period as pretender, Medina, however, remaining loyal to him until he died, in 1691. It was in this year that Yahya ibn Barakat came to Mecca as Emir of the Damascus pilgrims, "no Sherif for many years before or ever since having been an Emir al Hajj."[1]

The East India Company at this time was collecting information about the ports with which their merchantmen traded, and the chaplain of the Company, the Rev. John Ovington, published in London, in 1696, his secondhand but diligent account of the Red Sea ports under the title, *A Voyage to Suratt*.[2] Of Jedda he says that it is

the principal port in this sea belonging to the grand signior. . . . It is the sea-port to Mecca . . . and the land about that place is so useless and unprofitable and unfit for any improvements, that it seems to be accurs'd by nature and debarr'd of Heaven's blessings, by a constant scarcity of all things, unless they are imported from other kingdoms. Therefore is the Grand Signior obliged to very great expenses for its support, to furnish out a maintenance for it yearly from Egypt and send from there twenty or twenty-five sail of large ships, laden with provisions, money, etc. for its subsistence and the support of trade. Jedda flourishes in a constant traffick from India, Persia, and other parts of Arabia and the Abyssinian shore. . . . Hither the Arabians bring their coffee, which is bought here by the Turks and shipped for the Sues. . . . Hither likewise resort every year hoggees [*hajjis*] from all parts . . . and as soon as they are arrived . . . they instantly strip themselves, out of a humour of mortification and set out with only a longee [*lungi*] about their middle.

In the train of pilgrims about this time, probably in 1685 or 1686,[3] came a simple Englishman, Joseph Pitts of Oxford,

[1] Al Hussaini, *Kitab Tandhid al Uqud*.
[2] Reprinted by Oxford University Press in 1929.
[3] Sir William Foster, *The Red Sea at the Close of the Seventeenth Century*, Introduction, p. 11.

who had been captured at the age of fifteen. Describing the pilgrimage, he said:

The Sultan of Mecca, who is of the race of Mahomet, does not think himself too good to clean the *Beat* [that is, the *Bait*, or house of God, in the temple of Mecca]. He and his favourites first wash it with the holy water Zemzem, and after that with sweet water. The stairs which were brought to enter in at the door being removed, the people crowd under the door to receive the sweepings of the water on their bodies, and the besoms or brooms, with which the *Beat* is cleaned are broken to pieces, and thrown out amongst the mob; when he that gets a small stick or sprig of it, keeps it as a sacred relic. Every year the covering of the *Beat* is renewed, and sent from *Grand Cairo* by order of the Grand Signior; and when the caravan goes with the pilgrims to Mecca, the new covering is carried upon two camels, which do no other work all the year long. It is received with extreme joy, some kissing the camels and bidding them welcome. The old covering being pulled down, the new one is put up by the Sultan of Mecca; and he cutting the old covering in pieces, sells them at a great price to the Hadgees.[1]

At Mecca are thousands of blue pigeons, which none will affright or abuse, much less kill them, whence they are so very tame that they will pick meat out of one's hand, and I myself have fed them. They are called the pigeons of the prophet, and come in great flocks to the temple, where they are usually fed by the Hadgees. . . . The pilgrims, before they receive the honourable title of Hadgee, again put on their mortifying habit, and go to a hill called Gibbelel Orphat, or the mountain of knowledge, where there are said to meet no less than 70,000 persons every year. . . .

. . . the three days being expired they all return to Mecca, where they must not stay above ten or twelve days, during which a great fair is held, in which is sold all sorts of East India goods. Almost every one now buys a shroud of fine linen to be buried in, for the advantage of having it dipped in the holy water; and this they are sure to carry with them wherever they go. The evening before they go from Mecca, every one takes a solemn leave of the *Beat Allah*, from which they retire backwards, holding up their hands and offering up their petition with their eyes fixed on the building till they have lost sight of it and then they burst into tears.

---

[1] This practice of distributing the covering in pieces is continued. I received a section, embroidered in gold lettering, to say, "Whoever visits this House he will receive security and bread" (words of the Koran).

The Sherif Said's reign, begun in 1687, was chequered by interregnums.

Two foreign travellers who were in Jedda in the autumn of 1700, William Daniel, an Englishman, and Charles Jacques Poucet, a Frenchman, have left accounts of their visit and of Sherif Said's intransigence.[1] Daniel was an eye-witness of how

> the Grand Sheriffs treated the Grand Seigniour's Bashaw, he coming in person before the city, accompanied with 2000 horse and demanded of the Bashaw (who was my only friend) 100,000 chiqueens; adding that his master, the Grand Seigniour, was the son of a Christian whore, and he would not own him to be a protector of the Mahomedan religion (since he had made a peace with those unbelievers, the Christians) but that he would marry his daughter to the King of Morocco. Upon which the Bashaw was forced to send him the money to save his head; and I, very melancholy, returned to my lodging.

The Frenchman arrived in Jedda on the 5th of December, a few days after the incident related above.[2] He describes, however, the visit of the Sherif, who was still camped outside the walls. He says:

> The Sherif was a man of about sixty years of age, of a majestick presence, and of a somewhat ghastly look. He has a slit in his underlip on the right side. His subjects and neighbours do not much commend his sweetness and clemency. He obliged the Bacha, who resides at Jedda for the grand signior, to give him fifteen thousand crowns of gold, and threatened him with military execution if he did not forthwith obey.

Poucet describes how the Sherif took taxes from the Turkish merchants, and says that

> the Cherif—a fierce and haughty man—has withdrawn his subjection to the grand Signior, whom he calls by way of contempt, "*ebon mamlouq*," as much as to say, "son of a slave."

From 1705 Abdul Karim ibn Muhammad ruled until deposed in 1711, returning for a short time in 1715, when he retired to live with the Harb tribe and thence went to Egypt, dying there of plague in 1718.

In 1706 there had been an incident in Medina caused by a gift from the Shah to the Shrine of a golden bowl, full of amber, and decorated with precious stones. It was handed

---

[1] *The Red Sea at the Close of the Seventeenth Century.*   [2] *Ibid.*, pp. 74, 158.

over to the caretakers until leave was received from the Sherif and the Sultan to hang it in the Shrine, but later, when looked for, it had gone. The Eunuchs of the Shrine and the caretakers were all suspected, and one of the former confessed after torture. The inquisitor sent from Istanbul found some of the gold and amber, which he took to Istanbul to be remodelled. Whether it was ever returned is not recorded.

The Sherif Said died in 1716 and was succeeded, for a year and a quarter only, by his son Abdilla,[1] whose meanness was his undoing. He stopped nearly all payments to his family and to his soldiers, and there are many stories of his ludicrous pettiness in money matters, a vice which soon rendered him totally unacceptable, his brother Ali replacing him, following an abdication which was imposed by his whole family. Suddenly taking courage, however, Abdilla killed Ali. In consequence there were many disorders in the city, until the pilgrim caravans, with their military escorts, began to arrive.

The Pasha of the Damascus caravan, as the senior of the visiting Ottomans, pronounced in favour of Yahya ibn Barakat ibn Muhammad ibn Barakat, who had for a time been Governor of a district in Syria near Damascus, once been Emir of the Hajj, and was doubtless thought to be broken to Turkish ways, a consideration in which the Pasha was at fault. His vacillating rule lasted only a year and a half, when Mubarak ibn Ahmad was nominated as his successor.

The latter began collecting followers from the Ataiba tribe of Nejd and from the Thuqaif about Taif, and decided to advance on Mecca in three columns to meet at Arafat. There Yahya went out to meet him, but was outnumbered and defeated after a fight and pursuit lasting all one night and until noon of the following day.

The new Sherif maintained order well, until in 1720 a third of Jedda was destroyed by fire, a number of the oldest shrines and seminaries being burnt. The Sherif contributed so largely to the relief of the people of Jedda that he was in consequence forced to reduce the subsidies of his family and sell much of his personal property. Unable to maintain order in Medina or among the tribes, and lacking money with which to pay his

---

[1] 'Abdilla' was the Ottoman Turkish and Hashimite family usage for the name Abdilillah.

soldiers adequately, he was replaced by Yahya ibn Barakat, who returned from Turkey with the pilgrims.

The new ruler adopted an aggressive policy towards the sherifs of the Dhawu Zaid, being well supported by the Turkish troops of Ali Pasha. The Dhawu Zaid, on the other hand, sought the support of the Thuqaif tribe near Taif, but Yahya suborned some of their guides, and through them uncovered a correspondence between Zaid and some of the notables in Mecca, whose houses were thereupon looted and destroyed by order of Ali Pasha, the Turkish agent and commander.

The Sherif Yahya and Ali Pasha fought Mubarak at Arafat, in a running fight ending at Jebel al Khatoon, where Ali Pasha was wounded in the thigh, and the Turkish cavalry were halted, many of the soldiers being killed by the bedouin. Both sides, however, retreated, Mubarak to Taif, and Ali and Yahya to Mecca, from where, mustering a new force, Yahya advanced once more and temporarily drove out Mubarak. A few days later the forces were paid off, and Ali Pasha retired to Jedda, where he died of the effects of his wound.

Mubarak at once began raising fresh forces, and the new Pasha, Ismail, and the notables of Mecca, decided to call upon Yahya to resign in favour of his son Barakat, whom, however, they only supported for eighteen days. Mubarak thus at last entered Mecca and ruled for five months, in the latter days of which he was in continuous dispute with his former supporter, Sherif Abdilla ibn Said, and with Muhsin ibn Abdulla.

The former had written to the Sultan informing him that the killing of the Turkish soldiers was owing to Mubarak, and that he himself had protected the survivors, that having at first promised Mubarak to persuade his rival Muhsin to leave Mecca, he had subsequently changed his views. When, as a result, letters arrived by hand of the Ottoman Pasha, who had reached Medina, naming Abdilla as Sherif, the Qadhi refused at first to register them on the grounds that they were illegal, and only the actual firman itself acceptable. The Ottoman officers and Muhsin, however, brought pressure to bear on him to legalize them, for the sake of peace, Muhsin being already prepared to fight. Thus Mubarak was forced to leave Mecca, making for the Yemen where he died in 1727, and Abdilla ibn Said came to power, holding it until the end of his life.

THE BEGINNINGS OF THE DHAWU AUN CLAN

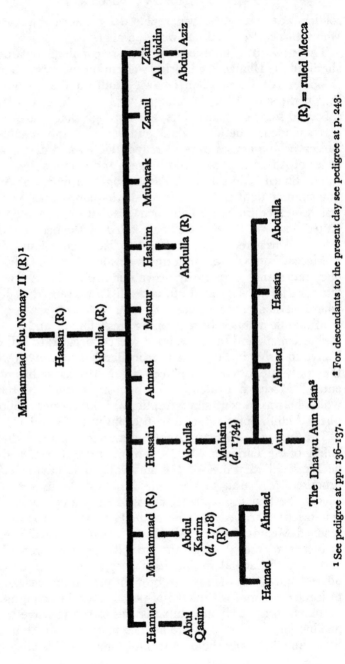

Muhammad Abu Nomay II (R)[1]

The Dhawu Aun Clan[2]

(R) = ruled Mecca

[1] See pedigree at pp. 136-137.

[2] For descendants to the present day see pedigree at p. 243.

Chapter X

ABDILLA IBN SAID
AND OTHER GREAT-GRANDSONS OF ZAID
(A.D. 1716–71)

THE SHERIFS WHO WERE OPPOSED TO ABDILLA'S ACCESSION went out to meet Othman Pasha, the Emir of the Damascus Pilgrims, on his way from Medina to Mecca in order to complain to him of the appointment of the new Sherif, and to say, more particularly, that Abdilla had not paid them their allowances. Othman told the new Sherif that he, the Pasha, could provide the family with plenty of money, and himself listed ten of the sherifs who had complained, and whom, he held, should be paid.

In spite of intrigues intensified upon his attempt to institute regular taxation of the merchants, Abdilla continued to rule successfully. His control over the tribes was strengthened by victories in Al Yamama, in Central Arabia, in 1727, where the Dhafir tribe was utterly defeated, few but women and children surviving the battles.

Al Hussaini relates that in about July 1727 a foreign Minister and his suite arrived in Jedda and were disliked by the Turks. The foreigners soon found their Muslim servants unsatisfactory, and, wishing to be rid of them, they approached Abu Bekr Pasha, the Governor of Jedda, who took no action, the servants being returned to them; but a rumour was spread that the foreigners had killed them, and a mob entered the aliens' house, killing eight of them, and looting all their belongings. The Governor, who was terrified of the consequences, found and returned most of the looted property, and hanged the ringleaders of the mob. The Sherif of Mecca, the Qadhi, and the Sheikh al Islam then arrived, and the people quietened down.

When Abdilla died in 1730, Muhammad his son, aged only twenty, was away leading an expedition in the Yemen, but his uncles and his brother managed to persuade the Qadhi to proclaim his appointment. Masoud ibn Said, his uncle, volunteered to be his Wezir, and the start of the reign was propitious; but before long he had quarrelled with the Wezir, and there was trouble with the Dhawu Barakat clan. One of the latter, being ordered for some minor offence to leave Mecca, instead sought refuge with a sherif of the Abādila clan, one Abdul Aziz ibn Zaid-al-Abidin, inside the city. The Sherif was furious, surrounded the house with his men, who opened fire. The sherifs inside replied, and then sortied, going to Muhammad to demand redress, which was rated at twenty-five horses, twenty-five slaves, sixty camels, and the Ruler to ride to their house and apologize.

A few days later there was a similar incident. A slave of the Sherif Abdul Muin was wanted for murder of a Hanbalite student, and Muhammad's slaves, passing Abdul Muin's house, saw the man in question, talking with Abdul Muin's slaves. They agreed between them to arrest him, but he escaped them and ran into the house. Hearing shouts in the street the sherifs inside came out and drove off the Ruler's slaves. The Sherif with his armed men about him came to the attack, but the leading men of Mecca also hurried to the scene with their armed servants to intervene. Thus the Sherif's family were embittered by him, and turned more and more to his uncle Masoud, the Wezir. Many of the sherifs left Mecca for Taif, and were followed by Masoud, where they ejected the garrison and proclaimed Masoud Sherif of Mecca. Their fight with Muhammad, for which they had secured some tribal reinforcements, took place at Arafat, where he was defeated, although the sherifs on his side fought fiercely and several were killed in his cause. Muhammad had only reigned for a year and a half and was still popular with many of his people.

During this, the first reign of Muhammad, there had occurred one of those not infrequent complaints of desecration of the Shrine by an unknown Persian, which, it was generally agreed by the sherifs, had in fact been staged by hired agents of the Turks. The Mufti refused to accept a charge against an unknown man or men, and the Sherif remained in his house, refusing to be impressed by the agitation of the mob, which, without waiting for the Mufti's agreement, forced their demand, that all Persians should leave the city, on the Wezir. Town-criers proclaimed the popular order, and the Persians indeed left, but only a few days later all of them returned with the incoming pilgrim caravan.

Masoud, the Wezir, was now Ruler of Mecca, but the Thuqaif tribe mobilized against him, and within three months he was defeated by them in the hills near Taif, and so Muhammad once more returned to the rulership.

At this time, in 1733, Hussain Agha, "an unbearable man," Sardar of the janizaries at Mecca, making an excursion with his family, was attacked because his soldiers had beaten an Arab and he had refused to punish them or give redress. He took refuge in a wayside building, and the Sherif, receiving a report of the matter, at once went to the scene. The Sardar was putting his head out of a first-floor window, to talk to the Sherif, when a bullet killed him instantly. The janizaries were much incensed and the Sardar's officers wrote angry reports to Egypt, the Sherif remaining aloof from them in his palace. Fortunately a Turkish Wezir, Mushir Abu Bekr Pasha, arrived at this time and quietened his people down.

The Turkish officials, however, now backed Masoud, who was still camped at Wadi al Marr, giving him money to raise supporters from the Thuqaif and from other tribes, while Muhammad relied upon his personal guards, his slaves, and the Yemenis.

Both Muhammad and Masoud separately appealed to Abu Bekr Pasha, who refused to make any decision without an order from Istanbul. Masoud thereupon prepared to fight, while Muhammad visited the Pasha at Jedda and made one more effort to obtain his intervention. Failing, he returned to Mecca, his force encountering that of Masoud outside the city—defeated them, but, although at first successful outside Mecca, he was later defeated inside it, and so after an hour's fight Masoud resumed the rulership.

The sherifs in council at this time decided that all resident foreigners should leave Mecca, since they were filling posts which might have been held by Meccans, many being employed as clerks, by the officials of the Government. Most of the Moroccans, Turks, and Egyptians therefore left with the returning caravans. The Indians, Uzbeks, Kashmiris, and

Persians, however, stayed, but, being again and insistently ordered to leave, most of them in the end did so. "The town was noticeably emptier and everything cheap and easy to find."[1]

The Sherif also ordered that there should be no smoking in public, as tobacco had become very popular with men and women of all classes, who even smoked outside the door of his house. Further, the Ulama being in agreement with him, all coffee-shops and tobacco-shops were closed. Meanwhile Muhammad was not idle, and had persuaded the Ataiba tribesmen to support him.

Masoud, fearful of the tribes, his treasury nearly empty, the Al Barakat and Al Hassan clans of the sherifs, together with a number of the Turks, all ill-disposed towards him, did his best to propitiate his family, many of whom continued to support Muhammad and had secretly sent him welcoming messages on his arrival near Mecca. With the expenditure of his last remaining money Masoud raised sufficient men to cut off Muhammad from Jedda and prevent supplies reaching him, so that an intermediary, the Wezir Sulaiman Pasha, was able to make peace between them.

The Sherif was shortly afterwards obliged to send an expedition to subjugate the sherifs of the Al Hassan clan, descended from Hassan al Aghan, who unexpectedly laid claim to the Sherifate of Mecca, and menaced the pilgrims from the Yemen. Their scouts were encountered five days' march from Mecca, while the main force slipped away into the hills of the Jebel Bani Sulaim, where they were besieged, eventually surrendering their chieftain, Sheikh Asaf, who was taken in chains to Mecca, he and his family dying there from smallpox a few years later.

Masoud improved and enlarged the Sherif's Palace, the Dar al Sa'ada, originally built by Hassan ibn Hussain ibn Abi Nomay, but he remembered to give it two massive towers in which he placed guns.

Medina now drew the Sherif's attention. A quarrel between the Egyptian Sheikh of the Haram and the Turkish garrison there had split both the townsmen and the Harb tribe into two camps, and when the Sherif of Mecca's slave cavalry were sent by him to restore order they failed so signally that he angrily closed the Red Sea ports to them, cutting off their retreat to

[1] Al Hussaini, *Kitab Tandhid al Uqud.*

Mecca, and ordered them into the field once more. The down-travelling pilgrim escorts restored order: on their arrival at Medina, the Sheikh al Haram was dismissed and sent to Egypt, and the city once more placed under the Sherif's control, his own troops furnishing the garrison.

In 1744 a special messenger to the Sherif of Mecca, one Sayid Nasrullah ibn al Hussain al Ja'afari, arrived from Nadir Shah, informing him that he had taken Basra, Erbil, Kirkuk, and Nejef, but not Baghdad "because it was walled, and the Wali a friend"; that he had surrounded and besieged Mosul, and that the Sunni Ulama of Baghdad had acknowledged the existence of the Ja'afariya, or Shiah, rite as the fifth rite of Islam.

The Sherif sent Nadir Shah's letter to the Sublime Porte, and the reply from the Sultan, arriving with the next caravan of pilgrims, merely ordered the sending of the Persian messenger to him in Istanbul. In the meanwhile Abu Bekr Pasha, Governor of Jedda, told the Sherif that he had heard from his nephew, Ahmad Pasha, who was commanding the troops at Erzerum, that peace between Nadir Shah and the Ottomans had in fact not been signed, that on the contrary Nadir Shah had been defeated, so that an. Ottoman victory was being everywhere celebrated, as it should now be celebrated in the Hijaz. The Sherif hesitated, but at last consented to do so. The Pasha next demanded the handing over of the Persian messenger to be killed, but this the Sherif refused, ordering instead a sermon reviling the Shiahs, in order that it might be publicly known that he was not in favour of them. The Shah's messenger, handed over on a promise of immunity, was, however, eventually executed on his arrival in Istanbul.

In Mecca contrary rumours as to the defeat of the Shah or of the Ottomans, and of peace or of war between them, continued to arrive for some time.

In 1746 came news of a fight between

the English and the French in Bengal, the English being the aggressors, until the French King sent forty ships and the English withdrew to Deccan, demolishing the port of Madras, where the French found a vast treasure left by them in the citadel.[1]

[1] Ibn Zaini Dahlan, *Al Jadawil al Mardhiya*.

The following year it was reported that Nadir Shah, the slave of Tahmasp, had been killed by his guards, and a letter came from Ahmad Pasha, of Baghdad, to the Sherif, informing him that peace with Persia was restored. Nadir Shah had, in fact, been assassinated on June 19, 1747, but by Persians who overcame his Afghan bodyguard.

The Yemenite soldiers of the Sherif at Qunfidha rebelled against his commander and agent there on the grounds that he had failed to give them their supplies. They took their dues by force and retreated into the Yemen, pursued by the Sherif's men, who failed to overtake them before they entered Yemeni territory at Lahoya. The Imam ordered the soldiers, whom the Sherif maintained had taken more than their dues, to repay 2200 riyals, and promised to send them back "when things were quieter." The Sherif, much obliged for his tact, sent presents to the Imam, including several mares and a white slave of great value.

The Sherif Masoud died on February 18, 1752, and was succeeded by his brother Masaad. The Dhawu Barakat clan alone objected to the new Sherif, and secretly sent messages of sympathy to his nephew Muhammad ibn Abdilla, many of them leaving Mecca for Wadi al Murr. Masaad wrote propitiatory messages to them, asking them to return to Mecca, but they stubbornly refused his appeals.

Masaad was still ignorant of Muhammad's desire to oust him, but, coming later to hear of it, he sent a brother to raise the tribes about Taif, who found that Muhammad had already gathered the Ataiba and was camped with them at Al Sail, half-way up the mountain slopes, from where he marched across to Taif, thus forestalling him. Announcing himself as Sherif, Muhammad advanced on Mecca, the fight taking place at Duqm al Wabr, where Muhammad was beaten and his baggage train looted. A few weeks later he again advanced on Mecca from Taif, the two armies camping opposite to each other for the night. In the morning it was found that Muhammad, having left his camp fires burning, was in fact advancing on Mecca. Masaad sent his fastest cavalry in pursuit, which overtook him at Wadi al Minhana, where after a two hours' fight Muhammad was again defeated.

An intermediary, Sayid Abdulla al Fa'ar, made peace

between the two parties, but on the condition that the Sherif granted subsidies to the disaffected sherifs. The Emirs of the Damascene and Egyptian pilgrims, however, supported the Sherifate of Mubarak ibn Muhammad ibn Abdilla, to which a number of the sherifs, unknown to Masaad, had already agreed. The house of Masaad was surrounded and the proclamation of Mubarak was read, without, however, the support of a Royal Firman. Nevertheless, Ahmad, Masaad's brother, led his troops into lower Mecca, and the Sherif himself sortied, and between them they cleared the remainder of the city.

Mubarak hastily sent a plea for pardon before fleeing to Wadi al Marr, whence he was fetched and imprisoned, dying a few years later. Abdulla al Fa'ar was then deported to the Yemen, where he was well received by the Imam, who eventually intervened with the Sherif for his return to Mecca, but no sooner was he there than, with the help of the same Emir of the Damascus pilgrims, he began his intrigues once more.

Largely owing to his encouragement, Abdulla Pasha al Sharchi called a council, on the pretence of discussing projects for improving the water-supply of Mecca, and vehemently attacked the Sherif, pretending that he had diverted for his own use water for the pilgrims; ordering his arrest, he announced that his brother Ja'afar was to be his successor. Ja'afar, a mild man, released his brother as soon as the pilgrim trains had left, abdicated in his favour, and, buying at once some gardens in Taif, removed there and cultivated them until he died five years later, in 1764.

About this time the merchants of the Hijaz began to find that their ships were often subjected to customs dues and port rules on the Indian shores, which, irking them, led to an appeal on their behalf by the Sherif. In November 1766 the following letter was received in London from Mr John Murray at Istanbul, addressed to the Right Hon. the Earl of Shelburne.

CONSTANTINOPLE,
October 16, 1766

MY LORD,

. . . The enclosed is a copy of a paper sent me by the Reis Effendi to desire that I would procure a letter to the Governor of Bender Minai and Bender Surat, not to molest the subjects of the Turks in their commerce in those parts. I promised to send it

to your Lordship; but I have searched and examined all the
books and maps of geography and cannot find Bender Minai, nor
can I find when these places were under the Dominion of the
Turks if they don't assume the Dominion over all the Maho-
metans.

I can no better describe the Sherif of Mecca, who makes this
request of the Porte, than by calling him the Pope of the Maho-
metan Law. . . .

I have the Honour to be with
the greatest regard and esteem,
My Lord,
Your Lordship's
most obedient and most humble servant,
JOHN MURRAY

The paper enclosed was in Italian, headed "Sostanza d'un
articolo contenunto nella Lettera del dottissimo Sherif dell'
Mecca."[1] Lord Shelburne replied in December 1766, and
referred the matter to the East India Company, which was
required to give the "strictest orders to prevent any interruption to the Turks in carrying on their trade to those parts in
the same manner that they have hitherto done."

One Ahmad Abdul Karim ibn Muhammad Ya'ali, supported
by the Dhawu Barakat, who desired to appoint Abdulla ibn
Hussain ibn Yahya ibn Barakat as Sherif, now collected their
forces, determining to take Jedda first, and then, with the help
of money from there, collect larger forces and attack Mecca.
Resisted by the people of Jedda, who closed their gates and
opened fire on them, they retired from their siesta to some
near-by reed huts. Meanwhile the defenders, using lighted
arrows, set fire to the huts. The new pretender and his forces,
after this defeat, returned to Wadi al Marr, and he himself left
for Egypt to obtain the Governor's backing and support from
the next escort of the downward Egyptian pilgrim caravan.

Masaad, forewarned, was able to arrange with his friend the
Emir of the Damascus pilgrims that he would stay until after
the Egyptian caravan had left, and so Abdulla ibn Hussain,
failing in his first plan, was forced to spend his money on
raising men to fight for him after the Damascus pilgrims had
left. The battle took place on the hills of Al Maala and Al

---

[1] Public Record Office: State Papers Foreign; Turkey (S.P. 97/43, f. 79).

Mu'abda, on the outskirts of Mecca itself. The Silahdar, or chief of the ordnance to Masaad, was the hero of the day, finally knocking one Sayid Ridha, who was heavily armoured, off his horse altogether and killing him with the weight of a mace blow. Abdulla, retreating to the Wadi al Marr, sent a request to the Ruler for pardon, and weakly it was given him; whereupon, without any hesitation, he went to Egypt to complain once more to the Governor, Ali Beg, who furnished him with 3000 men and thirty cannon and full supplies in three ships, the commander having had strict orders to support Abdulla and supplant Masaad; but it so happened that on the very day that the expedition sailed Masaad fell sick, dying on April 29, 1770, before the troops reached the Arabian shores.

In the time of Masoud, and again in Masaad's reign, Puritan Wahhābis of Central Arabia had approached the Sherifs for leave to make the pilgrimage, a request which both Sherifs refused, just as their successors, Ahmad and Sarur, were to do, in spite of the Wahhābis offering to send their learned men to argue their case.

In 1770—the exact date is not given—it is recorded that there was a "long tailed star like a lance in length from soon after sunset until sunrise." The people were upset and irritated by it, and some said later that it was an omen of the coming of the Wahhābis, basing this on lines in a poem by Al Fasi "the astrologer."[1]

Before he died Masaad had taken care to obtain the formal agreement, by a council of the sherifs, to the appointment of his brother Abdulla ibn Said, who was thereupon announced as the new Sherif, when, without hesitation, his brother Ahmad claimed it, and so forcibly made his demand that Abdulla abdicated in his favour.

The Egyptian expedition that was intended to place Abdulla ibn Hussain on the throne had by now reached Medina, and an attempt at a loyal defence led by the new Sherif's Governor there met with his instant execution. Abdulla ibn Hussain, encouraged by news of the force's arrival, began collecting tribesmen round his headquarters in the Wadi al Marr, while Sherif Ahmad, having little hope of winning, sent the women and children of the Dhawu Zaid to Taif for safety, and gathered

[1] Ibn Zaini Dahlan, *Khulasat al Kalam.*

his soldiers and tribesmen in Mecca. When the joint forces of Abdulla ibn Hussain and the Ottomans reached the outskirts of Mecca and pointed their guns at the city, on July 12, 1770, he felt obliged to send a message of submission, and retreated on Taif. Thus Abdulla ibn Hussain, of the Dhawu Barakat, was proclaimed Sherif of Mecca, and the Dhawu Zaid candidate was once more defeated.

Soon after Abdulla's succession he was attacked by a dervish, who stabbed him in the thigh as he was riding into the city, but, finding that the man was insane, he humanely released him.

Measures were now taken to drive Ahmad out of Taif, who, retreating into the Thuqaif country, raised followers sufficient in number to raid down to Jebel Arafat, where he was defeated, so that he was obliged to sue for peace and safe-conduct. Presents were exchanged—supplies for his journey against some mares—and then Ahmad set off for Lith, on the Red Sea, south of Jedda, where he remained until the Ottoman force had returned to Egypt. He then again advanced, supported by the Thuqaif tribe, led by their Sheikh, Rabia. The fight was going against him when Rabia was killed, and his men, suddenly inspirited by a desire for revenge, took Abdulla in the rear and, carrying all before them, entered Mecca.

Ahmad, contrary to the chivalrous traditions of the Sherifs, at once ordered all the houses of the Dhawu Barakat to be looted and then destroyed by fire. Some of the Barakat now took refuge in Jedda, and together with the Ottoman Sanjak there determined to resist Ahmad's force sent to capture it. Ahmad went in person to take part in the siege of Jedda, and sent messages to the Kathuda, promising him great rewards if he would corrupt the soldiers' loyalty, an offer he accepted, advising him to attack the Yemen gate, which he had arranged should be undefended.

The Sanjak, thus left with only the citadel, escaped through a small gate on the sea-side of the fort, and, riding with a small party through the shallow water unnoticed, made good his escape to Rabigh, on the coast north of Jedda. Abdulla ibn Hussain, hearing of his departure, followed his example and accompanied him to Yanbu', from where he set out for Egypt, staying there until he died. Ahmad's men then looted Jedda to such good purpose that there was a famine in Mecca, which continued until new supplies came at the end of the year.

At the same time the Imam of the Yemen had cut off supplies of coffee owing to a dispute over the amount of the taxes on it, so that the Sherif was obliged to send Abdulla al Fa'ar on a mission to him. As Ahmad was unable to control the country-side and insecurity increased, his reign was soon unpopular. The members of his family, if they admired his determination in the field, were no admirers of his administration in peace. In 1771, endeavouring perhaps in his rough-and-ready fashion to mend matters, he decided to replace his Wezir in Jedda, Yusif Qabil, sending soldiers with orders to bring him to Mecca in manacles. There was no secrecy about this, and the young sherif Sarur, aged seventeen, nephew of the ruler, hearing of the plan in his *diwan* and incensed at his uncle's methods, mounted a fast camel and rode at once to Jedda to warn Al Qabil.

When the Sherif's men arrived Sarur halted them, saying that he had given his protection to Al Qabil. In the end he agreed to their taking him, but only on condition that Sarur went with them, and that no punishment was to take place until they had reached Mecca. On the way they broke away from the soldiers and galloped to Wadi al Marr, from where Sarur wrote to his uncle to tell him that he had decided to fight him. Propitiatory letters from Ahmad had no effect on him, and he continued to muster tribesmen, requiring the Ataiba to meet him at Al Sail. With three hundred horsemen he led the tribesmen to Wadi al Minhana, and, after a two hours' fight against Ahmad and his troops, completely over-came them, entering Mecca victoriously on the 5th of February, 1773, at the age of eighteen.

THE DHAWU ZAID CLAN

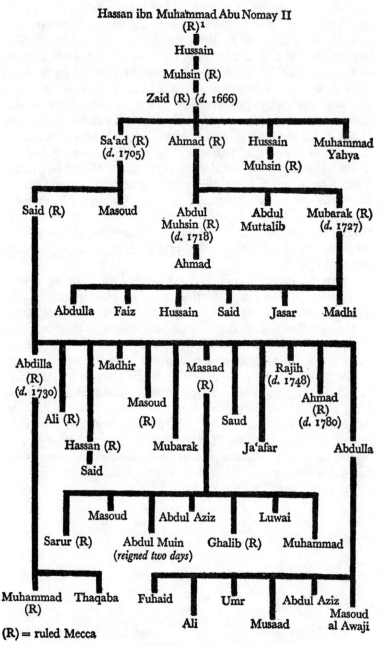

Hassan ibn Muhammad Abu Nomay II (R)[1]

Hussain

Muhsin (R)

Zaid (R) (*d.* 1666)

- Sa'ad (R) (*d.* 1705)
- Ahmad (R)
- Hussain — Muhsin (R)
- Muhammad Yahya

- Said (R)
- Masoud
- Abdul Muhsin (R) (*d.* 1718)
- Abdul Muttalib
- Mubarak (R) (*d.* 1727)

Ahmad

- Abdulla
- Faiz
- Hussain
- Said
- Jasar
- Madhi

- Abdilla (R) (*d.* 1730)
- Madhir
- Masaad (R)
- Rajih (*d.* 1748)

- Ali (R)
- Masoud (R)
- Saud
- Ahmad (R) (*d.* 1780)

- Hassan (R)
- Mubarak
- Ja'afar
- Abdulla

Said

- Masoud
- Abdul Aziz
- Luwai

- Sarur (R)
- Abdul Muin (*reigned two days*)
- Ghalib (R)
- Muhammad

- Muhammad (R)
- Thaqaba
- Fuhaid
- Umr
- Abdul Aziz

- Ali
- Musaad
- Masoud al Awaji

(R) = ruled Mecca

Note. For continuation of the Dhawu Zaid clan see pedigree at p. 190.
[1] See pedigree at pp. 136–137.

Chapter XI

SARUR AND HIS BROTHER GHALIB
(A.D. 1771–1810)

THE BEGINNING OF THE NEW YOUNG SHERIF'S RULE WAS far from tranquil. His uncle Ahmad at once and persistently contested Sarur's seizure of power, constantly rousing his followers to attack, the first fight taking place at Birkat Salman only twenty days after the change of rulership, when Ahmad was defeated and fled the field.

As the soldiers in Mecca refused to accompany Sarur until they had been paid the amounts owed them by his uncle, he was obliged to go unescorted, save by his personal followers, to the pilgrimage ceremony at Arafat.

There was still a strong party among the sherifs in favour of Ahmad, a number of whom were constantly visiting the Turkish representative, hoping for his assistance to unseat Sarur. Fortunately for the young Sherif the Pasha was from the first well disposed, and refused to move against him without orders from Istanbul. After the pilgrimage the unpaid soldiers, mutinous and encouraged by Ahmad, who had promised them all their back pay, and more, if he were restored, opened fire on the Sherif's house. Sarur called the nomads remaining in Mecca after the pilgrimage to his side, and, having sent his father's slave Mithgal Agha to the Egyptian Emir-al-Hajj to appeal for ammunition, once more defeated and captured Ahmad, whom he deported from Mecca with all his followers —but not far enough away, for no less than fifteen fights with Ahmad took place in the five years following Sarur's accession, his uncle using Taif as a base for expeditions against Mecca. The mischievous Abdulla al Fa'ar was busy on Ahmad's behalf, making a particular endeavour to win over the Turkish Emirs who came to Mecca at the pilgrimage season. They remained firmly opposed to the return of Ahmad, and eventually

Abdulla al Fa'ar was arrested and deported to Qunfidha. From this place he was rescued by the crew of a Yemeni ship in the pay of the Emir of Lohaya, very much to the annoyance of Sarur, by whom angry letters were sent to the Imam, who in the end ordered the return of the mischief-maker to the Sherif. He was again and more securely imprisoned at Qunfidha, this time dying there, "some say by strangling."[1]

Eventually, in 1779, Sarur imprisoned his uncle Ahmad, with his two sons, at Yanbu', from where, as he was ill, he was later transferred to Jedda, dying there in 1780.

Sarur was then able to turn to deal with the bedouin highway robbers. He used to ride out himself, with only a few followers quickly mustered, in order to surprise them. Some of his opponents in Mecca saw in these sorties an opportunity to waylay and kill him, but, one of their number giving them away to Sarur, he sent out to confirm the man's story and, finding that a party were indeed waiting, armed, for him, he ordered his men to arrest them all. Some escaped, but one Musaad al Awaji, his son, and twenty of their Negroes were taken, four of the Negroes being executed, Musaad having his hand cut off, and the rest being deported to India.

In 1779 the Sultan of Morocco sent his daughter, escorted by several of her brothers carrying wedding gifts, to be married to the young Sarur, and his prestige was thereby increased.

After the pilgrimage Murad Beg, the Egyptian Sanjak, who had seemed ill-disposed to Sarur, was held up during his return journey by the Harb tribe. Having hostages from the Harb, he at once made them sit on iron pegs and refused to pay the subsidy which they were to take back to their tribe from him as a condition of a peaceful passage of the pilgrims.

The Harb sheikhs believed that the subsidies for them had been paid in fact to Sarur, and when a little later in the year Sarur visited Medina—and in spite of a strong escort of 500 bedouin, 5000 of his own men, and 500 sherifs and their personal followers—the Harb made great difficulties for him, obstinately negotiating under arms for three days, without coming to an agreement, until he was obliged to fight them. Some neutral sheikhs arbitrating, he settled for a payment of 14,000 piastres and forty hostages to be given in return. Even

---

[1] Ibn Zaini Dahlan, *Al Jadawil al Mardhiya.*

then the Harb tried to avoid sending the hostages, and one sheikh who should have been included did not come until Sarur sent a force to bring him, and so, when at last he had them all assembled, he manacled them. The Harb, on hearing this after his entry to Medina, mobilized again, cutting off his retreat to Mecca and sending back the pilgrim caravans.

Worse was to follow. Some of the notables of Medina were discovered to be in league with the Harb and encouraging them. Fighting began inside the city, Sarur endeavouring to storm the citadel by sending his Negroes with scaling-ladders; but the place did not fall easily, and the fighting lasted a week. Finally he released the hostages, but sent to Mecca most of the prisoners taken from the citadel at Medina.

He wisely took the precaution of letting it be known in Medina that he would return through the Harb country, but actually took the far more difficult road farther east, and, running short of water, was only saved by some loyal nomads. Hardly had he reached Taif when news came that his Wezir in Medina had been attacked there and forced to surrender. At the same time the Harb took Yanbuʿ and captured his Governor in that port. Sarur now planned a serious campaign against the Harb, recruited some six thousand of the Ataiba nomads, three thousand Hudhail and Thuqaif, and two thousand of his own guards—the whole force, together with the sherifs and their bodyguards and slaves, being about twelve thousand strong. No less than one hundred and fifty craftsmen and engineers and seven thousand camels were included in the baggage train.

Some of the Hudhail cameleers refused to continue beyond Khalais, and in a fracas the Sherif was shot at by one of them, the bullet only just missing him. Frightened at what might be the outcome of this incident, the Hudhail all left the camp at once, and when he sent one of his family after them to persuade them to return, they only answered him, "If you want to be Emir of Mecca come with us—we are on our way to take Mecca now." Sarur was obliged to turn, pursue, and defeat them. They begged for mercy, which he granted, but it was too late and too unpropitious a beginning for him to continue his campaign.

In 1785 the Emir of the Damascus pilgrims was Ahmad

Jazzar Pasha, who commanded at Acre and resisted Napoleon. Ever since then he had claimed to be a Sherif by descent on both sides, and sometimes announced that in addition he was the awaited Mahdi, the last Imam. On his return journey he too suffered attacks by the Harb, catching some of their raiders, whose sheikhs came to ask for their pardon, to which the Pasha agreed on condition that he branded them on the cheeks. The whole tribe, hearing this, set upon the caravan, which was utterly destroyed save for the crazy Ahmad Pasha and a few exceptionally well-mounted horsemen, who with him galloped for Medina.

The Sherif now assembled an even greater force than in the previous year with which to attack the Harb. As it advanced slowly, the Harb believed that the Sherif was fearful of joining battle, and themselves began the attack, attempting to destroy the Ataiba advance-guard. The Sherif at once sent word that the head of a Harbi tribesman was worth to him five *mishkash*. Soon there were piles of heads in front of his tent. The same was then offered for prisoners, and soon five hundred men of the Harb were brought to him. He returned victorious in time to find that unusually lavish alms had been sent from India from Morocco, and from Muhammad Ali.

Shortly after a particularly brilliant circumcision party for his sons and nephews, given on his return from the victory over the Harb, Sarur fell sick. Twice he fainted, and after the second time he lived only four days, dying on September 20, 1788, aged thirty-four. Decisive and handsome, feared and admired, he had shown very great promise and was already of great repute when he died. Even seventy years later his name endured. Charles Didier, who visited the Hejaz in 1854 with Richard Burton, called Sarur "a Louis XI of the Hejaz,"[1] and added that he was of extreme generosity, of proved bravery, severely just yet forgiving towards his personal enemies; his policy included the removing of arbitrary taxes and improving the administration.

Sarur was succeeded by Ghalib, his younger brother. Ghalib was a colossal man, most skilful at arms when young, with an engaging manner, whom Didier says "was sweet and circumspect, absolute in power until the coming of the Wahhābis."

[1] *Séjour chez le grand-chérif de la Mecque*, p. 171.

On the other hand, the Jewish traveller styling himself Ali Bey al Abbassi (really Domingo Badia y Leiblich), who was travelling for the French Government,[1] says that he was an ill-educated egoist and that the English, having interests in trading with India through him, regarded him as their best friend. He used to send ships to trade with Mokha, Muscat, and Surat, and he claimed "the island of Suakim, also Massawa, although under the name of the Sultan of Turkey."[2]

His early days were marred by intrigues against him by some of his brothers and other relatives, whom he drove out of the city, most of them escaping to Taif. Even his nephew young Abdulla ibn Sarur, aged twelve, joining in the baiting of the new Sherif and, giving refuge to a prisoner who escaped through a water-channel to his house, was arrested and after a few days sent back to his mother. The escaped prisoner, a cadet of the family, in gratitude to young Abdulla, made off to Istanbul, where he asked the Sultan, who was impressed by his earnestness, to appoint Abdulla Emir of Mecca.

Far more serious than this family skirmishing was the threat from Central Arabia. In the time of the Sherif Masoud the Wahhābi Puritans of Central Arabia, considered in Mecca to be dangerous fanatics and non-Muslims, had asked leave to make the pilgrimage and had been refused, and when they sent some thirty of their holy men to discuss and describe their beliefs they had been turned back. The Qadhi of Mecca had more than once publicly denounced them as infidels. When Sherif Masaad was in power they renewed their request and were again refused. When Ahmad became Sherif in turn they had once more wished to send a deputation of holy men to argue their case, and were again refused permission. So when Sarur took over the rule in Mecca they again asked for permission to make the pilgrimage and received the reply that they might do so on condition that they paid exactly what the Persians paid and in addition sent a hundred mares a year, a condition they in turn refused. Now that Ghalib had taken over they tried once more, but Ghalib firmly denounced their ways and threatened to raid them, which he began to do in 1790 and continued for the next fifteen years, there being

---

[1] *Voyages en Afrique et en Asie pendant les années 1803 à 1807*, vol. ii, p. 421 *et seq.*
[2] *Ibid.*, vol. iii, p. 5.

innumerable fights between them. The first expedition, lasting some six months, commanded by Abdul Aziz ibn Musaad, Ghalib's brother, reached Anaiza, in the Qasim province of Central Arabia. The second raid, commanded by Ghalib in person, was equally successful, and notable for his protracted occupation of Al Sha'ara in Al Qasim, and for his use of field-guns. Marches to Taraba, Ranya, and Bisha, led by Abdul Aziz, to restore order in those districts where the Wahhābi influence was already making headway, were also successful.

Pilgrims crossing Arabia had long complained of increasingly heavy taxation by the Wahhābis and soon they ceased to come at all. The Sherif sent missives to Istanbul in 1793 and 1798 asking for munitions and support to deal with what he termed "the Wahhābi threat," but the Sublime Porte was silent.

The Wahhābi numbers in the field were astonishingly and frighteningly large. In 1797 the Sherif Luwaih reported from Nejd to Ghalib that the Wahhābis "come on like locusts or streams out of the hills after rain," which the ruler doubted for the moment, but two days later saw for himself, becoming involved in a fight in which the fatal casualties on both sides totalled some two thousand, more than forty sherifs being killed and Ghalib forced to withdraw to Mecca. An expedition was now sent from Baghdad, via Al Hasa, against Daraya, the Wahhābi capital, supported by the Shammar, Dhafir, and Muntafiq tribes, but returned after a short siege.

The Sublime Porte had, in fact, other and more serious troubles on hand than the Wahhābi threat to Mecca. A firman was received in Mecca at the end of 1798 ordering the fortification of the holy land of the Hijaz in view of possible invasion by the French, so the walls of Jedda were hastily repaired, the people given military training each evening, and all put in readiness to repel Bonaparte.[1] In November 1799 Said Hamid Agha, the Ottoman Wezir at Jedda, wrote to the English Commander at Aden, imploring him to send a force very quickly—"Come with the speed of a horse"—to prevent the French advancing southward towards the Hijaz and the Yemen. The Commanding Officer, Lieutenant-Colonel Murray, in forwarding the letter to the British Naval Officer in command in the Red Sea, added that the Sherif of Mecca had already

[1] C. Snouck Hurgronje, *Mekka*, vol. iii, p. 145.

offered troops to Admiral Blankett and that the French were reported to be collecting native sailing-boats at Suez. It now became a concern of the British military to collect stores and transport animals on the coast of the Red Sea. A native political agent, one Mirza Mehmendy Khan, was sent to Jedda from the Persian Gulf by the Bombay Government in May 1801, and General Baird and Sir Home Popham, who had been specially appointed by the Secret Committee of the India Office to visit the Sherif of Mecca and the Arabian princes, visited the Sherif, who came to meet them at Jedda. Home Popham had already sent a letter ashore for the Sherif:[1]

The undersigned Home Popham, Knight of the Most Sovereign Order of St John of Jerusalem and Captain of His Majesty's Ship *Romney*, has the honor to inform His Holiness, the Sheriff of Mecca of his arrival in Judda this day, with powers from the Honorable the East India Company in England given him in consequence of directions from the Right Honorable Henry Dundas one of His Majesty's Principal Secretaries of State to renew and enter into ties of intimate friendship and alliance with His Holiness the Sheriff of Mecca; which he has no doubt will be highly agreeable to His Holiness, as promising great advantage to him in a commercial and political point of view. His Holiness must be convinced that the object of His Brittanick Majesty and his powerful and intimate friend and ally the Grand Seignior is to drive the French out of Egypt and for this purpose it must be very satisfactory both to the King of Great Britain and the Ottoman Porte to find a zealous and proper co-operation on the part of His Holiness to conquer a set of plunderers and regicides who have waged war against religion and studied to overthrow all civil order, and every government who is weak enough to attend to the promises of their Secret Agents independant of the satisfaction it must be to His Imperial Majesty the Grand Seignior that he has given the most cordial assistance to British Arms; it may be the means of his entering immediately into commercial treaties; so very lucrative to his subjects in all their operations with India; for which purpose Sir Home Popham has full powers to treat whenever His Holiness will allow him the honor of an interview.

Given under my hand on board His Majesty's Ship *Romney* in Judda harbour this 21st day of May 1801.

HOME POPHAM

[1] India Office, Factory Records, Egypt and the Red Sea, vol. vi, folio 83.

The Sherif had already, however, acquired a reputation among them before their landing at Jedda "for something equivocal in his behaviour."[1]

They were nevertheless welcomed, saluted with gunfire, and presented with sable and ermine pelisses, shawls and arms, but the Sherif sought refuge in his allegiance to the Ottoman Sultan, with whom he suggested that their Government correspond.

A temporary truce with the Wahhābis had been arranged in 1799, which was celebrated by the passage of a great pilgrim caravan across Nejd, part of the way under the personal escort of Saud,[2] and in 1800 Saud with a great number of his men made the pilgrimage. In 1801 the treaty was flagrantly violated by a Wahhābi occupation of Hali, on the Red Sea coast, by the sack of Kerbela, in Iraq, and by attacks on the Persian pilgrims. Moreover, in spite of Saud's agreement with the Sherif, he was everywhere sending his agents into the areas which had been specifically reserved to the Sherif.[3]

Meanwhile, seeing the weakness of the Ottomans in the Hijaz, the British in India were persisting in their efforts to strengthen their relations both with the Sherif and the Imam of Sana. Wellington, then Marquis Wellesley and Governor and Captain-General over all the British Possessions in the East, etc., wrote his renewed instructions in October 1801 to Home Popham, whom he had now furnished with twelve of his own bodyguard and a company of sepoys as an escort:

> From the general tenor of my information I am inclined to believe that these powers, particularly the Sherif of Mecca and the Imaum of Senna [Sana] are nearly, if not altogether independent of the Porte. . . .

But he warned Home Popham that

> the State of the present Sherif's power renders it more especially necessary to use every degree of caution with regard to interference in the internal affairs of the country.

---

[1] India Office Records, Home Miscellaneous 477, p. 55. From the subsequent letters in this series from the political agent it appears that he became prejudiced against Sherif Ghalib, and even proposed to the British authorities, who were shocked by the suggestion, the deposition of the Sherif in favour of Abdulla ibn Sarur. The agent was removed—apparently only just in time, for his relations were daily worsening—in the first week of August 1801.

[2] Saud ibn Abdul Aziz Muhammad ibn Saud, the son of the Wahhābi chieftain.

[3] J. L. Burckhardt, *Notes on the Bedouins and Wahabys*, p. 326 *et seq.*

When Popham arrived, however, the Sherif stayed where he was at Taif and only replied to his request to see him again by saying that if he had anything to communicate he could send it in a letter. In his same report to India from Jedda, dated June 30, 1802, Popham says, laconically, that "the Turkish Pasha at Mecca was poisoned by the Sherif." But Popham had already disquietened Wellington by his unauthorized negotiations in Egypt, both with regard to Egypt and to the Hijaz. The Ottoman Viceroy, like the Sherif, had referred him to Istanbul, where in any case there was a British Ambassador in residence, and his mission was in consequence ending in failure.

Ghalib succeeded in recapturing Hali, and kept a small garrison there, which was overwhelmed again in 1802. And he now sent his brother-in-law, Othman al Madhaifi, with a party of sherifs to negotiate a renewal of the truce, which the Wahhābis had broken. Othman alone saw Saud and at once treacherously agreed to aid him; Saud promised to make him his Emir of the tribes of Taif and Mecca. The Sherifian delegates, not having seen Saud until the last day of their stay, knew nothing of this secret agreement, although during the return journey they noticed Othman's strangely changed attitude. One day from Taif he asked them to precede him, and, remaining with the tribes in this area, in which he lived, he called upon them to join him in attacking Taif. His first advance was defeated by the Governor of Taif, the Sherif's brother Abdul Muin, and he retreated to his own fort, to raise yet more men. The Sherif himself now arrived from Mecca with reinforcements and with Abdul Muin made an attack on Othman's fort, Al Abaqla. But reinforcements for Othman from Bisha and the south begat threats of an attack on Mecca itself, so that the Sherif was obliged to return to his capital and reduce in numbers the forces defending Taif. Hearing that he had gone, the people gave up the outer forts, and Othman was enabled to take the place, killing men, women, and children, even those who had sought refuge in the Friday mosque. The capture of Qunfidha, on the coast, by Othman quickly followed. There were no more than two hundred survivors, and the town was completely looted. Encouraged by the news of these victories, Saud himself took the field and advanced towards Mecca in open war against the Sherif and against the Turks. In Mecca and the villages of the Hijaz the town criers proclaimed *jihad* against the Wahhābi infidels, and announced that volunteers to form the Sherif's army were to join at once. It was the year 1802, and this was the first serious attempt at invasion and occupation by men from outside the Hijaz since the days of the Elephant, the attack by the Abyssinians in the year of the Prophet's birth.

At the last pilgrimage before the final invasion Ghalib tried to persuade the Emirs of the pilgrim caravans to lend him their active support, but they were only anxious to be gone in safety. The headquarters of Saud and Othman were now fixed at Al Hussainiya, where many of the richest Meccans had summer houses, only an hour and a half's ride to the south of the city. Their light troops harassed the eastern suburbs, and, occupying the quarter of Al Mu'abda, entered and held the Sherif's Palace there, from where they raided into the city itself. The Sherif bravely kept up resistance and laid mines to drive out the enemy and prevent their incursions, but the Wahhābis cut off the sweet-water supply from Arafat and reduced the inhabitants to rationing the brackish well-water.

After two months the people began to suffer severely from the lack of provisions and good water. Some of them ventured out by night to gather what they could, and some received corn in exchange for grass brought by them for the Sherif's horses at his headquarters. Soon they were reduced to eating cats and dogs, and Ghalib's provisions for his soldiers ran so low that he had no alternative but to leave Mecca. He burnt what he could not carry away with him of his property in his Palaces and left with his family and soldiers for Jedda. Early in May 1803 the Wahhābis entered Mecca, and to the astonishment of the inhabitants preserved good order. Saud ordered the shops to open and normal life to be resumed. He told the assembled Ulama that he had seen the Prophet Muhammad in a dream, who had threatened him that he should not survive three days if grain were forcibly taken from the inhabitants. On the other hand, severe punishment was promised for laxity. The Meccans were obliged to conform to Wahhābi practice, not smoking in public, laying aside their silken dresses, and praying regularly. Heaps of Persian pipes collected in the city

were burnt before Saud's headquarters and the sale of tobacco
was forbidden. The mention of the Sultan's name in the prayers was prohibited. As soon as he could Saud turned his arms against
Jedda, where Ghalib had taken refuge. The town was besieged
for eleven days, and then, as his people fought bravely, having
secure walls and sea communication with the outer world for
supplies, Saud despaired of taking it and raised his siege,
retiring from there to Nejd.

No sooner had he gone, in July 1803, than the Sherif Ghalib
re-entered Mecca, the small Wahhābi garrison of the forts
surrendering.

Abdul Muin, his brother, who had been acting as Governor
of Mecca, at once made his submission to Ghalib. The *modus
vivendi* was that customs dues at Jedda for all true Wahhābis
were waived by the Sherif, who was to remain in possession of
Mecca and all the towns of the Hijaz. Saud, however, attacked
some of his tribes, the Harb in particular resisting fiercely,
which so exasperated the Wahhābis that they treated them
worse than any other tribes. The Bani Subh, of the Harb,
even succeeded in avoiding surrender, taking to the higher
mountains. The other tribes and Medina finally surrendered
in the spring of 1804. The Prophet's tomb was stripped of its
treasure and the same measures taken as at Mecca, the inhabitants being made to answer their names at prayer roll-call five
times a day, absentees being severely beaten in public. The
Wahhābi chieftain, Abdul Aziz, did not live to see the capture
of Medina, having been assassinated by a Persian whose relatives the Wahhābis had killed.

After 1803 no regular pilgrim caravans came to Mecca, and
the *mahmal* from Cairo in that year was accompanied by only
four hundred soldiers under Sherif Pasha, who had been
appointed Wali of Jedda by the Sublime Porte.

Outside Mecca, except near the armies, insecurity prevailed
everywhere. At the close of 1804 the Asiris suddenly issued
from their mountains under their chief, Abu Noqta, swept over
the coastal plains from Lohaya and Hodaida as far north as
Qunfidha, plundering those towns. Nevertheless the Sherif's
power was still great, through his name and venerable office,
as was his personal influence over many of the bedouin tribes.

His garrison at Jedda was strong in numbers and morale, and the Wahhābis never entered it. Moreover, Ghalib's generosity was proverbial, and Saud often said that it made him blush to receive such liberal presents. At Mecca, therefore, Ghalib's power balanced that of Saud.

In the course of 1805 Othman al Madhaifi made several attempts to seize Jedda by surprise, without the formal authority of Saud, but the inhabitants, including the foreigners who happened to be there, took up arms and frustrated his designs. Although the Hijaz was tranquil except for Othman al Madhaifi's occasional raids, it had lost its principal source of income, the pilgrimage, owing to the pilgrims' fear of the Wahhābis.

So from 1806 to 1810 Ghalib's power gradually declined, while the Porte remained inactive, in spite of Wahhābi attacks on the Mesopotamian tribes, until there came a raid, in 1810, on Damascus itself. All the border peoples of the lands surrounding the peninsula had become terrified of the farouche Puritans of the desert, whose appearance lent heightened colour to the townsmen's fears.

Ali Bey al Abbassi, the Spanish pilgrim of 1807, who saw the Wahhābis entering Mecca for the pilgrimage of that year, described them as

> a mass of men all naked except for loincloths, a few with another cloth over a shoulder, the remainder entirely naked, but armed with rifles [*fusils à mèche*] or a dagger. At the sight of the torrent of naked and armed men every one fled and hid. There were some few horsemen, naked but with spears, shouting prayers confusedly, each in his own way. The children, the usual guides, came to conduct them, and there was not a grown Meccan to be seen. So they began to pass by and kiss the Black Stone, as it were a swarming of bees.[1]

Among them, he adds, "were many men with heads beautiful enough to be compared with those of Apollo, Antinous, and other gladiators."

The Sherif watched from his castle on the hillside and kept his Turks and Negro soldiers in their quarters, while the tide of desert manhood swept into Mecca and out again, their pilgrimage completed without incident between them. In

---

[1] Ali Bey al Abbasi, *Voyages en Afrique et en Asia pendant les années 1803 à 1807*.

these years appeal after appeal reached the Sultan of the Ottomans without success, for war in Europe had reached Turkish lands, his janizaries were half-mutinous, his 'nizam,' or new army, untried. In despair, he turned to the ambitious military Viceroy and Pasha of Egypt, Muhammad Ali, a native of Kavalla, in Thrace, whom he feared more than he loved. To be the liberator of the Holy Places would suit Muhammad Ali's book, his seeking after fame, and the lesser evil of his aggrandisement might be redressed later.

He had in fact ordered him to invade the Hijaz in 1804, and promised him the Pashalic of Damascus for one of his sons as soon as he did so, but the Viceroy had been too heavily engaged in warfare with the Mamelukes.

Once more, in 1810, orders were sent to him, this time to be put into execution.

THE DHAWU ZAID CLAN (continued)[1]

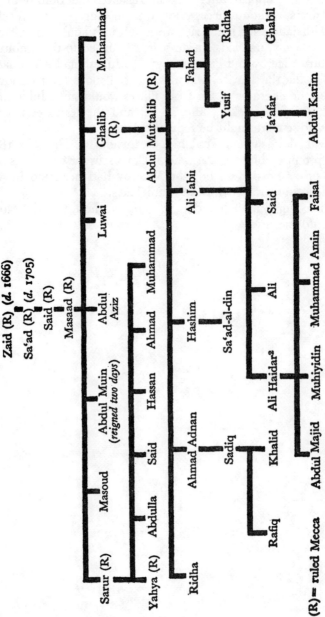

(R) = ruled Mecca

[1] See also pedigree at p.176.
[2] En secondes noces he married an Englishwoman, having by her two daughters. For his life see *A Prince of Arabia*, by G. Stitt (Allen and Unwin, 1947).

Chapter XII

GHALIB, THE WAHHĀBIS, AND THE EGYPTIAN TURKS

(A.D. 1810–13)

WHEN SHERIF GHALIB HEARD THAT MUHAMMAD ALI WAS making preparations for invasion of the Hijaz, and that he was assembling a greater force than any other Pasha who had previously come to the country, he thought it advisable to begin secret correspondence with him, and to affirm that although irresistible circumstances had hitherto obliged him to connive at Wahhābism he was ready to throw off its yoke at the first appearance of a large Turkish army on the shores of the Hijaz. In the course of this correspondence he gave the Pasha much information about the Wahhābis, the disposition of the Hijaz bedouin, and the best mode of attack.[1]

To the leading merchant of Cairo, Sayid Muhammad al Mahrouky, who had himself often been at Mecca and was deeply concerned in the Red Sea trade, Muhammad Ali entrusted the political conduct of the war and the necessary arrangements to be made with the bedouin near the Red Sea coast. Muhammad Ali was of too suspicious a character to place much confidence in the assurances of Ghalib, whose political talents were well known; but it was necessary to soothe the apprehensions that the Sherif might entertain of a foreign invader. The fairest promises were therefore made to him; that his authority in Hijaz should be respected; that the custom duties of Jedda, his chief source of revenue, would be left in his hands; while at the same time the Egyptian soldiers destined for the expedition were encouraged by the reports spread among them 'secretly,' but deliberately, that Sherif Ghalib, with all his force, would join them on their arrival in the Hijaz.

[1] For the history of the campaign see J. L. Burckhardt, *Notes on the Bedouins and Wahabys*, which has been largely used as source.

The state of Egypt was not tranquil enough to permit the absence of Muhammad Ali himself, for in the southern part of Upper Egypt the Mamelukes still continued a teasing guerrilla warfare with the Pasha's troops, so that Tousoun Bey, Muhammad Ali's second son, was placed in command of this the first expedition against the Wahhābis, which became ready for departure at the end of August 1811. Tousoun Bey, although still a boy of seventeen, had given proofs of unusual courage in the Mameluke war, and his friends believed that he would be able to undertake the command. Ahmad Agha, the Treasurer, or Khaznadar, of Muhammad Ali, was, however, sent with Tousoun, as being of equal bravery but graver counsel. The Agha's achievements in the wars against the Mamelukes and the Arabs of the Sudan had exalted him in the eyes of his masters, and his utter disregard of human life and his boasting procured him in Egypt the nickname of Bonaparte, which he had proudly adopted as surname.

Burckhardt says that he was a brave soldier, but that he was also strongly addicted to "drunkenness and lusts of the vilest kind." To these two commanders was joined Al Mahrouky, a prosperous and shrewd merchant of Cairo, whose role was to be diplomatic agent with the Sherif and with the bedouin. Two of the Ulamas of Cairo, Sheikh al Mehdi and Sheikh al Tahtawi, likewise embarked with the troops, that by their controversial learning, as it was said in Cairo, they might convince the Wahhābis of the errors which they had adopted in their faith.

The expedition was of two parts. There was, firstly, the infantry, composed principally of Arnaut soldiers, amounting to fifteen hundred or two thousand effective men, under Salah Agha and Umar Agha, that embarked at Suez for Yanbu', on the new-built ships well stacked with provisions, and, secondly, the cavalry, with Tousoun Bey and Ahmad Bonaparte, a body of about eight hundred Turkish horsemen and a party of bedouin under the command of Shadid, Sheikh of the Huwaitat tribe, that proceeded by land.

The flotilla anchored off Yanbu' in October 1811 and the troops, landing at a short distance from that place, took possession of it after a feeble resistance lasting less than two days. A fortnight afterwards the cavalry arrived by land, not having met with any opposition from the tribes, who had been conciliated by considerable sums of money. The taking of Yanbuʻ was proclaimed as a victory over the Wahhābis, and as a favourable omen for the future success of the expedition. The troops, however, remained inactive for several months there; the infantry at the port of Yanbuʻ, and the cavalry, with the bedouin, at Yanbuʻ el Nakhl, headquarters of the Juhaina tribe, and distant from the seaport six hours. This period of delay was passed in negotiation, for Tousoun Bey found that the Hijaz was not by any means in such a state as he had expected from the representations made to him by Sherif Ghalib. The bedouin, and especially those of the two great tribes of Harb and Juhaina, whatever might be their dislike of the Wahhābis and their desire to participate again in the profits from the passing pilgrims, had been completely overawed by the power and vigilance of Saud, the Wahhābi chief, and would not dare to stir until the Turks had some more decided advantage, for the taking of Yanbuʻ alone could not be reckoned of much importance in a war against Central Arabia.

When the Turkish expedition arrived, Yanbu' had not been garrisoned by Wahhābis, the Sherif Ghalib having there a Governor and about one hundred soldiers who had made some show of resistance until the inhabitants themselves obliged them to retreat, fearing that the town might be destroyed in an assault of Egyptian troops. The Sherif remained a quiet spectator of this beginning of the war, writing letters to Tousoun Bey, in which he excused himself for not joining him on account of the smallness of his force and his dread of the Wahhābis; but he again and again solemnly declared that he would throw off the mask and openly attack them as soon as the Turkish leaders should gain any important advantage. Meanwhile he strengthened the garrisons of Jedda and Mecca, and, when urged by Saud to join him against the invaders, excused himself by expressing his fears of a sudden maritime attack on Jedda, which might lead to the capture of Mecca. It was thus clearly the Sherif's plan either to temporize, and then to fall upon whichever party should suffer the first signal defeat, or, if that did not happen, to wait until the two parties were weakened by the length of the war and then to drive them both out of his dominions.

The only Hijaz bedouin whom Tousoun Bey was able to detach from the Wahhābis were a few clans of the Juhaina in the neighbourhood of Yanbu', while the greater part of that tribe and the whole of the Harb, who bordered upon their territories, remained quite insensible to his diplomacy.

It became necessary, however, to begin the campaign, lest the people of Hijaz, as well as the enemy, should regard inactivity as an outcome of fear and negotiation as a proof of weakness. To march towards Mecca or Jedda would have obliged the Sherif to declare himself at once for one party or the other, a decision from which Tousoun Bey had more to dread than the Wahhābis. He therefore considered the capture of Medina, six days distant from Yanbu'. Medina was the best-fortified town of the Hijaz, the rampart of that province against Nejd, the possession of which opened or obstructed the passage of the Syrian pilgrim caravans, and the Sherif Ghalib, when he learned of this design, formally promised to declare against Saud whenever it was successful.

Having left a garrison at Yanbu', Tousoun Bey began his advance towards Medina in January 1812. After a slight skirmish he entered Bedr, a village two days distant from Yanbu', occupied by the Harb tribe. Bedr is situated at the entrance of the mountains which it is necessary to pass through on the way to Medina, so some resistance was expected from the Harb, who held the passes through those mountains; but nothing was known of the presence of any Wahhābi troops. Tousoun therefore left only a small garrison at Bedr, and went on with his army to Safra, a market-place of the Harb tribe eight hours from Bedr; there, after some sharp fighting, a body of that tribe gave way. Four hours' march on from Safra the road leads through a ravine, from forty to sixty yards across, between steep and rugged mountains, at the entrance of which is the village of Judaida, among groves of palm-trees, the principal settlement of the Bani Harb. Here in former times the Syrian pilgrim caravan had often been obliged to pay considerable sums for the privilege of passing unmolested.

In this defile, which caravans take about one hour to traverse, the Turkish army was suddenly assailed by the Harb tribe, but after some hot firing, the Turks believed that they had obtained the advantage and so pursued the Arabs far into the ravine when, on a sudden, the mountains on both sides were thickly covered with the Wahhābi troops, who had arrived the day before from Nejd and of whom the Turks had not had the slightest information. The Wahhābis, commanded by Abdulla and Faisal, the sons of Saud, amounted to some ten thousand infantry and camel-riders, and from six to eight hundred horsemen. By retreating into the village of Judaida, and fortifying themselves there, the Turks might have withstood the attack and obtained an honourable capitulation, as the number of the enemy rendered it impossible for them to remain long upon the same spot. But on the first cry of alarm the Turkish infantry fell back, and the cavalry, ordered to cover their retreat, soon joined in the flight; while their nimble enemies, pressing them from behind and outrunning them along the mountain-side, poured incessant volleys upon them. Tousoun did not forfeit his reputation for bravery, and, accompanied at first by only two horsemen of his personal suite, he endeavoured to rally his troops, hastening to the rear, and himself plunging into the enemy's ranks to make them desist from the pursuit.

Burckhardt says, "Persons who were present assured me that while tears gushed from his eyes, Tousoun exclaimed to the fugitive Turks, 'Will none of you stand by me?'" About twenty horsemen at last joined him; when luckily at the same time the Wahhābis became much engaged in seizing the baggage of his army, thus slackening their pursuit. When the Turks had regained the open space beyond the entrance of the defile, their cavalry rallied, and in some degree protected the others. Even so, had the Wahhābis pushed forward over the mountains the whole body of Turks would have been annihilated; but they contented themselves with taking all the Turkish baggage, four field-pieces, almost every one of their camels, and much booty, which they found in the girdles of the Arnauts, who had enriched themselves by despoiling Mamelukes in Egypt. About twelve hundred men of Tousoun's force were killed on that day, and he was obliged to retreat to Bedr, set the camp there on fire—not having any means of removing it—and abandon, for the same reason, his military chest, returning to Baraika Bay, west of Bedr, where several of his ships lay at anchor. There he embarked with a few attendants and proceeded to

Yanbu' by sea, the rest of his troops arriving some days after in great distress. Fortunately for them, the Wahhābis, imagining that a strong Turkish corps was entrenched at Bedr, did not immediately follow up their success; and thus all who were sufficiently strong to perform the journey finally reached Yanbu'.

When the Wahhābis discovered that their enemies had secured themselves in Yanbu' they sent out parties of troops to scour the country up to its very walls. The Sherif, immediately after he received this intelligence that the Turkish expedition had failed, joined the Wahhābis in person at Bedr. It was at first proposed to storm Yanbu'; but this project was abandoned from fear of the Arab inhabitants, who, in doubt, would fight with desperation, as they had espoused the Turkish interests with cordiality. The Wahhābis found it useless therefore to blockade the town any longer, and retreated to the interior, but remained ready to assemble again at short notice whenever the Turks should venture a second time to lead an army into the open country. On their way they ordered the Harb bedouin to harass the Turks and cut off all supplies from the town.

Reverting to the account of the danger in which Tousoun was placed, when all his people had forsaken him except two horsemen, Burckhardt records an anecdote respecting one of those brave soldiers called Ibrahim Agha, acting as chief of Tousoun's Mamelukes.[1] Ibrahim Agha was a young man of about twenty years, a native of Edinburgh, whose real name was Thomas Keith. Having been taken prisoner at the last English expedition against Egypt, together with many others of his regiment, the 72nd Highlanders, in which he served as a gunsmith, he was obliged to become a Muslim, and was purchased as a slave from the soldier who had made him prisoner, by the doughty but vicious Ahmad Agha Bonaparte. A favourite Sicilian slave of his master having quarrelled with the young Scotsman, blows followed; swords were drawn, and the Sicilian fell. Ibraham Agha escaped from the wrath of Ahmad Bonaparte, and implored the protection of Muhammad Ali's wife, who befriended him and caused her son Tousoun Bey to engage him in his service. Tousoun, in one of those capricious fits of ill-humour to which despots are subject, gave

---

[1] J. L. Burckhardt, *Notes on the Bedouins and Wahabys*, p. 351.

orders that the young Scotsman should be put to death for some trifling neglect of duty; but the brave fellow with his sword defended the entrance of his room for half an hour against several assailants, then threw himself out of the window, and again escaped to his kind protectress, who soon reconciled him to his master. Tousoun Bey at length became sensible to Ibrahim's merit as a brave soldier, made him chief of his slaves, and, after his valorous conduct at Judaida, promoted him to the office of treasurer, the second post in rank at the court of a Pasha. He fought bravely at Medina and later at Taraba, and was appointed governor of Medina in April 1815, until two months after, in the very week of Waterloo, when hastening with two hundred and fifty horsemen to the assistance of Tousoun Bey, then encamped in the province of Qasim, in Central Arabia, he was overtaken by a superior number of Wahhābis and shared the fate of his troops, who were all killed. In this last action the gallant young man killed four Wahhābis with his own hand, and Abdulla Ibn Saud confessed that Tousoun Bey and his faithful Scottish treasurer were the two bravest men of the Turkish army.

The losses which they had sustained now began to dishearten the invading troops. Salah Agha and Umar Agha, the two leaders of the infantry, both declared that they could not fight any longer in the Hijaz, and Tousoun Bey therefore resolved to send them back to Egypt; but for their voyage to Cairo they recruited their escort from soldiers also discontented with the Pasha. On reaching the city they assumed such an aggressive attitude that Muhammad Ali had to exert the greatest artfulness to induce them, by threats as well as by presents, to quit Egypt, and, having pillaged the richest districts of Upper Egypt, they embarked at Alexandria with considerable treasure.

The troops of Tousoun Bey had had severe losses in horses owing to the fatiguing land-journey even before their arrival at Yanbu', and they were later forsaken by most of the bedouin horsemen who had accompanied them. Moreover, about two hundred horses were killed at Judaida, and when the army returned to Yanbu' those that could be mustered did not exceed that same number. Scarcity of food also obliged the owners of the remaining horses to sell them, and the cavalrymen were sent back to Cairo in order to be freshly mounted there.

As soon as Tousoun's failure was known every effort was made to prepare for a new expedition. Muhammad Ali sent large sums of money to his son for distribution among the neighbouring bedouin sheikhs, with the hope of detaching them from the side of the Wahhābis. The whole spring and summer of 1812 were spent in these endeavours, while daily reinforcements of troops and ammunition arrived at Yanbu'. Al Mahrouky, the merchant-diplomat, succeeded at last, by large payments in gold, in gaining over a considerable number of the Harb, including the important clans of that tribe called Bani Salim and Bani Subh, who held the pass of Safra and Judaida. Even Sherif Ghalib, when he was convinced that Muhammad Ali had resolved to prolong the contest, resumed his former policy, and assured Tousoun Bey that he had only joined the Wahhābis at Bedr from fear, renewing his offer of opening the gates of Jedda and Mecca to the Turkish troops as soon as the latter should have taken Medina.

By October 1812 Tousoun thought himself sufficiently strong to make his second attempt upon Medina. The bedouin on the road had become his allies and many individuals of the Juhaina tribe had enlisted under his banner, while news that the Wahhābis in Nejd were inactive encouraged his hope of success. He transferred his own headquarters to Bedr, and Ahmad Bonaparte took the command of the troops, who advanced through the pass which had been the scene of the defeat, and, leaving a strong garrison at Judaida, arrived without a skirmish before the walls of Medina, which, having been occupied by the Wahhābis since the previous year, was well guarded and stocked with provisions for a long siege.

The chief of the Wahhābis had remained inactive, but the victory at Judaida had extended his influence over all the Northern Arabs, and in 1812 he collected tribute even from bedouin near Baghdad, Aleppo, and Damascus. Having sold at Mecca the plunder obtained at Judaida, he had returned to Daraya, and his soldiers were so elated by their victory and so much despised the Turks for their conduct in the field that they considered it in their power to defeat them again at any time. Thus Saud probably expected that Medina would make a long resistance and that want of provisions would force the Turks at last to retreat; in which case he foresaw that the Harb would abandon their foreign allies, who, in their turn, might be easily annihilated.

After some light skirmishing with the Wahhābi garrison Ahmad Bonaparte entered the suburbs of Medina and drove the Wahhābis into the inner town, whence, on the approach of the Turks, they expelled the inhabitants. The inner town was defended by a strong and high wall and a fortified castle, to batter down which the Turks had nothing but light field-pieces. During a siege of fifteen days the garrison made several sorties, and the Turks laid a mine, but in so open a manner that the Wahhābis found a means to counter it. The laying of a second mine was attended with greater success, and in the middle of November 1812, while the Wahhābis were engaged in their midday prayers, part of the wall was blown up and the Arnauts rushed into the town. The defenders on the walls, surprised, fled towards the citadel, about one thousand of them being butchered in the streets, while the whole town was plundered. Only fifty Turks were killed. The Scotsman Thomas Keith, or Ibrahim Agha, evinced his usual intrepidity, being the very first man to enter the breach. About fifteen hundred Wahhābis had sought refuge in the castle, which the Turks were unable to take, not having proper battering artillery, and the building, situated on a solid rock, was proof against any mine. But after three weeks, their provisions being exhausted, the Wahhābis capitulated on the promise of Ahmad Bonaparte to grant them safe-conduct: he also agreed that they should carry off unmolested all their baggage and that camels should be provided for those who wished to return to Nejd.

When the garrison marched out they found only fifty camels instead of the three hundred that had been promised them, and thus they were obliged to leave behind the greater part of their baggage, carrying on their own backs whatever was most valuable; but no sooner had they left the town than the Turkish soldiers pursued, stripped, and killed as many of them as they could reach, and few, other than those mounted on camels, escaped.

The treacherous behaviour of the Turks at Medina was unwise, since they were contending with a bold and forthright enemy known for the most scrupulous observance of good faith and for executing verbal promises of safe-conduct once given.

Ahmad Bonaparte collected the skulls of all the Wahhābis killed at Medina and constructed with them a kind of tower on the high road to Yanbu', and stationed a guard over it; notwithstanding which, the Arabs, and even the people of Medina, succeeded in removing from time to time most of those ghastly memorials.

After the taking of Medina an expedition of one thousand horse and five hundred foot-soldiers was sent through Yanbu' to Jedda and Mecca. They were commanded by Mustafa Bey, brother-in-law of Muhammad Ali, and who, like Ahmad Bonaparte, had formerly distinguished himself by his fanatic severity towards rebels in Egypt.

Sherif Ghalib had at last been impressed by the fall of Medina, and sent messengers to the Turkish leader inviting him to his towns. A few hundred men were detached to Jedda, while the principal corps advanced towards Mecca, where Othman al Mudhaifi was then commander of the Wahhābi forces; but he found himself not sufficiently strong to offer battle, and retired towards Taif a few hours before the Turks entered Mecca in January 1813. The property of the Meccans was respected, as it had formerly been respected by the Wah-hābis, and Ghalib now joined the Turks with above one thousand Arabs and black slaves. A fortnight after the deliverance of Mecca from the Wahhābis an attack was made on Taif, and some skirmishing began before the town. Othman al Mudhaifi at once fled, and Sherif Ghalib, with the Turkish commander, Mustafa Bey, entered the place, which the Wahhābis had held for ten years and which had suffered from them more than any other town in Hijaz.

The new commander, Mustafa Bey, intoxicated with success and with the raisin wine of Taif, thus believed himself able to subdue the Wahhābis. The town of Taraba, distant from Taif about seventy miles in an easterly direction, was one of their principal strongholds, connecting the Wahhābis of Nejd with those of the Asir and Yemen mountains. At Taraba were the Baqoum tribe, who since the Wahhābi wars with Sherif Ghalib had fortified their town with a strong wall and a ditch, and the thick gardens of date-trees in which it was situated served as a screen and an additional defence. Mustafa Bey pushed on towards Taraba, but was opposed and obliged to return to Taif with a loss of four or five hundred men. Meanwhile Othman al Mudhaifi was not inactive: he scoured the country with his light cavalry, cut off many stragglers, often intercepted communication with Mecca, and during the whole summer of 1812 greatly embarrassed the garrison of Taif. Sherif Ghalib demonstrated his goodwill by offering five thousand dollars as a reward for the capture of Othman al Mudhaifi. The personal enmity to his brother-in-law, who had been the main cause of all his misfortunes with the Wahhābis, here overcame his judgment, and he did not reflect that if the bedouin about Mecca should lose their chief the Turks would find it easier to establish themselves in the country and deprive him of his own authority.

In September 1812 Othman al Mudhaifi halted during one of his excursions at a small castle which he had built in the mountains, four or five hours eastward of Taif. The Sherif, informed of his being there, detached a strong party of troops from Taif, who surrounded the place and soon managed to set it on fire. Othman al Mudhaifi with about thirty followers, dressed like poor bedouin, rushed upon the enemy and cut their way through them; a wound, however, disabled his mare, and she could not carry him far. Hastening off on foot, he escaped from his pursuers; but next day, seeking refuge in the tent of an Ataibi nomad, he was seized and carried before the Sherif, who paid the promised reward to the bedouin and loaded his prisoner with chains, who was at once dispatched to Jedda and Cairo and finally to Istanbul; where the youngest son of Muhammad Ali presented the captive to his sovereign, together with the keys of the holy cities and many valuable offerings. As may be supposed, Othman al Mudhaifi was beheaded soon after his arrival, and the Wahhābis thus lost their most active and daring partisan in Hijaz.

The whole Hijaz was now reduced to obedience. The pilgrim caravan from Cairo arrived in Mecca in November 1812 with the former traditional ceremony, although the caravan from Syria could not yet pass through the deserts, as the forts on that route and the water reservoirs attached to them had not been repaired or stores been provided.

Ahmad Bonaparte returned to Cairo, and Tousoun Bey, created Pasha of Jedda, came to Mecca as a pilgrim in the winter of 1812, leaving the Divan Effendi, an officer of Muhammad Ali's court, as his Governor of Medina.

Although the five towns of the Hijaz—Mecca, Medina, Taif, Jedda, and Yanbu'—were now in the hands of the Turks, the Wahhābi power was still unbroken. The tribes of Nejd still acknowledged the supremacy of Saud, and the Turks, whenever they encountered the bedouin in open country, were always defeated. Muhammad Ali Pasha therefore decided to visit the scene of action and strike a signal blow that would establish his authority on a permanent footing in Arabia, and incidentally enable him to claim for himself the merit of the conquest. Moreover, his sovereign had peremptorily commanded him to place himself at the head of the troops in that country; and as all Egypt since 1811 was under complete subjection, he had no excuse for further delay. He embarked at Suez with two thousand infantrymen, while a corps of cavalry, equal in numbers, accompanied by a train of eight thousand camels went by land about the same time. Tousoun Pasha was employed in collecting his troops at Mecca when his father arrived at Jedda in September 1813. Sherif Ghalib happened to be there, and repaired on board the Pasha's vessel to compliment him even before his landing. It was on this occasion that they swore upon the Koran never to attempt anything contrary to the interest, safety, or life one of the other—a vow which they solemnly and publicly renewed some weeks after in the Temple at Mecca by express desire of the Sherif. The Sherif likewise settled with the Pasha some difficulties which had arisen between him and the Turkish Governor of Jedda; for although since the sixteenth century it had been an established rule that the customs of Jedda should be divided between the Turkish Pasha of that place and the ruler of Mecca, Ghalib had appropriated them to his own use exclusively, and the Pasha now promised not to interfere with his full possession of them. Thus, once more, far from being overwhelmed by the presence of an invader, the Sherifs had adroitly used their circumstances to secure advantages and even a greater degree of freedom.

Muhammad Ali, having arrived at Mecca, bestowed presents on the Ulama and distributed alms to the poor. He began repairs to the Temple and devoted large sums for its service, as well as for the ornamenting of it. But his first and most urgent business at that time was to provide for the transport of his supplies from Jedda to Mecca and on to Taif. Jedda had become the great depository of provisions and ammunition for the army. The whole shipping of that port, and of Yanbu', was employed in the transport business; but, even so, it was not sufficient, and Muhammad Ali had to contract with the Imam of Muscat for the hire of twenty ships for a year.

He had wished that a small frigate, the only ship-of-war belonging to him, which was at Alexandria should have been taken round by the Cape of Good Hope into the Red Sea; but the English Government would not grant permission, knowing that the ship, badly manned as it was, would probably be lost in seas unknown to Turkish navigators and the loss attributed by the Turks to the secret orders of the English. Then an Englishman residing in Egypt proposed to convey the ship at high water to Cairo, and then upon rollers across the desert to Suez, and seemed confident the undertaking was practicable; but his project deviated too much from the usual routine of things to be adopted.

It was found yet more difficult to convey provisions the short distance between Jedda and Mecca than to send them from Egypt to Jedda. Most of the camels used for the expeditions to the Hijaz had perished soon after their arrival, and by the continual passage of baggage caravans the herbage near the road was soon consumed, so that the camels had no food, except a small quantity of beans in the evening; and of this scanty allowance some was purloined by the drivers, Egyptian peasants who had been forced from their homes, and sold by them to the Hijaz bedouin. Of the eight thousand camels which Muhammad Ali sent by land, only five hundred remained alive three months after their arrival. The number in use could scarcely supply the daily wants of the troops at Mecca and Taif, and the Pasha offered so little money to the bedouin that few of them would bring their camels to his service.

On his arrival, however, at Mecca, finding the case urgent, he pressed the Sherif to use all his influence with the neighbouring Arabs to induce them to furnish as many camels as possible; and for this purpose a large sum of money was advanced, to be distributed among the sheikhs. But a nomad chief, having no despotic power in his tribe, cannot forcibly take away the camel of his meanest subject, and thus, although a second advance of money was demanded from the Pasha, no camels appeared.

The Pasha, who during his first visit to Mecca had been on friendly terms with the Sherif, now became cooler in his manner. The Sherif, on his side, complained that the customs of Jedda, notwithstanding the promises of Muhammad Ali, were withheld from his officers, and each party soon accused the other of intriguing against it. The intimate connexion of the Sherif with all the neighbouring tribes, who, since the capture of Othman al Mudhaifi, looked upon him as their protector against both Wahhābis and Ottomans, excited additional suspicion in the Pasha's mind, and he became persuaded that as long as the Sherif retained his authority he himself could have no chance of pursuing his operations with success. Muhammad Ali interpreted his firman from the Sultan as allowing him to act towards the Sherif as he should think expedient, and either to leave him at the head of the Government or to depose and take him prisoner.

It now became his principal object to arrest and imprison him, but this was a difficult undertaking. Ghalib had with him at Mecca about fifteen hundred fighting men, and other troops at Taif and at Jedda. The neighbouring Arabs were all more inclined to favour Ghalib than the Pasha, against whom it would have been easy to excite their hostility. At Mecca the Sherif inhabited a strongly built palace on the slope of a hill, upon which was a fort that communicated with the palace by a subterranean passage, a castle that had been built by his elder brother, Sarur, and newly fortified by himself when he heard of Muhammad Ali's preparations for invading Arabia. The place was well supplied with provisions and the water in its cisterns was abundant. A garrison of eight hundred picked men, with a dozen heavy guns, constantly defended it. The whole town was dominated by the castle, which was deemed impregnable against the means possessed by Muhammad Ali. Many other of Ghalib's troops, such as the sherifs with their personal body-guardsmen, armed slaves, and mercenary soldiers from Yemen, remained quartered in the town itself or acted as his escorts.

It is certain that if Ghalib had violated his solemn promise and attacked the Pasha, who had at that time but twelve hundred men at Mecca, he might with the assistance of the bedouin have driven him from the town, but his bitterest enemies could never prove him guilty of having broken a promise.

Ghalib no longer visited the Pasha on a friendly footing as before, and whenever he went to see him at his residence, a large school-house near the shrine, he was accompanied by several hundred soldiers; and at last he discontinued his visits altogether, never quitting his palace but on Fridays, when he went to prayers.

Muhammad Ali in vain attempted to throw him off his guard. He visited him twice, attended only by a few officers, thinking that Ghalib would return this visit in a similar manner; he had even resolved to seize him in the Shrine itself, but was dissuaded from so strong a measure by the Qadhi, recently arrived from Istanbul, who strenuously maintained its inviolability.

Nearly a fortnight elapsed, during which Muhammad Ali made daily efforts, in vain, to accomplish his design. At last he devised a suitable stratagem. He directed his son Tousoun Pasha, who was then at Jedda, to come at a late hour on a certain evening to Mecca. Etiquette rendered it necessary that the Sherif should go to salute him; for the omission of such a ceremony would, according to the Turkish notions, have been equivalent to a declaration of war. Ghalib, wishing to pay his visit before any new plans could be devised against him, went at an early hour on the morning after Tousoun's arrival, and called at his house, attended only by a small party. This had been foreseen; and on the day before his son's arrival, Muhammad Ali ordered about a hundred soldiers to conceal themselves in different rooms adjoining the courtyard of the house where Tousoun was to stay; this they did in such a manner as not to excite any public observation. When Ghalib arrived the attendants conducted him upstairs under pretence that Tousoun was fatigued by his journey, and the Sherif's principal officers were directed to stay below. He entered the Pasha's room and conversed with him for some time, but, when preparing to depart, was informed by Abdin Bey, a commander of the Arnauts, that he must remain as a prisoner; the hidden soldiers rushed from their lurking-places, and Abdin Bey, with Tousoun Pasha, obliged the Sherif to show himself at a window and order his people below to return home "as no harm was intended."

When this was publicly known the two sons of Ghalib took refuge with their troops in the castle and prepared for defence. The Sherif manifested great coolness. "Had I proved a traitor myself, this would not have happened," he said to Tousoun, in the presence of the Pasha's officers; and when a firman, whether true or forged has not been ascertained, was exhibited, requiring his appearance at Istanbul, he replied, "God's will be done: I have spent my whole life in wars with the Sultan's enemies, and cannot therefore be afraid to appear before him." But as long as the castle remained in the hands of Ghalib's sons the business was but half done. The Sherif was accordingly forced to write a note to his sons, ordering them to surrender the castle to Muhammad Ali; but he did not sign this order until he was threatened with the loss of his head.

Next day the Turks entered the castle, and the garrison dispersed themselves among the neighbouring bedouin or went to join the Wahhābis. The Qadhi, together with an officer of the Pasha and another belonging to the Sherif, was appointed to make an inventory of the whole property of the Sherif, and for this purpose his different palaces at Mecca were closely searched. The amount of all that they found was estimated at about sixteen purses, or two hundred and fifty thousand pounds sterling.

After a few days' captivity at Mecca, the Sherif was sent in November to Jedda, where he was detained on board a ship in the harbour, and then embarked for Kosseir. Arriving in Upper Egypt on the 1st of January 1814, Burckhardt, who met him there on his arrival, says that his spirit seemed unbroken; he spoke boldly and with great dignity, but never mentioned the name either of Muhammad Ali or of Tousoun. He had with him a dozen eunuchs, a few Arab servants, and two of his sons, who had voluntarily joined him at Jedda. Among the few articles of his baggage was a handsome chessboard, and it was said that he passed some hours every day in playing chess with his favourite eunuch.

At Cairo Ghalib received his women, who had been sent by way of Suez, together with his property as it was found in his palaces at Mecca; for Muhammad Ali had received orders not to withhold any part of it. One of his sons died at Alexandria; the other followed his father to Salonica, which the Porte had assigned for his residence, and where he received a monthly pension corresponding to his rank. Some female slaves, a younger son, and a sister of Ghalib remained at Mecca. The Sherif himself and all his household died of the plague—which was everywhere in the Middle East then—at Salonica in the summer of 1816.[1]

Abdulla ibn Sarur, a cousin of Sherif Ghalib, was seized at Mecca the day after that chief's imprisonment, and likewise forwarded to Cairo. He succeeded in escaping, but was retaken and brought back by the bedouin of Suez. As he had always been at enmity with Ghalib, no motive could be assigned for his seizure except that he had a strong party at Mecca, and by orders of the Porte he was soon after liberated.

Sherif Ghalib during his government of Mecca had shown bravery in fighting against the Wahhābis as well as against his own relations, who often opposed him. His intimate knowledge of the bedouin and their politics, his eloquence and penetration, eminently qualified him for the government of Mecca; but his levying of great fines for small offences in the latter part of his reign had caused him to be less liked. Many persons suspected that he had privately remitted considerable sums of money or articles of value to the East Indies, particularly to Bombay, with which port he was long engaged in commercial intercourse, and Muhammad Ali himself insinuated that the Sherif had intended to take refuge at Bombay; but the care with which he fortified and stored his castle at Mecca rather proved that he had been determined to resist and even to fight the Turks within the precincts of the holy city.

[1] His son Abdul Muttalib later erected a domed tomb, which was seen by his great-grandson, His Excellency the Sherif Abdul Majid, in 1912, but it is not now to be seen, having been built over after 1922.

Chapter XIII

THE WAR AGAINST THE WAHHĀBIS OF
CENTRAL ARABIA
(A.D. 1813–14)

THE SEIZURE OF SHERIF GHALIB TERRIFIED BOTH MECCANS and bedouin. Several chiefs of the latter, whom he had introduced to Muhammad Ali, and with whom negotiation had begun, fled from Mecca and returned to Taraba. All Ghalib's friends at Mecca, and several powerful families with their adherents, left the city and took refuge in the tents of their bedouin neighbours. Among these was Sherif Rajih, a distant relation of Ghalib and the most conspicuous man in the Hijaz for justice and liberality. Muhammad Ali had given to him the command of a few hundred bedouin and had charged him to procure others as recruits in his service, but on the day when Ghalib was seized Rajih left Mecca and went with all his people to Daraya, the capital of Saud, who, being glad to have such a redoubtable ally, gave him a large sum of money and appointed him in the room of Othman al Mudhaifi as Emir al Umara, or chief of the chiefs of the Hijaz bedouin.

After the imprisonment of Ghalib there was stagnation in the political affairs of the country. Their treachery had alienated from the Turks even those who were most strongly opposed to the Wahhābis, and Muhammad Ali's situation became critical. The best-informed persons thought that if he had resolved to seize the Sherif he should have waited until some powerful bedouin sheikhs had joined him, and then should engage them to commit actual hostilities against the Wahhābis, which might have rendered it difficult or impossible for them afterwards to abandon the Pasha's cause. Muhammad Ali, no doubt, judged the Sherif's intentions by his own, and, fearing that he might himself fall a victim to treachery were he to allow Ghalib time for the execution of his designs, took action first.

But in this he was wrong. Ghalib was no particular friend of the Ottomans; but, on the other hand, he equally disliked the domination of the Wahhābis. His project was doubtless to let each party weaken the other, without thought of personal treachery towards the Pasha, to preserve whose safety he had made a solemn vow.

A man of the Sherifian family, Yahya ibn Sarur, a nephew of Ghalib and formerly his antagonist, was now appointed Governor of Mecca by Muhammad Ali, who knew him to be without marked talents and wished him to be no more than a cipher. The Pasha took into his own hands all Sherif Ghalib's income at Jedda and Mecca, allowing Yahya a monthly stipend; so that he became, in fact, one of Muhammad Ali's own officers.

At this time Muhammad Ali had no other object than to forward provisions from Jedda to Mecca and Taif. Having collected a small quantity at the latter place, he resolved to strike a decisive blow against his enemies, who had been emboldened by his long inactivity to carry off camels from the very gates of Taif and the neighbourhood of Mecca, while the bedouins were beginning to show contempt for the power of the Pasha, whom they now detested for his treachery.

Among the enemies of the Turks near Mecca none had evinced more determined hostility than the Baqoum Arabs, who had on a former occasion defeated Mustafa Bey. Most of Ghalib's troops had taken refuge in Taraba after the capture of their master, and Sherif Rajih had fixed his headquarters there and was joined by Ali al Mudhaifi, brother of Othman, himself a man of influence in his own country. Thus Taraba became a point of union for all the southern Wahhābis, just as Daraya was of the northern.

The Baqoum Arabs, of whom some are shepherds and some cultivators, were headed by a remarkable widow named Ghalia, whose husband had been one of the chief men of Taraba. She herself possessed more wealth than any family in the neighbourhood, and she now distributed money and provisions among all the poor of her tribe who declared themselves ready to fight the Turks. As the old lady was celebrated for sound judgment and an accurate knowledge of the interests of the surrounding tribes, her voice not only was heard in council, but generally prevailed; and she actually governed the Baqoum, although they had a nominal sheikh, called Ibn Khorshan. From the first defeat of Mustafa Bey, near Taraba, the fame of the widow Ghalia spread over the whole country. The Turkish soldiers' fears soon magnified her influence; they regarded her as chief of the united Wahhābis, and reported absurd stories about her powers as a sorceress and the bestowing of her personal favours on all the Wahhābi leaders, who, by that means, were rendered invincible in battle. These reports discouraged the Ottomans and inspired the bedouin with confidence, contributing to the failure of Tousoun Pasha's expedition.

Muhammad Ali determined to try a second attack about the end of October or beginning of November 1813, sending two thousand men to take possession of Taraba. The country between that town and Taif was in the hands of hostile tribes, the Bani Sa'ad, Al Nasara, and particularly the Ataiba. These had appeared to be neutral when the Sherif governed, and several of their sheikhs had even come to Mecca that they might negotiate with the Pasha; but as soon as he seized the Sherif they all returned to their highlands and began to raid Taif and the Turkish troops.

When on Muhammad Ali's orders Tousoun marched from Taif he took with him provisions for thirty days, most of which time he consumed in warfare against the Ataiba, whom he hunted about in their deserts, reducing some of their lesser clans to subjection. On his arrival before Taraba he had thus only three days' allowance of provisions remaining. The troops were therefore immediately ordered to attack the place; but the Arabs defended their walls with spirit, being animated by the weird exhortations of Ghalia, while the Turks, having no prospect of a rich booty, much fatigued by their marches, and terrified by the sound of strange incantations, were easily repulsed.

Tousoun commanded a second attack to be made the next day, but his troops openly refused to contend with Ghalia, and his officers represented to him the exhausted condition of the army and the want of provisions, emphasizing to him that in case of a second repulse they would all perish from famine. They thus induced him to change the order for attack into one for a retreat towards Taif. The bedouin, aware of his situation, issued from the town as soon as he began to retreat, pressed closely upon his soldiers, gained the passes through which his road lay, and harassed his men so severely that at last the Turks broke, abandoning their baggage, tents, guns, and provisions. More than seven hundred men were killed in this retreat, and many died from want of water and provisions. The army was saved from annihilation by about a hundred horsemen who accompanied Tousoun. The bedouin infantry were unable to withstand the charge of the heavy Egyptian cavalry, which, however, had small opportunity of acting decisively in those hilly and rocky districts.

After four days of hardship and many hairbreadth escapes Tousoun Pasha arrived at Taif with the remains of his army. The failure of his expedition may be chiefly ascribed to want of camels for the transport of his men and of provisions. Nor were any spare camels left at Taif to furnish him with fresh supplies. With no other advantage than some experience derived from these misfortunes, Muhammad Ali was obliged after this signal defeat to resume his former occupation of sending caravans backward and forward between Jedda, Mecca, and Taif, being convinced that any operations against his enemies could best be directed from the last-mentioned place.

The Wahhābis, having pursued the Turks to within a day's journey from Taif, returned to Taraba, and again put into practice their harassing of the Pasha's caravans by flying excursions. These caravans could not pass through the country without escorts so large that, before arrival at their destination, they consumed one-third of the food carried.

In November 1813 the pilgrimage was performed with particular pomp. Sulaiman Pasha of Damascus had come with the Syrian caravan through the desert without any obstacle; although the bedouin through whose territories his road lay obliged him to pay the passage-toll for the whole previous ten years, during which there had been a suspension of the Syrian pilgrimage to the Hijaz. Great numbers of pilgrims from Asia Minor and Istanbul had come by Suez and Jedda to Mecca, and the inhabitants of the holy cities rejoiced to see the revival of their customary source of income, of which they had been

partly deprived by the Wahhābis. Several thousand camels
were sent to Muhammad Ali with the caravan from Cairo and
a large reinforcement for the troops, while Mustafa Bey was
ordered back to Egypt that he might thence procure fresh
horses in place of the great number that he had lost. During the
winter of 1813 and the beginning of 1814 the Turkish army
thus remained inactive, except for recruiting its men and
replenishing its stores.

Every expedition against the enemy having failed, except
that in which Medina was taken, the Pasha thought it necessary
to attempt a diversion or a new plan, the success of which
might encourage his troops and draw off the attention of the
Wahhābis from the main point of attack. A naval expedition
was therefore fitted out at Jedda, carrying fifteen hundred foot-
soldiers and numerous transports loaded with provisions.
Hussain Agha and Saym Oglu were entrusted with the command of this force. They proceeded to Qunfidha, seven
marches south of Jedda. This seaport had formerly been part
of Sherif Ghalib's territory, but during the last five years it
had been in the possession of Tami, Sheikh of the Asir tribes,
the strongest south of Mecca and the most enthusiastic adherents of the Wahhābis. The position of Qunfidha seemed
good for directing attacks on the mountaineers of Asir in
concert with the garrison of Taif, and as the place might be
easily supplied with provisions its capture would be a step
towards the conquest of Yemen, the riches of which no doubt
strongly attracted Muhammad Ali; so the plan was not injudi-
ciously contrived. Qunfidha, where Tami kept only a small
garrison, was taken in March 1814 without bloodshed; but
most of the inhabitants had fled. A corps of four hundred
cavalry set out from Jedda on the seashore, as soon as the capture of the town became known. Qunfidha was sufficiently
defended by a wall to resist an enemy who, like the Wahhābis,
had no guns; but it had no water within its walls, and the wells
which supply it are three hours distant near the mountains.
Fortifications should have been constructed about these wells,
and the road from them to the town of Qunfidha protected by
a line of towers or batteries, as the Turks had abundance of
artillery with them, but these precautions were neglected.

One hundred and fifty Arnauts had been placed near the

wells of Qunfidha; not so much to guard them against the enemy as to prevent the neighbouring Arabs and country people from watering their cattle. After the Turks had remained at Qunfidha about a month, perfectly inactive, they were surprised early in May by a corps of from eight to ten thousand Wahhābis, under the personal command of Tami. The Arnauts near the wells were first attacked. Some of them fought bravely till night; the others fled towards the town and spread consternation. Without attempting resistance from within the walls, the panic-struck commander and most of his troops ran towards the ships that lay in the harbour, while the Wahhābis entered the town and killed numbers of soldiers and servants belonging to the Turkish army who had not been able to save themselves in the ships' boats or who were not able to swim. Many others were actually slain in the water close to the vessels by the Wahhābis, who swam after them—their swords in their teeth—and fought them in the sea, and the Turkish commander was no sooner safe on board ship himself than he ordered the sails to be hoisted, and abandoned to certain death all who had not by then climbed aboard a ship.

The Wahhābis never found again such booty as rewarded them at Qunfidha. The whole baggage, considerable stores, and all the guns became their property, few of the Turks carrying away more than the clothes which they wore. But the most valuable part of the plunder was hundreds of horses and a considerable number of camels. The ships being badly supplied with water and provisions, many of the Turkish soldiers and sailors died on the short passage to Jedda. A few soldiers who had stayed to fight during the day at Qunfidha contrived to escape by night, twelve of them reaching Mecca, where they were rewarded by Muhammad Ali and allowed to enter another corps, since they had all resolved never to serve again under the command of Saym Oglu.

About the time of the disastrous expedition to Qunfidha, Muhammad Ali had gone to Taif on account of its better climate and that he might be nearer to the scene of action and to the bedouin, with whom he again wished to establish amicable relations. In June 1814 a body of fifteen hundred soldiers, the best infantry of Egypt, arrived from Cairo under Hassan Pasha, a celebrated Arnaut chief and a faithful adherent of

Muhammad Ali, whose fortunes he had shared even before Muhammad became Pasha of Egypt, and who had lately shown his zeal during a short revolution headed by Latif Pasha while the Pasha was absent from Cairo. This man, once a Mameluke of Muhammad Ali, had been sent with Ismail Pasha to present the keys of Mecca and Medina to the Sultan, by whom he was created a pasha of two tails[1] in compliment to his patron, Muhammad Ali, but a report became current at Cairo that Muhammad Ali was dead, and the conduct of Latif Pasha then gave reason for suspicion that he intended to seize the government. It was publicly rumoured that he had received from the Porte a firman authorizing him to do so whenever an opportunity should offer. The Deputy-Governor, with Hassan Pasha, immediately adopted measures to check this revolution, and for three days they besieged the palace of Latif Pasha, who was taken soon after, already disguised in the dress of a peasant, and beheaded.

On his arrival in Hijaz Hassan Pasha was sent by Muhammad Ali to establish his headquarters at a village with important wells eight or nine hours eastward of Taif on the road to Taraba, beyond the crest of the mountain chain. Meanwhile Tousoun Pasha, who had incurred his father's displeasure by his ill-considered attack on Taraba, remained at Mecca.

Discontent was universal among the Turkish soldiers, who had spent their savings on the necessaries of life, being paid in Egyptian piastres, so much less valuable in the Hijaz than at Cairo; by having this money they lost one-third of their pay. Many sold their fire-arms and clothes, and all in general suffered much distress. Many soldiers, camel-drivers, servants, and artisans forfeited their pay, and embarked at Jedda and Yanbu' for Cairo; but Muhammad Ali soon forbade such a proceeding under severe penalties. By this prohibition they were much annoyed, a Turkish soldier being then at all times a volunteer and able to retire from the service whenever he pleased. Many left their quarters at Taif and Mecca and came privately to Jedda, hoping that they might escape on board some vessel, but when detected they were marched back in chains to their headquarters. To these causes of complaint were to be added

---

[1] Military pashas were of one, two, or three tails, the tails being those of yaks, which were fastened to a standard, thereby denoting their rank and presence; three represented the highest rank, one the lowest.

the unwholesome air and the bad water of the Hijaz. Despondency, arising from illness, without any hope of relief, became general; and Muhammad Ali neglected the means of encouraging them and reviving their spirit by increasing their pay or distributing rewards among the few who had distinguished themselves.

Muhammad Ali was perhaps the only person of his own court and army who did not despair of ultimate success, knowing that his downfall and expulsion from Egypt must be certain if he should not gain some signal advantage in Arabia.

Since his arrival at Taif he had endeavoured to reopen a friendly intercourse with the bedouin, and in this respect partially succeeded by means of money and patience. In August 1814 the tribes of Hudhail, Thuqaif, Bani Sa'ad, and part of the Ataiba entered into a new alliance with him, the three first roaming between Mecca and Taif, and the Ataiba farther eastward. Their sheikhs had come to headquarters, and above five hundred of their men had enlisted under the banners of Muhammad Ali, who allowed them nearly double as much pay as his own soldiers received. In August 1814 bedouin chiefs arrived daily at his headquarters and were sure of being presented with clothes and money. Many of them took the money, returned to their tents, and informed the Wahhābis of all they had seen at Taif; others remained neutral; and the Pasha, for the sake of gaining over a few, gave fair words and presents to all, listening to their discourses and often deceitful assurances with an unusual degree of patience and apparent good-humour.

Those sons of the desert addressed him in the most democratic and unceremonious manner, as is their custom, calling him merely by his name, Muhammad Ali. One, an Ataiba tribesman, it is related, presented himself before the Pasha, kissed his beard, and exclaimed, "I have abandoned the religion of the Muslims [or "True Believers," as the Wahhābis styled themselves]; I have adopted the religion of the heretics [so the Wahhābis entitled all those Muhammadans who were not of their own creed]; I have adopted the religion of Muhammad Ali." This unintended blunder caused a general laugh; and the Pasha answered through his interpreter—for he but imperfectly understood Arabic—"I hope you will always be a staunch heretic."

So even Sherif Rajih, who had taken the lead among Muhammad Ali's enemies and had personally distinguished himself on the Wahhābi side during the attack on Tousoun Pasha on Taraba, now made proposals for returning to Muhammad Ali's side. Hitherto the Pasha's conduct showed that Sherif Ghalib was the only individual personally disliked by him among the chieftains of the Hijaz, and Rajih could clearly prove that he had only abandoned the Pasha's cause from the fear of sharing Ghalib's fate. In September he came to Taif, and Muhammad Ali received him most graciously, and again placed him at the head of his bedouin soldiers.

Besides his condescending policy adopted in his intercourse with the bedouin, Muhammad Ali had done all in his power to conciliate the inhabitants of the Hijaz itself. Many small duties levied by the Sherif were abolished; the customs at Jedda upon various articles, particularly coffee, were diminished; great sums were distributed among the needy and poor of all descriptions, besides quantities of corn. The learned men and those who held offices about the mosques and schools received donations; the holy places at Mecca were repaired, and during his residence there the Pasha observed most scrupulously the minute and tedious rites prescribed for those who visit the Ka'aba, although at Cairo he had never taken any pains to conceal his scepticism. The Turkish soldiers throughout the Hijaz were ordered to abstain from any insulting language towards the natives, and were severely punished whenever they indulged in those tyrannical acts they so frequently practised in Egypt. No soldier could venture to take things by force, or at half-price, from the market; for, on complaint to the Pasha or his officers, the natives were always the favoured party. Thus the strong prejudice of the Arabs against all foreigners became gradually weaker, and the Pasha obtained credit for justice and charity.

In May 1814 Saud died of a fever and the Wahhābis lost an indefatigable leader. It is said that his last words were addressed to his son Abdulla, advising him "never to engage the Turks in open plains"—a principle which, if strictly followed, would have ensured to his people the recovery of the

Hijaz. Abdulla, his eldest son, to whom the principal Wah-hābi chiefs had already paid homage during Saud's lifetime, thus became heir to the supreme authority. Some dispute, however, arose because Saud had several brothers who claimed part of his treasure, and one of these brothers, Abdulla, was supported by a strong part of the Ulama of Darayah. However, after some short hostilities Abdulla, the son of Saud, was acknowledged the Wahhābi chief. His courage and skill in war exceeded that of his father; but he did not know so well as Saud how to manage the tribes under him or the great sheikhs, some of whom began to assume airs of independence. The southern Wahhābis, who were now most exposed to attacks, did not receive support from the northern tribes, whose cavalry might have assisted them; and even the southern sheikhs were at variance with each other, and the Pasha had therefore to contend against single tribes rather than a combined force. This want of union, perhaps, may be ascribed to the contempt in which the Turkish troops were held by their enemies.

In September 1814 the Pasha's forces were distributed as follows: About two hundred men were with Ibrahim Agha, the seal-bearer of Muhammad Ali, at Mecca, where also were one hundred and fifty Arabian soldiers under Sherif Yahya. Between three and four hundred men, commanded by Divan Effendi, were at Medina; one hundred formed the garrison of Yanbu', and two hundred were stationed at Jedda. Tousoun Pasha, with three hundred and fifty men, was encamped between Yanbu' and Medina. Muhammad Ali had with him at Taif three hundred Turks, of whom about one hundred were cavalry. Hassan Pasha, commanding in the interior, had one thousand of his Arnauts, and his brother, Abdin Bey, commanding the advanced posts of the army, had twelve hundred Arnauts and four hundred cavalrymen who had just arrived from Cairo. These advanced posts had pushed forward three or four days' journey southward of Taif into the territory of the Bani Nasara tribe and towards Zahran, where the sheikh of the Ghamid Arabs was the principal opponent of the Turks. They had the advantage of being quartered in a fertile country furnishing a sufficiency of corn and barley for their wants: thus they became independent of the magazines at Taif.

Daily reinforcements arrived from Egypt, but were scarcely sufficient to recruit the ranks which had been so much weakened by disease and by unsuccessful encounters with the Wahhābis, and the number of troops which Muhammad Ali had in Egypt was too small to admit of many large drafts for the Hijaz, for he could not lessen their number without exposing Egypt to attacks, which, if he were weak, he expected at once from Istanbul, from the Mamelukes, or from England.

When it became known in those countries which furnished the greater proportion of soldiers to the Turkish Pashas—namely Albania, Rumelia, and the coast of Asia Minor—that the campaign in Hijaz was so extremely distressing to the troops engaged in it, very few recruits came to Egypt; and Muhammad Ali was obliged to keep in those countries his own recruiting officers, who could not accomplish their object without expending considerable sums. The Pasha's army consisted of no more than 35,000 men, 20,000 of whom were in Hijaz and 15,000 in Egypt.

To defend the holy cities and overawe the neighbouring provinces a small force of between four and five thousand men was quite sufficient, with the help of four hundred bedouin, collected from different tribes, and whose pay was twice as much as that allowed to the Turks; but with this army the Wahhābis could not be conquered, although the Pasha at his departure from Cairo had solemnly promised to his sovereign that he would bring them into subjection. Nor, notwithstanding all the Pasha's efforts, had the want of camels been supplied; the road from Taif to Mecca and thence to Jedda was literally strewed with the carcasses of dead camels, showing that a continual renewal of the baggage train was absolutely necessary. In the suburb of Mecca called Al Mu'abda, where the caravans from Jedda and Taif halted, so pestilential a stench was produced by the hundreds of dead camels that, on application made by the inhabitants, numerous poor Negro pilgrims were hired to fetch dry grass from the adjoining mountains; a quantity of this was piled over each dead camel and set on fire, so that the carcasses were consumed to ashes. At a moderate calculation, from the beginning of the war in 1811 up to this period thirty thousand camels belonging to the army had perished in Hijaz, and few remained in Egypt.

Large supplies had been sought in the Negro countries as far as Sennar, but the transport of provisions from Genne to Kosseir and from Cairo to Suez required such numbers that few could be spared for the Hijaz service. The Pasha had sent an officer to Damascus to purchase camels among the Syrian bedouin, and these camels were expected at Mecca with the next pilgrim caravan, while Ibrahim Pasha had done all in his power to collect camels from among the Libyan tribes, which were likewise to be sent with the Egyptian pilgrim caravan to the Hijaz. Thus, until the time of their arrival only defensive measures were possible.

Meanwhile the Wahhābis made frequent incursions towards Taif and against the tribes which had espoused the cause of the Pasha, who, on his side, harassed the enemy's country, by means of cavalry sent out in small detachments. The Sherif Yahya with his Arabs made an expedition in August 1814 by the mountain route towards Qunfidha, and brought back valuable booty in camels and sheep, but he had no sooner returned to Mecca than Tami avenged himself by sending a corps of six hundred camel-riders of the Qahtan tribe towards Jedda.

The intercourse between Jedda and Mecca was therefore interrupted, but the Wahhābis, having accomplished their purpose of raiding, retreated to their homes. They had set out from a distance of at least fifteen days' march to plunder on this road, and their exact knowledge of the country enabled them to take such routes as brought them suddenly on their prey.

Ever since the taking of Medina the Turkish troops there had remained inactive, as the supplies sent to them from Yanbu' were scarcely sufficient for their daily use and for the inhabitants of the town. The near-by Harb tribes continued on amicable terms with the Turks; and the Sheikh of the Harb, Jazi, who had mainly assisted in taking the place, had gone in June 1814 on business to the Divan Effendi, commanding there. Being one day seated in full council with the latter, and unable to endure the vain Turk's idle bragging, he exclaimed in hearing of the whole company, "Be silent, O Divan Effendi, as everybody knows that it was I who paved the way for your entrance into this town, and were it not for this blade no Turk

would have ever entered Medina." The Turkish commander
was incensed at this address, insulted Jazi with the most
opprobrious terms, struck him, and caused him to be put in
chains. Next day it was reported that he had killed himself
in prison, certain proofs having been obtained that he was
carrying on a treasonable correspondence with the Wahhābis.
The consequence of such an event might have easily been
foretold. As soon as the Harb knew that their sheikh was
killed they shut the road through their mountains against the
caravans from Yanbu', and, without actually joining the
Wahhābis, they began hostilities against the Turkish outposts.

In hope of settling these disturbances Muhammad Ali
ordered his son Tousoun Pasha to proceed at once towards
Medina. He arrived at Bedr in September and found that the
Harb had strongly garrisoned the pass of Judaida and were
resolved to oppose his entrance by force. They boldly demanded
the life of the Divan Effendi as an expiation of the murder of
their sheikh. Fortunately the Divan Effendi died at that very
time, not without strong suspicion of poison. Their new sheikh
and minor chiefs received valuable presents; the price of
Jazi's blood was paid to his relations in compliance with the
bedouin custom, and peace was concluded with them.

Having passed the defile, Tousoun Pasha arrived at Medina,
in October 1814, with about three hundred foot-soldiers and
five hundred horse, most of the latter having just come from
Cairo.

About this time the affairs of the Turks assumed a more
favourable aspect throughout the Hijaz, and hopes were being
entertained that the Pasha might be able to conduct in person
some grand enterprise against the enemy, when another
defeat was experienced. Abdin Bey, with his Arnauts, occupied
districts in the province of Zahran, south of Taif. To prevent
the daily attacks of his enemies he had laid waste the country
within forty miles and totally destroyed whatever might be
serviceable for the passage of troops. He was encamped on one
side of this artificial desert, and the enemy sheikh, Bakhroudj,
was posted on the southern side of it. Bakhroudj early one
morning in September fell upon the sleeping Arnauts, who
scarcely waited to fire one shot, but abandoned their camp
and all that it contained. Some little resistance was made by

a few hundred soldiers from Rumelia under Mahou Beg, the Pasha's most active chief in the Hijaz, but they could not long contend against the overwhelming force of the Wahhābis, and the whole army owed its escape to a corps of cavalry commanded by a Syrian chief named Hussain Bey, who covered their retreat, in which Bakhroudj pursued them for two days. The Turks once more lost all their tents, artillery, baggage, and provisions: eight hundred Turkish foot-soldiers and eighty horsemen were killed; and it was not until the remainder of the army arrived at about four hours' distance from Taif that they ventured to take up a position. Here Abdin Bey received some reinforcements from Taif, and, as it was known that the Arabs had returned home, he advanced a second time, by the Pasha's orders, towards Zahran. But such a panic had seized the Turkish troops that half of them deserted, and Abdin Bey was obliged to halt and wait for reinforcements.

This last defeat had a depressing effect on the spirits of the troops. Abdin Bey had hitherto enjoyed the highest reputation for skill and courage, and his troops were certainly the best of the whole army; but the late disasters convinced his soldiers that further resistance against such numerous enemies as the Wahhābis would be vain, and there was not a man among the Turks who did not long to find himself again safe in Egypt. As the Turks, however, understand better almost than any other nation the need for a bold face in evil circumstances, they described their last defeat as a victory, because the horsemen had brought the heads of about sixty Wahhābis with them to Taif. While the army trembled within the walls of that town, guns were fired at Jedda to announce a victory, and Cairo was illuminated for three days to celebrate the glorious exploit of Abdin Bey.

Chapter XIV

THE WAR AGAINST THE WAHHĀBIS OF
CENTRAL ARABIA (*continued*)
(A.D. 1814–40)

SOON AFTER ABDIN BEY'S DEFEAT A WELCOME REINFORCE-
ment of cavalry arrived from Cairo. Horsemen had been
drawn from all the Libyan tribes of bedouin who encamp
during summer in the neighbourhood of the Nile valley, and
eight hundred of them had been dispatched to the Hijaz.
These were themselves bedouin, and well accustomed to the
system of warfare prevalent among the Wahhābis; their horses
were equally as trained to fatigue as the riders, and every horseman had a camel with him, carrying provisions for the most
distant expedition. Half of these horsemen had joined Tousoun
Pasha on his way to Medina; the others advanced to Taif, and
had no sooner arrived there than they distinguished themselves
by daring excursions against the Wahhābi tribes situated
several days' journey eastward of Taraba, being accompanied
by bedouin guides of those countries. They were all well
armed and known as good marksmen, and in one of their
excursions they brought away eight thousand sheep from a
Wahhābi encampment.

The pilgrim caravans duly arrived in November from Syria
and Egypt. With the former came three thousand camels,
which Muhammad Ali had purchased from the Syrian bedouin,
and another one thousand taken by Tousoun Pasha from
passing caravans. The Egyptian caravan likewise brought
about two thousand five hundred camels, besides a reinforcement of one thousand Turkish horsemen. And that these
might be all employed for military purposes the whole caravan
was detained at Mecca, and the *mahmal* sent, after the pilgrimage was over, by sea to Suez.

The Pasha came down from Taif to assist in the ceremony

of the pilgrimage and to meet Sulaiman, Pasha of Damascus, who had again accompanied the caravan from Syria. Muhammad Ali's favourite lady, the mother of Tousoun, had come by sea to perform the pilgrimage. Her retinue was as splendid as the wealth of Egypt could render it. Four hundred camels transported her baggage from Jedda to Mecca, and her tent, pitched at the foot of Mount Arafat, was magnificent in style and size. Several personages of high rank had come from Istanbul, and the pilgrimage was performed by about eighty thousand persons of all descriptions and nations. After the ceremony, the Syrian caravan generally remained a few days at Mecca, but Muhammad Ali protracted their stay ten days beyond the usual term, requiring all their camels—some twelve thousand—to carry provisions between Jedda and Mecca to supply his troops before they left.

When he had collected his whole effective strength between Mecca and Taif, and the state of his storehouses and the number of his camels at last raised in him hopes of success, he announced his intention of placing himself at the head of the army, which served to raise in some degree the spirits of his troops.

Taraba was again pointed out as the first object of attack, and well-appointed artillery, consisting of twelve field-pieces, encouraged the soldiers to believe that the walls of Taraba could not long remain standing and that no man would be required to scale the wall in the face of the enemy, as had been the case when Tousoun Pasha made his attack. Five hundred axes were provided for cutting down the palm-trees which impeded the approach to Taraba. Twenty masons and as many carpenters were attached to the army for the purpose of opening a mine which was to blow up the enemy at once. That the soldiers might be sure of success, a load of watermelon seeds was brought from Wadi Fatima[1] and carried in pomp through the town of Mecca, it being intended by the command, after the total demolition of Taraba, to sow these seeds on the spot where it had stood. But in the end these extensive preparations, so far from calming the minds of the soldiers, began to make them uneasy, as they proved what vast importance was attached to the taking of that place and the difficulty of the enterprise.

---

[1] Formerly known as Wadi al Marr.

As a further encouragement to the army thirteen bedouin captured on the Jedda road and accused of being Wahhābi robbers—although it afterwards appeared most clearly that they had only gone to Jedda to buy provisions—were executed on an open space outside Mecca before an immense multitude of people.

Following this strange sacrifice, and everything being now prepared for the expedition which was to decide the fate of the whole campaign, Ahmad Bonaparte left Mecca with the greater part of the infantry, and with full military pomp, on December 15, 1814. The Pasha intended to follow him with about twelve hundred cavalry on the 24th, when intelligence arrived that a strong Wahhābi force had been seen in the neighbourhood of Qunfidha advancing towards Jedda. This report excited great alarm. Bedouin scouts were dispatched to obtain information, and at Jedda considerable disorder prevailed, for it was expected that the Wahhābis, if they did not attack the town itself, would at least cut off its communication with Mecca. For some time water had been extremely scarce at Jedda; the Government cisterns were now hastily filled by compulsory measures, and the inhabitants drew their scanty supply from wells three hours' ride away. Every kind of provisions in Mecca rose 30 per cent. on the first rumour, but the people recovered from their panic when it was known that only a small troop of Tami's soldiers had pitched their tents near Qunfidha.

A few days after, news arrived that the Wahhābi tribes from Zahran had made an incursion into the territories of the bedouin allies of the Pasha and had completely sacked a fortified village where a garrison of Arnauts had been stationed, while Taraba was already in a state of full preparation and reinforcements were hastening from all quarters towards that town to defend it against the threatened attack.

On January 7, 1815, Muhammad Ali Pasha marched forth from Mecca with all the troops and camels that he could muster to join Hassan Pasha, Abdin Bey, Mahou Bey, Ahmad Bonaparte, Toupous Oglou, Sherif Rajih, and other chiefs of his army, already assembled at a point where sufficient provisions for fifty or sixty days had been collected. When he arrived at Zaima, the second station on the northern road from

Mecca to Taif, express messengers informed him that a considerable body of the enemy was advancing against his allies the Ataiba tribe. Muhammad Ali therefore hastened his march and dispatched Sherif Rajih with his bedouin soldiers and the Libyan horsemen to support the Ataiba. He found that the Wahhābis had possession of several watering-places, while the advanced Turkish soldiers carried the water for their own use upon camels from afar. The Wahhābi force was estimated to be about twenty-five thousand men, accompanied by five thousand camels, but wanting any artillery. All the chiefs of the Yemen mountains and of the south-eastern plain were with the Wahhābi army, as was Faisal, the son of Saud. In making a diversion against Qunfidha the Wahhābis had hoped to draw off the Pasha's attention from the main object of attack, and then fall unexpectedly upon the Turkish lines; so, when the Pasha's cavalry nevertheless approached, they remained upon their mountains and only sought to repulse an advance made into a valley where Muhammad Ali wished to plant one of his field-pieces. The whole of the next day was spent in fruitless excursions with this object by the Turkish cavalry.

Although but few lives were sacrificed, the Turks began to despair of success, while the Wahhābis entertained sanguine hopes of weakening the enemy by repeated defeats and finally destroying them. Fearing such a result, several Turkish soldiers, as well as bedouin in the Pasha's service, deserted from the army and hastened back to Mecca. Here, in excuse of their defection, they spread the news of a complete defeat, of the Pasha's death, and other disasters. Burckhardt says:

> The terror caused by these reports in Mecca can scarcely be imagined. Numerous stragglers belonging to the army, and Turkish hadjys preparing to return home; also Turkish merchants and such soldiers as were in the town, all expected to suffer death on the first arrival of the victorious Wahabys. Four hundred piastres were offered for a camel to convey a person to Djidda [Jedda]; but the few bedouin who possessed camels, removed them into the mountains on the first rumours of defeat. Several people left Mekka on foot that very evening, and endeavoured to reach Djidda by the next morning. Others joined the garrison in the castle, and put on bedouin rags that they might

not be supposed foreigners; but nobody prepared for defence, and Sherif Yahya himself, although he had not received any official report, was ready for a sudden flight to Djidda. For my own part, being convinced that if the Pasha had been defeated, the Wahaby light troops would intercept all fugitives on the Djidda road, and preclude the possibility of escape, I thought my safest asylum would be the great mosque, which, at all times, the Wahabys had respected as an inviolable sanctuary. Having put into a bag the few valuable articles that I possessed, along with a good provision of biscuit, I went accompanied by my slave and established myself in the mosque, where many poor hadjys had from the same motive taken up their residence. My biscuit, with the water of Zemzem found in the mosque, might have supplied my wants for some weeks. That the whole crowd of Turks did not follow this example, may be ascribed to their judging of the Wahabys by themselves; for they could never believe that in the hour of victory a soldier would regard any place as sacred. But our apprehensions proved to be founded on imaginary disasters; and, after a night of considerable anxiety, we were surprised and gratified the next morning by the official account stating the total defeat of the dreaded Wahabys.[1]

Muhammad Ali Pasha had learnt that he could have no chance of success as long as the enemy remained upon the mountain, and he likewise knew that if he were unsuccessful on the following day his career both in Hijaz and in Egypt would probably close for ever. He therefore sent during the night for all his reinforcements, and ordered two thousand of his infantry, together with the artillery, to take up a position on the flank of the Wahhābis. The next morning at an early hour he renewed the attack with his cavalry, and was again repulsed. He then assembled his officers, and commanded them to advance with their columns closer to the position of the Wahhābis than they had done before, and, after firing off their guns, to retreat in seeming disorder. This plan was accordingly executed. The Wahhābis, seeing the enemy fly, thought that the fortunate moment for completely crushing them had arrived; they left their stronghold on the mountain side and pursued the flying Turks over the plain. All happened as the Pasha had expected. When he thought the enemy sufficiently distant from the mountains, he rallied his

[1] *Notes on the Bedouins and Wahabys.*

cavalry, faced the pursuers, and the battle was soon decided in his favour.

The Turkish infantry now turned the position of the Arabs. Sherif Rajih, who had just arrived with his corps after having repulsed the enemy's feint attack upon the Ataiba, joined Muhammad Ali, beset the valley through which the Wahhābis were to retreat, and compelled them to fly in disorder. As soon as Muhammad Ali saw the enemy running he proclaimed among his troops that six dollars would be given for every Wahhābi head. In a few hours five thousand were piled up before him: in one narrow valley fifteen hundred Wahhābis had been surrounded and cut to pieces. Their whole camp and baggage and most of their camels fell a prey to the Turks.

About three hundred Wahhābis were taken alive, who at the express command of Muhammad Ali were offered quarter, as very few of the enemy had condescended to beg for mercy. Sherif Rajih was dispatched with some cavalry in pursuit of the fugitives, and he was joined on his way by many of the neighbouring Arabs.

In this battle the Pasha fought in person at the moment when he ordered his cavalry to wheel about and face their pursuers. He deserved great credit for having known how to instil a soldierly spirit into troops who had relinquished all hopes of success. On his side no man distinguished himself more than Sherif Rajih; mounted upon a famous black mare and armed with his lance, he galloped far in advance of the army, and among crowds of the enemy, towards the tent of Faisal, the most conspicuous in the whole camp, and, striking his lance into the ground before it, defended himself with his sword against a number of Wahhābis until his friends approached and rescued him. Beyond the camels, no booty of great value was taken by the army. Rajih found in the tent of Faisal about two thousand dollars only. Many quarrels occurred between the Turkish soldiers and their allies the bedouin, who accompanied Rajih, respecting the division of plunder. The Pasha seemed inclined to favour the bedouin, and most of the camels fell to their lot. It was stated that the Turks lost on this day between four and five hundred men.

The complete defeat of the Wahhābis may be attributed

entirely to their having descended from the mountain into the plain, where they had no means of resisting the Turkish cavalry. Saud, in the last words which he addressed to his son, had cautioned him against such a proceeding. But the contempt in which the Wahhābis held the Turkish troops, the desire of terminating the campaign, and perhaps the hope of securing the person of Muhammad Ali himself made them forget the system of warfare which they had hitherto adopted, and their astonishment on finding themselves so suddenly overpowered rendered them incapable of resistance.

Messengers were immediately dispatched to Istanbul and Cairo with intelligence of the victory, and the Turks everywhere became elated. Meanwhile the natives of Hijaz, although glad to be secured against a second Wahhābi conquest, grieved to see Arabians vanquished by Turks, and shuddered at the cruelties which these victors had practised both during and after the battle. The three hundred prisoners, to whom quarter had been promised, were sent by Muhammad Ali to Mecca. He celebrated his triumph by causing fifty of them to be impaled before the gates of Mecca; twelve suffered a like death at every one of the ten coffee-houses, halting-places between Mecca and Jedda; and the rest before the Mecca gate of Jedda, where dogs and vultures devoured their carcasses.

Four days after the battle Muhammad Ali arrived before Taraba, from which Faisal fled at his approach. The inhabitants, abandoned by their allies, capitulated; and the Pasha fixed his headquarters at that place for some time. The Turks plundered a few houses and carried off some handsome Arab women, who were, however, restored to their families by the Pasha's order. The famous Ghalia had taken refuge with the bedouin. She might, it was hoped, have been sent as a trophy to Istanbul, but no proposals could induce her to return or confide in the offers of the Turks.

Immediately after the victory the Pasha directed Sherif Yahya to proceed with his Arabs to Qunfidha, and he reinforced his corps with the troops of Mahou Bey. Orders also were sent to Jedda that several transports loaded with provisions might be dispatched to Qunfidha. As the strength of his enemies now lay in the southern countries, Muhammad Ali resolved to carry the war into their own territories and completely to exterminate them. Whatever provisions could be procured were loaded upon five thousand camels.

The main army also proceeded from Taraba southward towards Ranya, and after four marches from that place they arrived in the district of Bisha, a fertile valley belonging to the tribe of Bani Salim, whose chief, Ibn Shaqban, was a leading man among the Wahhābis. Here two small castles had been built by the express command of Saud.

The army remained about a fortnight at Bisha, the most important position in the country eastward of the Yemen mountains, and called by the northern nomads the key of Yemen. Here the Pasha was joined by many bedouin. All those who were discontented with the Wahhābis, and all the relations of those sheikhs who had been turned out of their situations, came now to seek redress from Muhammad Ali, who, imitating the system of Saud, changed everywhere the chiefs of tribes, by which means a strong party in his favour was created. News reached him here that Tami had again assembled a considerable army in his mountains, and he thereupon resolved to try the chance of battle a second time. It was towards his territory that Muhammad Ali now directed his march, taking a western course from Bisha.

On this march his army suffered the extremes of hunger and fatigue. Half of the camels had already perished before the arrival of the troops at Bisha, and many horses had shared the same fate. The vanguard cleared the road of every particle of stubble or blade of grass; so that those who came after found nothing but a barren desert. On the Turks' approach the Arabs fled in all directions, carrying off their cattle and provisions, while the bedouin themselves, who followed the army, took advantage of the general disorder and purloined many loads. At every halt a number of camels dropped, and their flesh was greedily devoured by the soldiers. The last biscuits had been distributed at Bisha, after which every man was left to supply himself as well as he could. The Pasha found it necessary to allow the troops an additional pay of one piastre per day, but this money was of little use in a place where as much corn made into bread as would satisfy a man's appetite once cost twelve piastres.

At two days' journey from Bisha they entered the mountainous country, which had been almost totally deserted by its people. Among the Shahran Arabs the Turks enjoyed a few days' repose. Here in one day a hundred horses died. The soldiers became dissatisfied, but, as they clearly saw that a retreat would lead to inevitable destruction, they still advanced. The Pasha commanded all his chiefs to dismount and to march on foot at the head of their respective columns. To his soldiers he promised a glorious booty from plunder in the towns of Yemen, thus endeavouring to keep up their spirits. A market was established at every halt, just before the Pasha's tent, where the allied bedouin sold to the troops whatever they had been able to carry off from the Arabs on the road, the Pasha himself presiding and enforcing strict order.

Near the territory of Asir the rugged mountains presented many obstacles to the passage of artillery. This territory the Turkish army entered twelve or fourteen days after they left Bisha, halting near the castle called Tor, which stood upon an elevated ground, surrounded by mountains. It had been built by Abu Noqta, the predecessor of Tami, and was deemed so strong that no Arab force could possibly take it. Here Tami had collected from eight to ten thousand men, and when the Pasha attacked the Asiris fired incessantly, and three hundred Turks were killed. Tami was seen on horseback in front of his men, animating them by war-songs, but, the field-pieces having been brought to bear on the second day, the Wahhābis gave way. Tami himself fled, although the last to quit the field. Considerable stores of provisions were found in the castle, which proved most serviceable to the army, likewise ammunition, the guns taken from Qunfidha the year before, and a large stock of matchlocks, then particularly esteemed by the Arabs.

The army, however, after such a long, fatiguing, and perilous march openly declared their desire of returning to Mecca. As the only means of calming his men, Muhammad Ali was obliged to promise that they should soon be sent back to Egypt; so instead of proceeding southward, he now directed his march towards Qunfidha. Tami, after the battle which he had lost, took refuge in the neighbourhood of Al Arish, at the house of a Sherif. The Sherif thought this a favourable opportunity for warding off a hostile invasion and of evincing his submission and repentance. Tami was put in chains, and a messenger dispatched to the Turkish headquarters with a letter in which the Sherif styled himself the "slave of Muhammad Ali," and asked how he should dispose of his prisoner. Sherif Rajih, who was then roaming about the mountains in search of the fugitive, received orders to take him back to Qunfidha, where the army now arrived to find that an abundant supply of provisions had been brought from Jedda by sea.

Muhammad Ali sent off a body of troops from Ranya to invade Zahran from the east, while Mahou Bey ascended the mountains from the east, and by a skilful manœuvre placed the Arabs of Bakhroudj between two fires, so that they were defeated and Bakhroudj himself taken and carried to Qunfidha. Here the Pasha remained several days, his two captives being lodged in tents close to his own, Tami's conduct inspiring the army with respect. The Pasha often conversed with him for amusement, as the tiger plays with his prey before he seizes it in his grasp; but Tami's dignified behaviour subdued the ferocity even of this Turk, and he promised to write in his favour and procure him permission from the Sultan to live in retirement in the mountains of Rumelia. Tami was a man of great natural powers; short in stature, with a long white beard, his eyes darting fire; sarcastic in general, but polite towards the Turkish chief. Bakhroudj, on the contrary, observed a sulky silence, convinced that Muhammad Ali would never forgive him; nor did the Pasha ever desire to see him. Finding his guards asleep one night, Bakhroudj seized a poniard, contrived to loosen his chains, and escaped from the camp, but was overtaken after he had killed two men and wounded another. Next day Muhammad Ali asked him by what right he had killed his soldiers. "Whenever I am not chained," replied Bakhroudj, "I act as I please." "I shall act in the same manner," said the Pasha; and to entertain his Turks, and at the same time to gratify his revenge, he immediately caused the unfortunate prisoner, bound as he was in chains, to be placed in the midst of his bodyguards, who were directed to wound him slightly with their sabres so that his torments might be prolonged. He at last expired without having uttered one complaint: his head was sent to Cairo and Istanbul along with

Tami, who, upon his arrival in the latter city, was instantly beheaded.[1]

From Qunfidha the Pasha proceeded to Mecca, which he reached on the 21st of March, fifteen days after he had left that city. Of the many thousands of camels originally with the army less than three hundred returned to Mecca, all the rest having perished on the road. Much of the baggage and ammunition was destroyed, there being no means of transporting it, and of the horses, only three hundred were brought back. Of four thousand Turks who set out from Mecca only fifteen hundred returned, all of whom were, from the highest in rank to the meanest, in rags, worn out with fatigue, and without money.

Muhammad Ali, according to the promise extorted from him at Qunfidha, permitted them all to embark at Jedda, except Hassan Pasha, whom he kept in the Hijaz with a few hundred Arnauts; and soon new reinforcements arrived from Egypt.

The strength of the Wahhābis was now considerably reduced, particularly in the south. Abdulla ibn Saud had returned to Daraya from Al Qásim on learning of the defeat of the Wahhābis by Muhammad Ali, apprehending a new attack from him. On his arrival at Mecca the Pasha assembled all the chief men and Ulama of the city, and read to them a letter which he had addressed to Abdulla ibn Saud, exhorting him to submission and offering terms of peace. He charged him to restore the treasures which his father had taken from the Prophet's tomb, at Medina, if he did not wish to share the same fate as his friends in the south. This letter was sent to Daraya by a Turkish soldier accompanied by some bedouin.

After a short stay at Mecca Muhammad Ali, having appointed Hassan Pasha Governor of that town, and left Hussain Bey, a cavalry chief, and Sherif Rajih in garrison at Taraba and Bisha, set out for Medina, where he arrived unexpectedly, on the 14th of April, with only thirty or forty attendants mounted upon dromedaries, having performed the whole journey by land.

When the news of Muhammad Ali's success became known

---

[1] In violation of the solemn promise made by Muhammad Ali, Tami, when he arrived at Cairo, was loaded with an immense chain about his neck, placed upon a camel, and then paraded through the streets with the head of Bakhroudj in a bag suspended from his shoulders.

to the northern tribes, many of their sheikhs made proposals
to Tousoun Pasha, who was then at Medina, offering to join
him against the Wahhābis, whose power was more severely
felt in the north than among the southern tribes. In March
most of the Al Qasim sheikhs came one after another to Medina
and assured Tousoun Pasha of their readiness to assist him.
He bestowed presents on them, and sent back with them four
hundred cavalry to garrison some of their villages. Tousoun
himself now conceived hopes of conquering Nejd. Notwithstanding his great personal courage so often displayed, he had
been always unfortunate in his Hijaz expeditions. He became
anxious to emulate his father in the glory he had acquired by
his late campaign, but he did not well calculate his means.
Muhammad Ali had not entrusted to his son's management
any considerable sums of money, knowing his liberality and
generous disposition, and perhaps unwilling that anyone
besides himself should acquire renown. Tousoun was therefore
much in want of camels and of food. He, however, resolved to
try his fortune, and left Medina at the end of March, setting
out for Hanakiya, a ruined village with walls, a home of the
Anaiza tribe three days' march on the road to Al Qasim. He
had with him about four hundred camels carrying provisions,
and between two and three hundred cavalry, with four hundred
foot-soldiers. He was followed by a few hundred bedouin,
chiefly of Harb and Mutair.

He remained some time at Hanakiya, and was still there
when his father arrived at Medina. The reason of Muhammad
Ali's visit to this sacred city was probably his wish to obtain
information respecting the affairs of the northern Hijaz and to
pay his devotions at the Prophet's tomb; but from Medina he
immediately sent orders directing Tousoun to return from
Hanakiya that he might concert measures with him. His son,
however, had determined on the expedition, and as soon as he
received Muhammad Ali's order, instead of obeying it, he set
out towards Al Qasim. As he was equal in rank to his father,
being like him a pasha of three tails, the latter perhaps was
wrong in making him feel too strongly his state of dependence.
The custom duties of Jedda, which by right belonged to the
Sherif and had been allotted to Tousoun, had been transferred
by the Porte to Muhammad Ali for the expenses of the war.

Of this amount Tousoun Pasha received merely a certain allowance by the day, like all the other chiefs of the army; and in placing the north of the Hijaz under his command, Muhammad Ali had associated with Tousoun a person of his own court, through whom all business was to be transacted, and whom Tousoun was advised to consult upon all occasions —as if his father thought him unfit for the high situation that he filled.

Soon after their arrival at Medina this person, as might be supposed, rendered himself disagreeable to his pupil, who, in a fit of anger, caused him to be beheaded. Great disorder then prevailed in the administration of affairs. The interests of the Turks with the surrounding Arabs were ill managed; the soldiers committed depredations. Tousoun, wanting camels, seized all the cattle that could be found among the bedouin; and Muhammad Ali, on his arrival, instead of taking offensive measures against the enemy, was fully occupied in repairing the mischief consequent upon the errors of his son. Two hundred and fifty horsemen, under the command of Thomas Keith, or Ibrahim Agha, were dispatched after Tousoun Pasha, as was likewise a detachment of infantry which had arrived from Yanbu', having as their chief Ahmad Bonaparte, just returned from Cairo. Tousoun, early in May, after a march of ten or eleven days from Medina, at last reached the province of Al Qasim. During this journey he attacked the Hataim bedouin and carried off five hundred of their camels, which he sent to Medina for the transport of provisions from Yanbu'. Upon his arrival at Rass, one of the principal towns of Al Qasim and defended by a wall, he was joined by the cavalry which had preceded him by some time, and the sheikhs of different districts in Al Qasim came to concert measures with him.

In the meanwhile Abdulla ibn Saud, with an army composed of bedouin and agriculturists of Nejd, likewise entered Al Qasim and fixed his headquarters only five hours distant from Khabra, where Tousoun Pasha had encamped. Here Tousoun found himself in a precarious situation.

He heard that his treasurer, Thomas Keith, had been surrounded on the road, and, notwithstanding a most gallant resistance, had been cut to pieces, together with all his horsemen. The fertile district of Al Qasim might have supplied provisions for a much larger army than his, but the light troops of the Wahhābis were hovering about the Turks, who depended wholly upon two or three villages for their daily food, which they foresaw must soon become extremely scarce. The road to Medina was occupied by the enemy, and no intelligence could be obtained respecting any steps taken by Muhammad Ali. He could not place much confidence in the bedouin who were with him, knowing that they would readily join the other party on the first defeat, and when he wished to end suspense by giving battle his officers and soldiery were unwilling. The superior numbers of the Wahhābis frightened them, and they felt convinced that in case of defeat not one of them could escape, and that it was prudent to compromise with the enemy rather than to fight, the more so as Muhammad Ali had empowered his son to make peace on favourable terms. Some bedouin were employed to sound the disposition of the enemy's chief, who sent one Habab to find out what were actually the designs of Tousoun.

Habab was well received by Tousoun, who immediately sent Yahya Effendi, his physician, a native of Syria who spoke Arabic better than any of the Turks, to negotiate with Abdulla. He was the bearer of some presents, and remained three days in the Wahhābi camp. As both parties desired peace, the negotiation was soon concluded, and one of Abdulla's courtiers waited upon Tousoun that he might ratify the treaty. In this Abdulla renounced all claim to the possession of the holy cities, affected to style himself a dutiful subject of the Sultan, and obtained a free passage for all his party through the Turkish dominions, which would enable him to perform the pilgrimage at pleasure. Tousoun Pasha abandoned to Abdulla ibn Saud those towns of Al Qasim which he held in his possession, and dismissed from his party all the sheikhs of that country who had already joined him. He likewise ceded to him all those bedouin tribes whose pasture grounds lay beyond Hanakiya, reserving to himself only those which resided between Hanakiya and Medina and in the territories of the holy cities. Nothing was said of the Southern Wahhābis; in consequence of this, immediately after Tousoun went away, Abdulla punished the bedouin, particularly the Mutair tribe, who had joined his enemies. As both parties apprehended treachery, some difficulties arose respecting the priority of departure. Abdulla at length consented to break up his camp but insisted that four of the Pasha's chief officers should be left with him as hostages until his arrival in a safe position, when he was to send them back. Tousoun, probably to conceal his own weakness, cavilled for some time on this point, and then returned from Khabra to Rass, and, after having been twenty-eight days in the province of Al Qasim, arrived at Medina about the end of June 1815. With him were two Wahhābis, envoys from Abdulla to Muhammad Ali, bearing the articles of peace and a letter from their chief to the Pasha and another for the Sultan.

Tousoun did not find his father at Medina, for, being convinced that the actual resources and means of war in those northern parts of the Hijaz were not sufficient to give him hope of success, Muhammad Ali had resolved on leaving the doubtful chance to his son rather than incur the risk of diminishing the reputation which he had himself acquired.

While Tousoun was absent not one messenger was ever dispatched to him by Muhammad Ali, so that he remained ignorant of all that was passing at Medina and other places. Muhammad Ali, besides, thought so little of his son's necessities that he left him without a single piastre, and when Tousoun arrived at Medina he was obliged to borrow money for his daily expenses. There was perhaps a sound reason why Muhammad Ali quitted Medina and finally the Hijaz. In February and March 1815 fears were entertained in Egypt of an attack to be made upon Alexandria by the Admiral of the Grand Seignior, who had arrived from the Sea of Marmara with a strong fleet and was cruising in the Greek Archipelago. Alexandria and Rosetta were reinforced with numerous troops, and the Governor of Cairo sent messengers in haste by land and sea to acquaint Muhammad Ali of these events.

On the 19th of May Salim Agha, Governor of Yanbu', received an express from Medina, ordering him on pain of death to have a ship ready for sailing on that very evening, and next day Muhammad Ali with a few of his suite, mounted upon dromedaries, arrived at Yanbu', and without waiting for refreshment on shore hastened to the ship and immediately set sail. The Pasha would not even allow the captain to keep along the coast, as is usual, although he knew that the ship

THE WAR AGAINST THE WAHHĀBIS 237

was but scantily supplied with water, but made him stand out into the open sea straight for Kosseir.

On his landing at that place he could not immediately procure either a horse or camel, so without loss of time mounted a riding-donkey, that he might proceed through the desert to Genne and hasten down the Nile. The dread of an attack upon Alexandria had, in the meantime, subsided, and he therefore travelled more leisurely towards his capital, which he reached in June 1815, after an absence of nearly two years, during which his health had considerably suffered from the climate of Arabia. He did not then know that peace had been concluded with the Wahhābis, but, in order that his arrival might be attended with enthusiasm, the taking of Daraya by Tousoun Pasha and the complete annihilation of the Wahhābis were announced.

In the month of August, after Muhammad Ali's return to Egypt, most of those very troops who had accompanied him in the Arabian campaign showed symptoms of insurrection. The corps of Mahou Bey and others began to pillage the capital, and the Pasha found it necessary to shut himself up in his castle at Cairo. Those troops to whom fine promises had been made in the Hijaz now found that regulations were proposed which would considerably reduce their pay and increase their fatigues. The Pasha desired to introduce the Nizam Jedid, or new and European system of discipline, a measure which had proved fatal to Sultan Salim; but when insurrection stopped its progress Muhammad Ali did not venture to punish the mutineers. The reputation which he had acquired in the Hijaz was found to have caused a change in his character. The affability that had distinguished him from other Pashas was converted into haughtiness; instead of a simple soldier-like establishment, he began to indulge in pomp and show and monopolized all the exports and imports for his own advantage, by which the labourers and manufacturers were materially injured.

The two envoys sent by Abdulla ibn Saud in the train of Tousoun Pasha to Medina arrived at Cairo in August, during this insurrection of the soldiers. One of them, named Abd al Aziz, was a relation of the great founder of the Wahhābi sect, Abd al Wahab; the other was an officer of Saud. They presented to Muhammad Ali the treaty made with his son Tousoun

Pasha. On their departure they were given a letter to Abdulla ibn Saud from the Pasha, written in a most ambiguous manner, respecting peace or war. It offered to confirm the treaty concluded with his son provided the Wahhābis would cede to him the province of Al Hasa, one of the most fertile and important of their dominions.

It now became manifest either that Tousoun Pasha had deceived the Wahhābis at Al Qasim or that Muhammad Ali had given proof of the contempt in which he held engagements. Tousoun, equal in rank with his father, had concluded a treaty, binding his whole party; and he had enjoyed the full benefit of that treaty in being allowed to save himself and his army from destruction. His father, however, seemed anxious to represent the matter under a different point of view at Istanbul, and as he had pledged himself to annihilate the Wahhābis by taking Daraya it was necessary to persuade his sovereign that he had not yet abandoned that object, and that the treaty concluded by his son should be merely considered as a temporary armistice.

On November 7, 1815, Tousoun Pasha arrived at Cairo with a few hundred soldiers. After his return to Medina from Central Arabia, communication was restored all over the Hijaz with the Wahhābis. Caravans came from Nejd to Medina and Mecca, and in December many Wahhābis attended the pilgrimage. No Turkish chief had exerted himself so much as Tousoun during this war or displayed more personal valour, but his efforts had always been unsuccessful. He was welcomed at Cairo with all the honours due to his rank and bravery, but on paying a visit to his father at Alexandria he was very coldly received.[1]

About the close of 1815 several Arab sheikhs from the Hijaz came to Cairo, claiming the Pasha's protection. They were relations of the sheikh whom Muhammad Ali had appointed chief of the Asir Arabs in place of Tami; but when he returned to Cairo Tami's party obliged the new sheikhs to fly, Hassan Pasha being unable to support them. Muhammad Ali received them politely at Cairo, gave them some presents, and sent them

[1] In September 1816 Tousoun Pasha died of the plague at Rosetta, where he commanded a large body of troops encamped there for the defence of the coast. In the same summer, in June, Sherif Ghalib and his household died of plague at Salonica.

back to Mecca, but could not at that time spare any troops for the Hijaz, being seriously engaged in preparations for defending the Mediterranean coast against an attack, which according to general report the English intended. He had already heard, while still in the Hijaz, of the first Peace of Paris and the fall of Napoleon Bonaparte, and had become apprehensive that England would send a large army from the South of France to Egypt, which he fondly supposed was the darling object of all European Powers. These apprehensions were renewed by the second Treaty of Paris. Afte some months the alarm subsided, and he again directed his views towards the Hijaz, intending to dispatch a powerful expedition to that country under his son Ibrahim Pasha. Circular letters were written in January 1816 to all the Arab sheikhs of the Hijaz, apprising them of Ibrahim's speedy departure, exhorting them to assist him, and assuring them that Muhammad Ali designed to revisit their territories himself in a short time, and crown his former victories by the taking of Daraya. In these letters no mention was made of the treaty concluded with Abdulla ibn Saud, nor had any answer yet arrived from the latter respecting Muhammad Ali's demand for the district of Al Hasa.

In March 1816 intelligence arrived from Mecca that disturbances had broken out to the south. The Turkish cavalry stationed at Bisha, Ranya, and Taraba had been withdrawn and only a few bedouin in the Pasha's service remained as the garrison of Taraba, while the Wahhābis gained daily in strength in those districts.

In August 1816 Ibrahim Pasha therefore left Cairo for the Hijaz with orders to attack Daraya, moving by way of Medina and Al Qasim. He was accompanied by about two thousand infantry, who went by Kosseir to Yanbu', and fifteen hundred Libyan bedouin horsemen, who went by land; these horsemen he had himself chosen from among the most warlike tribes in Upper Egypt. In his suite were two French officers, one of whom, a *chef d'escadre*, had been with Napoleon Bonaparte at Rochefort, but in consequence of orders to quit France had repaired to Egypt, where Muhammad Ali received him in a very flattering manner, besides several other French emigrants of the year 1815.

Taught by Tousoun's failure, Muhammad Ali enjoined

inaction on Ibrahim until he had secured the neutrality of the
Central Arabian tribes, and it was not until 1817 that he gave
the word to move eastward. Rass, the first walled town, gave
them pause for many months, and before he could take Daraya,
the Wahhābi capital, he had to send for reinforcements of guns
and men from Egypt, who in the end reduced it to the ruin it
is to-day. The Wahhābi ruler was sent to Istanbul to die there
by order of Sultan Mahmoud, Ibrahim took Al Hasa, the
eastern province, and all Central Arabia, making his headquarters at Buraida, in Al Qasim. Thus at last Nejd and the
Hijaz was under Egyptian military control, but Muhammad
Ali had no mind to waste his resources on barren possessions,
and Ibrahim was ordered to withdraw to Medina and garrison
the Hijaz. The Yemen Tihama, held since 1813, was handed
over to the Imam of the Yemen, but was reoccupied in 1832.

The Egyptians were represented at Mecca itself by a
'Muhafiz,' or governor-guardian, while the Ottomans, in
accordance with the old tradition, sent their Wali to Jedda;
thus between the two of them Yahya ibn Sarur, the Sherif,
had no share in the administration and little of the influence
that his ancestors had left to him. It was to the Egyptian
Pasha, the bestower of corn from the Jezira of Egypt, that the
Meccans looked for law and order and benevolent gifts.

Before Muhammad Ali left the Hijaz he ordered his Muhafiz
at Mecca to rely upon the advice of one Ahmad ibn Turki, of
Mecca—an intriguing creature whom Ghalib had sometimes
used on special missions—and to prefer him to Yahya.

Even after the death of Ahmad ibn Turki, in 1820, Yahya
was excluded from the administration by the Pasha, who dealt
with another go-between, one Shambar, of the Abādila clan
of the Sherifs, against whom the Bani Zaid division of his
family began to unite, both their Meccan and clan pride
combining to strengthen their hatred. At the beginning of
1827[1] Shambar was assassinated by Yahya inside the Temple.
Hurrying at once to his house Yahya prepared it for defence
against the Pasha, but, faced with his guns, Yahya gave way
and promised to travel to Egypt by land, actually making no
effort to go beyond the deserts of the Harb tribe.

The Pasha then lent his support to Abdul Muttalib, the son

[1] C. Snouck Hurgronje, *Mekka*, vol. i, p. 159.

of Ghalib, whom the Turks had removed to Salonica in 1815, and who therefore was accepted by the people as the new Sherif of Mecca.

As Yahya was with the Harb, and likely to attack, Abdul Muttalib took care to raise the tribes near Taif, and a conflict seemed certain when it became known that Muhammad Ali Pasha, in Egypt, had nominated a former fighting colleague of his, then in Egypt, the Sherif Muhammad ibn Abdul Muin ibn Aun, who two years earlier had helped the Egyptians to wrest Asir from the Wahhābis. He is described by Didier as wise and moderate, of diplomatic character, five foot seven inches, good-looking, with a prominent chin and fine teeth, his curls very long. When Didier saw him he wore a red, yellow, and green head-kerchief with a huge white turban above it, a flesh-coloured tunic, with a muslin shirt and undertrousers of nankeen embroidered in his harem; he wore a gold dagger and "carried a Persian sword in the Osmanli manner, but always had in his hand a camel stick with a crooked end." M. Bolta, who saw him in 1837, says:

> It is impossible but to be astonished and overwhelmed by the affable dignity and distinguished easiness of one who, bedouin by nature and by heart, has found by his own instinct the way to conduct himself in a totally new sphere. . . .

But M. Bolta was evidently not well acquainted with or had not given due consideration to the long family history or he would have been less astonished. Yahya and Abdul Muttalib, faced with this new move by the Egyptians, wished to join forces, but Yahya was captured by Egyptian cavalry when leaving Taif, and taken to Egypt, dying there in 1838.

The new Sherif, Muhammad, was able to subdue his tribes with large subsidies, Muhammad Ali Pasha having well provided him with money before he left Egypt. For a time Abdul Muttalib made abortive efforts to raise tribesmen, other sherifs, and their followers, but eventually he accompanied a northward-bound caravan to Damascus, in 1831, whence he made his way to Istanbul.

Muhammad ibn Aun was soon seen to be aiming at a greater measure of independence and power than had had his immediate predecessors, circumstances helping him. In 1841 cholera carried off the Eygptian Pasha in the Hijaz, and his successor immediately found himself in trouble with his irregular troops, who demanded arrears of salary which had not been paid by his predecessor.

Unable to bring them to order, he left for Egypt, and the Sherif managed to drive the rebellious Turkish soldiers to Jedda, whence, after some plundering of shops, they disappeared in various directions to settle here and there or make their way to other countries.

In 1833 the Sherif determined to bring back under his control the country about Bisha, Zahran, and Ghamid, which had been increasingly subject to raids by the Asiris. He made a demonstration as far as the frontiers of Asir, but, failing to receive the supplies and reinforcements which he had been promised by Ahmad Pasha, the Egyptian representative in the Hijaz, he returned in angry mood.[1] Both the Pasha and the Sherif blamed each other in letters which they wrote to Muhammad Ali Pasha, who ordered them both to Cairo.

Muhammad Ali agreed to the Pasha's suggestion that he should return to the Hijaz for three months without the Sherif, during which period he undertook to subdue the Asiris and restore order. The Sherif remained an involuntary guest in Egypt while the Pasha of Jedda protracted his own stay in the Hijaz and achieved no decisive result. But at least the main threat, from Nejd, was at an end, and the control of the Hijaz was restored to the Sublime Porte, so that the Viceroy of Egypt wished to bring his troops home. To do so expeditiously he sent back to the Hijaz, in 1840, the Sherif Muhammad ibn Aun, who promised to extricate them, and by successfully doing so once more proved the Sherifs' right to power.

[1] Didier gives at some length a verbatim report of a conversation between the Sherifs and Kurshid Agha, a "superior Turkish officer," which was, as he says, "a courteous declaration of war." The Sherif is described as "leaning on two serving men." When asked by the Pasha if he were ill he explained them as "the honour of my rank, all unworthy as I am." It was seemingly therefore at this time a custom at ceremonious entrances of the Sherif for him to have two supporters.

THE DHAWU AUN CLAN (continued)[1]

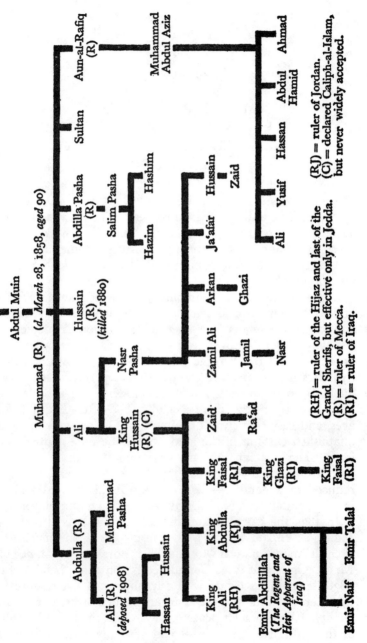

(RH) = ruler of the Hijaz and last of the
Grand Sherifs, but effective only in Jedda.
(R) = ruler of Mecca.
(RI) = ruler of Iraq.

(RJ) = ruler of Jordan.
(C) = declared Caliph-al-Islam,
but never widely accepted.

[1] See also pedigree at p. 164.

Chapter XV

MUHAMMAD IBN AUN
AND HIS RIVAL OF THE DHAWU ZAID CLAN,
ABDUL MUTTALIB IBN GHALIB
(A.D. 1840–81)

APART FROM THE INVASION FROM CENTRAL ARABIA, THE
Sherif Ghalib had had to contend with the repercussions
in the Red Sea of a war between Western Powers. A
Western emperor had sent agents and spies; another dispatched
to him special envoys, a native political agent, and military
purchasing officers.

In the end all his adroit diplomacy had failed him, and, falling
under Ottoman suspicion, he had been treacherously kidnapped
and deported, under the eyes of his powerless subjects, to
Istanbul by Muslim overlords, sure of their power in an army
of occupation. By 1840 the wild tide which had washed away
dynasties in Europe, and in Arabia had permitted the Wahhābis to go for a time over their borders, had subsided. It
must have seemed as if a peaceful period of trading, pilgrimages, and easy profit was once more beginning, and the long-
established customs of the land were to be once more in full
force. The Arabian Puritans were forgotten and the men of
that Ottoman Power which pretended to sovereignty were
reduced to a handful—the Pasha's own bodyguard and the
annual military escort of the Syrian and Egyptian pilgrims.

In 1835 the harmless appointment of one Yacoub Yusif, of
Jedda, as unpaid British Vice-Consul passed unremarked by
even the most fanatical Muslims. Nor does the acceptance of a
Mr A. Ogilvie as Vice-Consul Jedda, on the 4th of August,
1838, seem to have met with any objections, for doubtless it
was seen as nothing more than an augury of greater trading
facility. Who in such peaceful days—and in the very middle
of the Jedda summer, too—could stir himself to imagine its

significance? How could even Mr Ogilvie himself foresee or know himself to be the herald of overwhelming forces which were to disturb so much in so short a time, and make the idea of sanctuary, voluntary restraint, and the spiritual as out of date and odd as animism and pagan love had been to Christians and Muslims?

In less than a hundred years an offshoot people of his race, with their recruits from the European continent, having taken up the new inventions with fervent belief in their efficacy and making use of their country's great resources, were to loose them on the Old World and in Arabia heave up the imprisoned minerals with which to drive machines that could move faster than the swiftest animals and could soar thousands of feet into the air. When humdrum workers of machinery can outdo before our eyes the reputed miracles of the prophets then the servants of old religions perforce look to their codes with care and examine with anxiety their tenets.

At first nothing of this, or of the effects upon them to come, were guessed at by the Hijazis, and no complaints were made. Their fears were nearer and smaller, and small things loom large in the Hijaz.

The Sherif was well aware that in Istanbul the Sultan held as prisoner-guest the former Sherif's son Abdul Muttalib ibn Ghalib and that the Ottomans might manœuvre his succession if dissatisfied with the degree of his own loyalty to their requirement. Abdul Muttalib was the candidate of a rival clan, the Dhawu Zaid, and with their support in Mecca the change might be made without great difficulty by the order of the Sultan. But Muhammad ibn Aun had the support of the greater in power in the Hijaz, if lesser in name, the Viceroy of Egypt.

By 1844, however, the Sherif began to fall foul of the Sultan's agent, in spite of his diplomacy. Osman Pasha had been administrator of the Mosque at Medina, and his several years' experience in the country would give his words additional weight in Istanbul. The immediate cause of coolness between them arose from trouble in the district of the Harb tribe. A sheikh of one of its divisions, Ibn Rumi, revolted because the Pasha had failed to pay directly to him a subsidy which he had formerly received on account of the safe conduct of the pilgrims through his area. He signalled his displeasure by attacking the small Turkish garrison in the little port of Rabigh, the landing-place for Medina, which was happy to surrender in exchange for escort to his borders.

The Pasha sent for Ibn Rumi on the grounds that he would negotiate with him, and with a promise of safe-conduct he came, agreeing to protect the building of a fort and supply-depot on the road to Rabigh in exchange for a subsidy. The fort being at length finished, the Pasha sent one of his officers, Kurdi Osman, with an escort of cavalry to take over the guard-duty from Ibn Rumi. Arrived at Kalais, he sent cordial messages to Ibn Rumi and invited him to a banquet. After dinner a buffoon entertained the tribal guests, and while he did so Kurdi Osman made an excuse to leave the tent for a moment and gave the order for the taking dead or alive of his guests. His men cut the tent-ropes and caught the Arabs like fish in a net. After the slaughter a boy of twelve, brother of Ibn Rumi, remained unwounded, hidden by a chest, but when he leapt up to escape was overtaken, and his head cut off like the others. Another and younger boy, son of the Sheikh, was saved by Kurdi, but twenty-five of the Harbis had been killed, and the heads of five of the more important of them were sent to Mecca, there impaled on pikes, after necklaces had been made of their noses and ears to decorate the neck of the camel carrying the herald of the victory after dinner.

Ibn Aun had had excellent relations with the Harb tribe, and this stroke by the Turks was a blow to his prestige and a setback to his policy of strengthening his position with them. Nor was the effect at all what the Turks could wish, for the Harb became their convinced enemies. In the following decades there were innumerable incidents on the pilgrim road, and the Turkish pilgrim train could pass only by payment of very heavy subsidies. In the fifties and sixties of the century the Turks had almost continuous trouble in the Harb districts and at Rabigh, and by 1861 they were obliged to increase the payment to 250,000 francs annually. Thus uneasiness and feud grew up between the Turks and the Harb, largely owed to the killing of Ibn Rumi. And out of this grew the permanent spirit of mistrust which contributed to the ease with which the descendants of Muhammad ibn Aun were able to raise the tribesmen against the Ottomans in the Arab revolt.

Elsewhere the Sherif had had striking success. Marching into Al Qasim, the province of oases north of Riyadh, the new capital of Nejd, which had replaced Daraya after its destruction by the Egyptians, he defeated the forces of Faisal ibn Saud, the Wahhābi Emir, who was forced into paying tribute, and enabled a Sheikh of the Abda division of the Shammar tribe, who had been increasing his power, to cut adrift from Riyadh. Relying upon the support of the Sherif of Mecca, and behind the screen of autonomous Al Qasim, he consolidated his position of independence and became the founder of an Emirate of the Jebel Shammar, with its capital at Hail, that was to be famous in Europe for the bloodiness of its succession and the purity of its horses.

The Turks meanwhile sought to subdue the Yemen and overcome the tribes of the south. In 1842 Ashraf Bey had been sent as their commissioner, via Jedda, to reorganize the administration, and in the following year the Sherif Hussain, of Mokha, received an Imperial firman raising him to the rank of Pasha and placing him under the Sherif of Mecca. In 1848, however, he was attacked and defeated by the Imam of Sana, in the Upper Yemen, so that in May 1849 a Turkish military expedition was set under way via Jedda, accompanied by the Sherif Muhammad ibn Aun, who promised to neutralize by his influence the tribes of Asir, through whom the force would be obliged to pass. The expedition successfully reached Hodaida, where the Imam came to sign a convention whereby he agreed to receive a garrison in Sana and pay over a proportion of his revenue as tribute. Tawfiq Pasha, the Ottoman delegate and commander, the Sherif Muhammad ibn Aun, and the Imam entered Sana together, and at prayers the day after their arrival the name of the Sultan was substituted for that of the Imam. At the same moment an Arab was killed by a Turk after a quarrel in the market, and the population ran to arms and killed a large number of the Turkish soldiers. Tawfiq Pasha, who himself was wounded, supplanted the Imam and bought his safe retreat from the new one for 20,000 thalers. Thus the Turkish prestige was little, if at all, increased, but that of the Sherif was established. The Asiris were still his allies, and without him the Turks could not have passed into the Yemen, still less returned; he was successful in Nejd, and had there the alliance of the Shammari Emir; if his influence with the Harb was less, it was the Turks themselves who had lowered it, and it might yet be recovered; and he passed as being on good terms with the Viceroy of Egypt, Abbas Pasha.

In spite of this influence, or perhaps because of it and of intrigue by Abdul Muttalib ibn Ghalib at the Court of the Sultan in Istanbul, the Pasha of Jedda received orders in August 1852 to send Muhammad ibn Aun and his two eldest sons to Turkey. The sons were induced to visit Jedda on pretence of being shown some new military equipment, and the same day, as soon as they had gone, the Pasha's men surrounded the Sherif's palace, the artillerymen with their matches ready and lighted. The Sherif, who with an hour's warning could have raised the tribes and called about him all his numerous guards, realized that there was nothing to be done, and quietly embarked, Mansur ibn Yahya taking over the Sherifate from him until Abdul Muttalib ibn Ghalib, of the Dhawu Zaid, could arrive from the Court of the Sultan.

The new Sherif Abdul Muttalib was to find the intermediate ruler and Abdulla ibn Nasir, whom he had co-opted to help him, both waiting for him impatiently at Jedda, where they had sought refuge from the responsibility of dealing with the turmoil caused by Turkish insistence on the anti-slavery clause of the Hatti Humayun law. There had been rioting in the streets of Mecca, the Turks were unable to move about safely and freely in any of the towns of the Hijaz, and there were endless complaints from the Pasha on the one hand, and daily demands from the people on the other. Abdul Muttalib is described by Sir Richard Burton, Snouck Hurgronje, and M. Didier as very dark, almost black, in spite of vigorous denials by some of his descendants. M. Didier says:

> ... a grand old man of sixty, tall, but slender, with the grand manner, distinguished in every way, of very brown colour, almost black, fine skin, a long blue robe, a Kashmir turban, a magnificent dagger mounted in gold and set with shining brilliants in his waistband.

He found him a little too civilized, if anything. It is scarcely to be a matter for wonder, since he had spent twenty-five years at the Court in Istanbul. Events overtook him before he could become accustomed to the people from whom he had so long been absent. His prompt attempts to restore order were seen by the Turks as menacing military preparation against them, and when one day the Pasha received a ball through his fez his temper was not improved. Little help could be expected from Turkey, which was involved in the Crimean War. Fortunately the Pasha's return was ordered, but his relief was soon rumoured to have orders to depose Abdul Muttalib, who at once rode away to his summer palace, in Taif. Mecca relapsed into something like anarchy, the Sultan's name was no longer mentioned in the prayers, and the Turks were forced into an abortive attack on Taif. In the midst of all these troubles the Sultan's restoration of Muhammad ibn Aun was announced. He arrived on April 17, 1856, and a few days later Abdul Muttalib was secured and taken to Salonica, where his father Ghalib had died. His resistance had been much less than was anticipated, and a small reinforcement was actually preparing in Egypt, when the news came of his surrender after a skirmish near Bahra, on the road to Jedda from Mecca.

In Jedda the French Consul, M. Fresnel, had been attacked in 1851 and his assailant never arrested. In March of the same year, it is true, the French had sent to the port a sloop, the *Eurydice*, and her captain, Capitaine de Vaisseau Guerin, landed and demanded satisfaction, but was unsuccessful, both in that year and the following year, when he repeated his visit. In 1853 Admiral Laguerre arrived in the *Jeanne d'Arc*, with the sloop *Caiman*, and these naval visits were frequent; but it was useless to expect satisfaction while the state of affairs in Mecca was as disturbed as it had been under Abdul Muttalib ibn Ghalib, or to pursue matters under his successor, who was doing his utmost to restore order as it had been during his own former rule.

It thus fell out that it was publicly known that the Consul of France had been attacked in Jedda and no retribution taken or punishment given.

In March 1858 Muhammad ibn Aun died, aged ninety, and was succeeded by his son Abdulla, then in Istanbul as a member of the Sultan's Council of State. Accounts of the new Sherif agree that he was a cultured man with, as Snouck Hurgronje says, "adaptable comprehension of the foreign mind, a characteristic which distinguishes the Abādila,"[1] but sufficiently moulded by his youth in Arabia to be above all an Arab and 'Sherif.'

Before he arrived in the Hijaz an ugly event was to delay his ceremonious entry into Mecca until the autumn. News had reached Jedda of quite another kind. A steamship company had been formed to send vessels to ply for trade and passengers in the Red Sea. As this was debated and pondered over by the masters and crews of Arab sailing-ships, they became more and more alarmed. Many of the sailors were from the Hadhramaut or the Yemen and the remoter corners of the peninsula, places inviolate to all foreigners and their machines.

These wild lovers of their craft and of the seas, through constantly holding their own and others' lives in their hands and at the same time daily submitting in their frail ships to the whim of a violent element, acquire a different regard for life to that held by landsmen; and, visiting the diwans of their betters in Jedda, they heard more and more disturbing tales, and when they returned, to mend sails and caulk hulls with others on the shore, they argued until they knew that something evil to them and theirs was come upon them, something that if struck at early might be stayed. The subtle merchants and the more fanatic Muslims were all of one mind, and each worked upon the other; for to the British Consul had been added a French Consul, and foreigners in their outlandish clothes stalked the streets of Jedda, as by right, and planned what would alter all Arab economy without taking council of the people.

On June 15, 1858, in virtue of a judgment given by the British consular court, a Turkish flag was taken down on a sailing-boat, the *Irani*, owned by two British subjects, and replaced by the British flag. The execution of the judgment had been carried out by bluejackets from the steam-frigate H.M.S. *Cyclops*, which happened to be in the roadstead. The same evening about six o'clock Mr Page, the British Vice-Consul, was surprised and assassinated, his house being immediately looted by ruffians from the stews. The murderers then went to the French Consulate, but by the efforts of M. Emerat, the Chancellor, were prevented from entering at once. The colonel of the Turkish garrison was informed and

[1] *Mekka*, vol. i, p. 170.

refused to send any of the men—about a hundred—under his command without an order from his superior, Namiq Pasha, who was fifty miles away in Mecca.

The Consulate *kavass*, or head-porter, was wounded and M. Emerat, badly wounded, was saved and carried off by an Algerian, Hajji Muhammad. The mob then entered the house by the terrace and shot Mme Eveillard, the wife of the Consul, whose daughter was given a sabre-cut while defending her father, who was then killed. Mme Eveillard was saved by the wife of a soldier whom the family had tended a few days earlier. All the Christian foreigners on whom the crowd could lay hands—fourteen in number—were then killed and their houses gutted. A few survivors managed to swim out to the *Cyclops*.

The next day, while burying the dead, the Muslims were astonished to find that M. Emerat was not among them. A sentence of death was formally pronounced upon him for having killed two Muslims in the fight at the consulate, and true believers invited to search for him. Three days later Namiq Pasha entered Jedda at the head of a battalion.

In Istanbul the Turkish Foreign Minister promised the French and British Ambassadors that the Sultan's orders had gone to Jedda that his Governor there was to hold an inquiry, arrest and put to death the ringleaders, and take indemnities from the town, which were to be paid to those who had suffered. The three Governments agreed that special representatives were to be sent to Jedda to see that the Sultan's orders were carried out. The sloop *Duchayla* left Marseilles for Jedda in order to lend support to the commissioners and to the agent of the Ottoman Government. The British ship *Cyclops*, however, arrived first, and the captain immediately demanded the execution of the ringleaders. Namiq Pasha replied that they were under arrest, but awaited the Sultan's orders for execution. The captain of the *Cyclops* did not hesitate. He began to bombard. It might have gone on longer had not the Ottoman commissioner arrived with the order for execution. A party of British marines was landed, and at dawn on August the 5th eleven persons had their heads cut off by native executioners in front of the kiosk where they had met to decide upon the attack on the Consuls.

The matter of the indemnities was dealt with as soon as both the commissioners had arrived, which was not until the end of the year. The conduct of the inquiry was conducted on lines prompted by M. Emerat, the French Chancellor, who had been bravely saved and hidden by his faithful Algerian. The Pasha invited all the principal inhabitants to dine, and at the end of dinner announced that they were his permanent guests. The death sentences were subsequently pronounced on three chief offenders: the former Chief of Police, the Chief of the Hadhramis, and the Kaimakam. Their heads were sliced off, as in the former case, by local executioners at the kiosk where the massacre had been commended by them.[1] It was only after the murder of the Christians that consuls at Jedda were officially recognized and exequaturs given them. Even so, Mr G. E. Stanley, the British Consul, reported in 1864 (April 26) the difficulty he had in maintaining his position, the Governor-General refusing him rights over British subjects in Mecca or over their property when deceased. "The word Beit-al-Mal [Treasury] is synonymous with everything that is vile," he adds. He suggested the appointment of Muslim Consuls in the holy cities.

In 1861 a Turkish force sent from Hodaida to occupy Jizan, where the Asiris had long been defying the Ottomans, had its boats sunk and nearly every man in them killed without ever landing there. The Viceroy in Egypt thereupon decided to send a sufficient reinforcement to warrant permanent occupation of Jizan, Al Arish, and the neighbouring towns of Asir, but it was not until 1869 that the Sherif himself at his own risk decided to do what the Turks had not yet accomplished. The expedition assembled at Qunfidha, and the land force was accompanied by two British steamers with supplies and 850 Egyptians,[2] the greater part of the Hijaz regiment leaving with them. Thanks to the skill of the Sherif in his military dispositions and in his diplomacy, the Asiris gave way after a few skirmishes and agreed to evacuate Jizan and Al Arish and to pay an annual tribute, on condition that their chief was to be styled Emir al Umara, or Prince of Princes.[2]

---

[1] Outbreak at Jedda, 1858–59 (Foreign Office Print, December 31, 1859, and tomes viii and ix of the *Annuaire des deux mondes*).

[2] Public Record Office: Foreign Office, Embassy and Consular Archives; Turkey (F.O. 195/956) (Jedda, December 14, 1870).

Nevertheless, the Sherifate fell to a lower depth of humiliation than it had touched for centuries. The opening of a direct waterway from Istanbul by the cutting of the Suez Canal altered the political relations of the West with the East, and of the Sultan with the Sherif even more suddenly and strongly. Formerly tired columns of men which had already suffered casualties in their long desert marches would arrive long after the event which had caused their dispatch. From 1870 onward they could be sent by sea, and quickly supplied and reinforced by sea, through the Suez Canal. Thus, in 1872 the Turks were able to follow up the Sherif's expedition and reconquer the Yemen without his assistance.

At this time, from 1871 onward, there was no British Consul at Jedda; but a Consul, without salary, was appointed in February 1874 under the immediate superintendence of His Majesty's agent in Egypt. His instructions particularly mentioned that he was to report on the slave trade, and his letters show that it was indeed flourishing. His reports in 1875 tell of hundreds of slaves passing through the port in open daylight, the tax on them being ten piastres each. On June 20, for example, he related that he had "counted a batch of ninety-six slaves, boys and girls in a state of nudity, just landed and being drove through the gate into the City like a flock of sheep." He seems to have been assiduous in visiting the water-front and counting, as accurately as he could, this naked black merchandise of the Arabs.

In 1869 the Sherif had had to submit to the imposition of municipal organization, and his autonomy was being lessened day by day to the scorn of his subjects. In 1880 his brother and successor, "the mild and liberal" Hussain, fell a sacrifice at Jedda to an assassin "emboldened by popular contempt for politic princes," although the man never gave even at the moment of his execution any explanation of his motive. Doughty described Hussain, after being received by him at Taif, as

a man of pleasant face, with a sober alacrity of the eyes and humane demeanour; and he speaks with a mild and cheerful voice. . . . He seemed, as he sat, a manly tall personage of a brown colour; and large of breast and limb. The Sherif was clad in the citizen-wise of the Ottoman towns, in a long blue *jubba* of pale woollen cloth. He sat upright on his diwan, . . . with a comely sober countenance; and smoked tobacco in a pipe like the "old Turks." The simple earthen bowl was set in a saucer before him: his white jasmine stem was almost a spear's length.— He looked up pleasantly, and received me with a gracious gravity.[1]

This mild and just man fell by the knife at Jedda two years afterwards, and was tended and died in the arms of Dr Wortabet, the British Resident Officer of Health for the Red Sea.[2]

At this time the Sherif's guards or soldiers consisted of the 'Bisha' and 'Bawardi.' Doughty describes the Bisha as standing on the palace stairs and making "the reverence as we passed," and both corps were used as personal bodyguardsmen of the Sherif, living in and about the palace, although the Bawardi were more akin to a security force in the town. The Bisha were so called because they were recruited originally from Bisha. The Bawardi, or musketeers of the Sherif, and the Turkish soldiers both haled off malefactors to the same prison, Turks being tried by the Wali or Turkish judges, the Arabs by the Sherif, except when the case demanded trial by the Shari court. The unwritten stipulation that the Sherif judged only sherifs, bedouin, and Meccans by birth was, however, only valid in so far as personal circumstances could not be brought to bear, and there were many exceptions. The men of the Sherifs and the soldiers of the Wali or the Sanjak had access to the one prison. Snouck Hurgronje says[3] he himself knew of several cases of a man being tried by the Sherif and released by the Wali or arrested by the Wali demanding trial by the Sherif, and of decisions and judgments being variable and altered according to individual cases rather than any fast rules. Some energetic Walis acquired a right to supervise the work of the Bawardi as well as of their own garrisons.

The new Sherif who took over from Hussain was of the Dhawu Zaid, the elderly Abdul Muttalib, who had already ruled twice before, and who had to travel from Istanbul, where he had long been in exile at the Sultan's Court. The people of the Hijaz greeted him with sombre applause, impressed with

[1] C. M. Doughty, *Arabia Deserta*, vol. ii, p. 508.
[2] D. G. Hogarth, *Arabia*, p. 114.
[3] *Mekka*, pp. 182, *et seq.*

his great age, with his knowledge of the Court, and experience in his two former reigns, which only the very old could remember. His abruptness—for he soon expressed openly contempt for the rich Hadhrami merchants and for those who were too friendly in his view with the Franks—served to increase their respect rather than diminish it. All that he did at first seemed to them, says Snouck Hurgronje, to have been invested with a kind of medieval, mysterious touch. If he ordered three respectable men to be arrested at midnight for no other reason than that their sentiments were suspect to him, and then ordered them to be flogged there and then by torchlight until two of them died, that only seemed to show a new and thrilling plenitude of power.[1] One of the Abādila sherifs who had had a palace built opposite one of Abdul Muttalib's houses had to submit to its demolition for a trifling compensation. Some bedouin who had appealed to the Wali against ill-treatment by his guards were raided and a number killed, an act that made him more, not less, respected. He cancelled various licences given by his predecessor and sold them to others.

The rich were treated by him more severely than the poor, and he used Syrians and Muslim foreigners as his secretaries and administrators. But gradually the government of the ardent old man became insupportable to most of the sherifs and more influential men of Mecca. Petitions were drawn up and presented to the leading Abādila sherif and the Wali.

In November 1881 a new and more energetic commander, Othman Nuri Pasha, arrived with fresh troops, and in order that the Sherif's suspicions might not be aroused the old Wali, Izzat Pasha, was reappointed to the Hijaz. In fact, the new Wali had received orders from Istanbul to make sure that he secured the old Sherif and to prevent him from escaping to the bedouin or to Taif, since many of the people still greatly revered him and would have fought for him. He therefore ordered his men to surround the Sherif's summer house at Al Mathna without warning, guns being trained on it from the hills near by. The Abādila sherifs meanwhile quietly raised their men and stood by not far off, ready for action. At dawn the firman deposing him was read to him, and he was taken as a prisoner to Taif, and later from there to his house near Muna,

[1] *Mekka*, vol. i, p. 173.

where he was allowed to live until he died on the 29th of January 1886.

The ordinary people revered him until the end, but he himself admitted sometimes that the new days, of the telegraph, the steamboat, the breech-loader, left no room for him.

The whole populace went to his funeral in Mecca. Many of the people let themselves down from the roof-tops by ropes in order in that way, because of the great press, to come at his corpse and touch the body for the last time. Even the Wali and the new Sherif seemed to be carried away with emotion, and overwhelmed by the devotion of the people for their idol. So passed Abdul Muttalib, the reincarnation of the spirit of the Middle Ages, of Zaid and of the Qitada, of a tyrannous self-will, but of majestic stature, of lordly demeanour and assurance; it was as if not only he but the life and history of the Middle Ages were being buried too.

Chapter XVI

AUN-AL-RAFIQ, ALI, KING HUSSAIN, AND KING ALI OF THE HIJAZ

(A.D. 1882–1925)

I N SPITE OF THE REPRESENTATIONS AND HOPES OF THE WALI, the Sublime Porte nominated Aun-al-Rafiq and not his younger brother Abdilla, whom the Wali had recognized as successor to the Sherifate for the time being, and who therefore acted as ruler until the new Sherif arrived from Istanbul.

So ended the old régime, the uncontaminated Oriental life. From now onward there was an uneasy changing of age-old customs and competition in newness. Deference to the past and pride in continuity was become a sin in Istanbul and a folly to the ambitious. Rulers who would be popularly acclaimed lent themselves to the movement by forgoing something of their state in the hope of retaining their powers, and the *bravura* of the Sherif's Court was reduced in tone.

Portly pace and ostrich-feather fans, halberdiers, and trumpeters in the morning to announce the Sherif's rising for the dawn prayer, armoured Negroes, the great State umbrella over him, the press of swordsmen going before him, blind reciters of the Koran intoning in the corridors round him, largess thrown as he rode, the young lance-men bodyguard, the executioners, and even the Sherif's dress, the huge turbans, the hand-concealing wide sleeves, the gold-embroidered robes of the finest cloth—all such things of the age-old panoply were to go or be less used, reduced, or done away with in the next three reigns, in fifty years.

These days are known. Old men are alive who remember their beginning. The events in them, if not the *ambiance*, are closely recorded in many books and newspapers. It only remains to close the story.

Aun-al-Rafiq is described[1] as being at his succession fifty

---

[1] C. Snouck Hurgronje, *Mekka*, vol. i, p. 177.

years old and as typifying in his appearance the new age.
Instead of the scarlet and gold gown and great turban of his
predecessors, he habitually wore a small white turban and a
black dress, and when travelling used a nomad's kerchief and
fillet. He made his daily public reception a formality at which
he seldom spoke of politics or of the daily administrative
matters, reserving them for review with his Wezir and Treasurer, or when closeted with the Wali and the officers directly
concerned with the matter in hand. This new and comparative seclusion, to-day usual, but then astonishing, led to
his being thought and spoken of as a philosopher, that word in
Arabic signifying something more of the mystic and hermit-like
pensiveness than it does in the English tongue. What seemed
a strange retirement to the nomads and Meccan nobility, who
spend much of their day at the open coffee-hearth or in
diwans, where men come and go unbidden, was partly of
the new foreign manners, but mostly to shield himself from the
Turkish agents and cover an ardent nature irked by their
dominance.

The officers of the Ottomans took the whole of the port
customs dues, yielding up the Sherif's share in such a fashion
that it seemed not so much his of right but a salary in their
giving. They paid his own bodyguards, and, by the device of
calling in mediators allied to their cause whenever there
occurred a disagreement between them on a point of administration, further weakened his standing. Moreover, the Pasha
undertook public works, improving the Jedda water-supply,
rebuilding the Zubaida aqueduct, building a new Government
office and a barracks and guard-houses—all within the Sherif's
own province, and much to his secret annoyance. To make
matters worse, the Wali in no case permitted the trial by the
Sherif or his officers of anyone except members of his family,
nomads, and persons of non-Turkish blood actually born in
Mecca itself. He sought to control the caravan routes directly,
and undertook expeditions against the Harb tribe with a wholly
Turkish force and no advice from the Sherif.

At last the Sherif could bear this degree of interference no
longer and left for Medina with all the leading members of his
family, a number of the notables and merchants, the Mufti
of the Shafites, and a long train of minor judges and holy men.

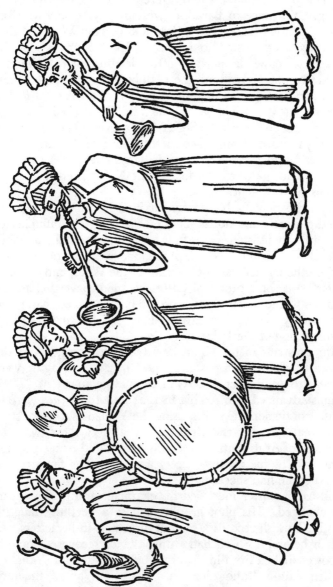

THE DAURA, OR STATE BAND, OF MECCA

After "Taskhilat wa qiyafat askariya," by Mahmoud Shawkat

This strange exodus was at night, and in the morning the wondering Turks found the houses of the nobles locked against them and only caretakers left. Here and there were placards reading, "Entrance to Paradise, without payment of a bribe, for he who rids Mecca of its cursed and corrupt Wali." From Medina couriers posted to Istanbul with the protests of the Sherif, that neither he nor any of the leading men of the city would return to Mecca until the Wali had gone from it for ever. The Sultan having long had amiable regards for Aun-al-Rafiq, the Porte at this point gave way and dispatched Othman Pasha to Aleppo. Thus the Sherif Aun-al-Rafiq and his people returned, removed from office the nominees of the late Pasha, and in triumph carved in stone in large characters over the Sherif's palace gateway, "Office of the Noble Emir and of his Glorious Government."

When the new Pasha, Jamal, arrived he was found to be more diplomatic and no less bent on subduing the influence of the Sherif. He insisted successfully on the release of the member of the Sherif's family, Abdilla ibn Zibn, who had been nominated by the former Pasha Governor of the Wadi, and restored to their posts some others of Othman's men; nevertheless, the Sherif's influence with his own people had become greater and he gradually resumed a larger share in the revenues and administration of the Hijaz.

Othman's rule of the Hijaz, or attempt to do so, marks the high-water of Ottoman power in the Hijaz. Never again were they able to administer directly or to so large an extent. Their columns advanced into Arabia in 1904 and 1905; they were to dispute frontiers in the south, using the Yemen as a vassal state when treating with the British; but always there was the hardening of Arab sentiment against them, and Aun's position at the end of his twenty-three-years reign was far stronger than when he had succeeded.

And as his power increased his character and even appearance changed. His photographs disclose a beetling haughtiness, the Turkish records a smooth directness in his letters. As so often before, a Sherif had with patience recovered some of the power filched from his Emirate by the Ottoman Walis.

When Aun-al-Rafiq died, in 1905, the Wali of the day, Ahmad Ratib Pasha, firmly recommended to the Porte Aun's nephew Ali ibn Abdulla ibn Muhammad ibn Aun, whom he had groomed to take the old Sherif's place. The eldest member of the family of Aun, Abdilla Pasha, brother of Aun al Rafiq, and then in Istanbul, was furious, and his scathing comments made subsequently some impression.

In Mecca itself the Wali showed his hand increasingly now that there was a new young Sherif appointed by his own influence, and his unpopularity carried in its train the Sherif of his choice. Thus, when at last in 1908 the Turkish Constitution was proclaimed, Ahmad Ratib Pasha, already marked down by the younger Turks as incurably of the old régime, was swept away to a humiliating oblivion, and with him the Sherif Ali, who, saving his fortune, sought refuge under British ægis in Egypt, while they proclaimed and announced the appointment of Abdilla Pasha. The new Sherif was very old but very happy. He had lived long enough to survive most of his family, and before he left he went to take last farewell of their graves, and there on his son's gravestone when he prostrated himself he was seized with an apoplectic stroke and a few days later died in his house at Emirgaun, on the Bosphorus, Sherif of Mecca in name, but no more.

Then there hurried to the *serai*, the office of the Wezir, and every door of influence the emissaries of Ali Haidar, of the Dhawu Zaid, and of Hussain ibn Ali, of the Dhawu Aun. Hussain was held to have shown a rebellious spirit in his youth, while the other had taken the extraordinary step of marrying an Englishwoman.[1] In the end it was Hussain who received the *khila'* and firman for Mecca.

The Sherif Hussain ibn Ali had been invited to Istanbul with his family in 1893, when he was thirty-seven years old. He had three sons just old enough to be put to school there: Ali, Abdulla, and Faisal. For fifteen years they lived in the Turkish capital, more or less prisoners of the Sultan, leaving it only by his command in the autumn of 1908, when Hussain was appointed Grand Sherif. Since he had left the Hijaz the railway to the holy cities had been inaugurated, with rejoicing, as a means of conveying the pilgrims easily to their spiritual journey's end, but Hussain and the sherifs must have remarked

---

[1] See Commander G. Stitt, *A Prince of Arabia* (Allen and Unwin, 1947). She is at present living in Cairo.

that it also meant that reinforcements of the Turkish army in the Hijaz could be sent with far greater celerity to Mecca. So far, in the autumn of 1908, the rails, laid by German engineers, had only reached Medina, and in fact, owing to the First World War, they never reached Mecca itself.

While the railway had been winding its way down into Arabia new thoughts and a fresh wave of Arab nationalism had been stirring everywhere in the Arab communities of the Ottoman Empire. The Constitution of 1908 had loosed abroad a stimulus to old hopes that travelled more quickly along the steam routes than they could have done heretofore, and seemed more important for being necessarily concealed from the Ottoman Government. Secret societies formed and re-formed themselves, one in favour of a Turco-Arab empire on the model of the Austro-Hungarian, another less ambitious, and several far more extreme in their objectives. Western visitors unwittingly stimulated by inquiry the Arab thoughts of an ideal independence, which nothing but old history justified, for secret societies were in themselves not enough, and one day the Arabs must pass to action if they would see complete freedom in fact.

It was in this atmosphere that Hussain travelled to Mecca in 1908. At first, he was considered to be loyal to the Turks, but, having sent expeditions into Asir and Al Qasim, he set about restoring the influence of the Sherifate, which had declined among the tribes under Ali, and, in consequence, was soon suspect by the Ottoman Pasha in the Hijaz.

In 1913 there took place an Arab congress in Paris which voted for measures of autonomy that the Ottomans appeared to accept, but sedulously undermined. The Committee of Union and Progress, in spite of its name, showed little interest in fostering Arab progress towards autonomy, and Abdulla, son of the Sherif and a Deputy in the Ottoman Parliament, took the bold step of approaching Lord Kitchener, the British Agent in Egypt, in February 1914 to sound him on the attitude of the British Government in the event of war between the Turks and the Arabs. He received no encouragement, and his request for machine-guns was refused, but his visits served to open the eyes of the British Government to the depths of the Arab feeling and of Arab-Turco animosity.

An English officer who visited Mecca in disguise described the scene at one of the first pilgrimages under the new Sherif:[1]

This . . . was the day of the festival. Every one was dressed in his smartest clothes and the whole camp presented a very picturesque appearance. In the morning we went to see the presentation of gifts to the Shareef. His camp, which was on an artificially raised platform, comprised four high marquees and many smaller tents. Lines of troops formed a passage and kept back the crowd. Bands paraded up and down the empty space left between them. The various grandees present arrived one after the other with their proper escorts and were received by the Shareef seated on a dais at the far end of the largest marquee. They included envoys from Moslem countries, the Governor of Mecca, some minor Mohammedan potentates from India and elsewhere, and other people of consequence. When all were assembled and seated, the Turkish Ambassador arrived with the Sultan's present carried on a gold dish. I cannot say of what the gift consisted, as it was covered with a cloth, but I was told that a few thousand in cash is the form it usually takes. The Shareef came to the edge of the platform to receive this visitor and escorted him within.

As soon as the ceremony was over, and the Turkish Ambassador had ridden away, the principal Meccans and pilgrims from foreign countries wishing to salute the Shareef passed in. He held in fact a sort of levee to which every one was admitted who cared to go. Masaudi went, but I declined to do so, fearing possible questions about myself which might be awkward.

The present Shareef, Sayyid Hussain, is a very popular man. From what I could see he fully deserves the estimation in which he is held. While quite alive to the dignity of his position, he endeavours to revive the old traditions of the Prophet and the earlier Caliphs, who were accessible to all and sundry, and put into actual practice the theory of equality and fraternity inculcated by the Koran.[2]

---

[1] A. J. B. Wavell, *A Modern Pilgrim in Mecca*, p. 209, *et seq.*

[2] Wavell, describing the reverence of the pilgrims and the seemingly demure conduct of the Meccans, admits that there is another side to the picture (*ibid.*, p. 126). He describes a manuscript book then popular in the Hijaz, and since his day printed in Cairo, without its theological digressions, as a straightforward anthology of amorous encounters compared with which the *Arabian Nights* is *petite bière*, and which would have been "considered unduly coarse in a pot-house in Gomorra" (p. 138).

In 1926 the Wahhābis tried to rectify Meccan habits, but among the multitude of pilgrims from foreign lands brought together for a short time there is inevitably laxness. The Meccans are proverbially happy-go-lucky in their morals.

Hussain's popularity, as so often before, disquieted the Ottoman officials in the Hijaz and the neighbouring Arab countries.

In their attempt to stamp out deflection from their failing Empire the Turks unwittingly encouraged revolt, bringing into being secret societies that planned all the more activity for being forbidden. What the Greeks had long ago achieved the Arabs were emulating in the years before the First World War. Their liberal clubs, forced underground, became fervent conspiracies, into which the Sherif of Mecca was drawn. The 'Union' society in Mesopotamia and the 'Freedom' society in Syria both sent secret messengers and corresponded with the Sherif as head of the Arabs in their sacred city and as a potential leader of revolt when the time came. There was no one else fitted to appeal to all the Arabs.

Eighteen years of political detention at the Turkish capital had taught Hussain its ways and weakness, and he at once set to work to restore, as unobtrusively as possible, the strength of his Emirate against the day of independence. But the issue was not as simple as it might seem to foreign observers. Since 1516 the Hijaz had known the Turks, who were Muslims too, with at their head a still powerful Emperor, or Hünkar, accepted as Caliph-al-Islam. Long years in Istanbul, and in many cases—like Hussain's sons—a necessarily Turkish education, had given the leading Sherifs Turkish veneer, Turkish was used bilingually with Arabic, a third of the Turkish Army were Arabs, the sacred relics of the Prophet brought out in his name in times of stress were reverently housed in the Serai at the Turkish capital, there were Turkish troops at the holy cities, and Turkish subsidies could not be overlooked. Moreover, it was still a widespread belief among Muslims of the simpler sort that the Sultan was in fact, as well as in title, "the Master of the World"; that the six infidel Sultans were his tributaries. Not to be represented at Istanbul was to be of no account. To have an ambassador there was to many who had no hearsay knowledge of other capitals a sign of submission. So this wedding of the greatest Muslim peoples could not be brought to an end in a day, and a coming war between Christian Powers would seem to many Muslims the last excuse to make for a divorce.

But the tide of revolt was rising in Syria and Mesopotamia, and when concrete proposals began to come in the Sherif sent his son Faisal to Damascus to discuss these projects as his representative. His reports were so favourable that Ali, the eldest son, was dispatched to Medina with orders to raise quietly troops from villagers and tribesmen and to hold them ready for action when Faisal called them. Abdulla, his second son, was told to sound the British by letter as to their attitude towards an Arab revolt.

When the First World War broke out, in August 1914, Lord Kitchener, British Agent in Egypt, was in England on leave and started back at once to return to his post, but he had not proceeded beyond Dover before he was recalled by the Prime Minister and appointed Secretary of State for War.

Sir Ronald Storrs, his Oriental Secretary, who had returned to Egypt without his chief, had not been idle. The frankness with which Abdulla had spoken to him a few months previously had exposed to him the wider implications of Arab discontent. He saw, perhaps more clearly than anyone else at the time, the possibility of turning it to useful account; and the consultations which, as Oriental Secretary, he had occasion to hold with the numerous Arab leaders residing in Egypt strengthened him in his view. He wrote privately to Lord Kitchener for authority to sound Abdulla about the Arabs coming into the war on the British side.

Kitchener adopted the suggestion at once, and directed Storrs to inquire specifically from Abdulla whether, in the event of Germany's prevailing upon Turkey to enter the war on her side, the Sherif of Mecca would follow Turkey or join Great Britain against her. These instructions were issued in the last week of September, about six weeks before the declaration of war on Turkey. It took Storrs a few days to find a reliable messenger who could be counted upon to travel secretly to the Hijaz and insinuate himself into Abdulla's presence without attracting notice. The messenger—an Egyptian known as Ali Effendi—arrived in Mecca about the middle of October, delivered his message, and returned to Cairo before the end of the month, bringing with him a written reply from Abdulla.

The arrival of a message from Kitchener placed the Sherif

in a delicate position. He had sought an opportunity to assert his authority in the Hijaz, even at the cost of a breach with the Turks, several months before the outbreak of the War, when his differences with the Turks related only to affairs in the Hijaz. Now that war had broken out and Turkey's participation seemed imminent, the problem had become very much broader and involved the future of all the Arab provinces of the Ottoman Empire. Two courses were open to him: to stand by Turkey in her hour of trial and earn her grateful recognition, or to rise against her and seek freedom at the point of the sword.

The two sons he consulted were of opposite minds. Faisal favoured the first alternative: he was convinced that France had designs on Syria and Great Britain on the southern regions of Iraq, and Kitchener's offer contained no guarantee against those dangers; moreover, he did not think that the Arabs were sufficiently prepared, and feared that a revolt would misfire. Abdulla thought otherwise. His admission to one of the secret Arab societies had given him an insight into the strength of the revolutionary feeling, and, being of an optimistic turn, he was confident that Damascus and Baghdad would respond handsomely to a call to revolt. He felt that the proper course would be not to reject Kitchener's offer as insufficient, but to find out by negotiation whether it was intended as an absolute guarantee of Arab independence.

The two brothers stuck tenaciously to their opinions in the whispered conferences to which their father kept summoning them. Hussain was inclined on the whole to share Faisal's views on the unpreparedness of the Arabs in the other provinces, yet Abdulla's insistence made him pause. Eventually he came to an interim decision. On the one hand, he would send emissaries to Syria and to the principal Arab rulers to discover the true state of their feelings and prepare and sound the leaders; and, on the other, he would give Kitchener just enough, but no more, encouragement to keep him in play. He composed a letter to Storrs for Abdulla to sign, in which he defined himself as being willing to come to an understanding with Great Britain, but unable yet to depart from the neutrality which his position in Islam bound him to observe. He hinted that he might find it possible to lead his immediate followers to revolt in the event of the Turks bringing matters to a head, provided that England were to promise effective support.

The letter reached Storrs before the end of October and was telegraphed to London at once. Its text must have reached Kitchener about the same time as a letter from his old friend Sir John Maxwell, who was then commanding the British Forces in Egypt, and who, writing from Cairo on the 16th of October, advised, "I do not know what the policy of the Foreign Office is, but I think the Arabs about Mecca and the Yemen ought to be approached and set against the Turks."

Maxwell had served long in the East, and his advice was weighty with Kitchener. On the 31st Kitchener telegraphed to the British Agencies in Cairo the text of a message to be dispatched to Abdulla in reply. The message opened with an announcement of the news of Turkey's entry into war. It contained a definite promise to Hussain that if he and his followers were to side with Great Britain against Turkey the British Government would guarantee his retention of the dignity of Grand Sherif with all the rights and privileges pertaining to it and would defend it against all external aggression. It held out a promise of support to the Arabs in general in their endeavour to secure freedom, on condition that they would ally themselves to England. It concluded with a hint that, in the event of the Sherif's being proclaimed Caliph, he could count on Britain's recognition.

This message reached Abdulla on November 16, at a critical juncture, and caused him the liveliest satisfaction. On the subject of the Hijaz it gave Hussain the very assurance he had solicited, while, on the question of the other Arab provinces, it opened out an alluring prospect of national liberation. The terms of the message were studiously general, it is true, but in the form in which it reached Abdulla it spoke of "the Arab nation" and of the "emancipation of the Arabs." Whatever these phrases may have meant to the preoccupied Kitchener when he used them, to the Sherif they conveyed an unmistakable invitation to foment a revolt of all Arabs. In that sense did he read the letter addressed to his son in the name of Kitchener, whose fame in the East was then greater than that of any living Englishman and whose word was accepted without question; and to that end from that time forward did he direct his activities.

He caused an answer to be sent to Cairo, in which Abdulla definitely committed his father to a policy of unavowed alliance with Great Britain. Abdulla stressed again the inability of the Sherif, before the requisite preparation, to commit any act of overt hostility against the Turks, and he asked for time in which to find his bearings, muster his forces, and then seize a favourable opportunity for a rupture. He promised Storrs that he would send a further communication in due course. This reply reached Cairo in the early days of December, and with it the first chapter in the Anglo-Arab conspiracy came to a close. The second chapter was to open eight months later, in the following July, as soon as Hussain had completed his inquiries among Arab leaders and his negotiations with them. It opened with a note from the Sherif to Sir Henry McMahon, British High Commissioner in Egypt, the first of an important series of diplomatic notes which make up what is known as the McMahon Correspondence.

In Mecca the Sherif was cautiously picking his way. Kitchener's offer of the 31st of October, which had reached him almost simultaneously with the issue of the call to *jihad* had brought him definitely round to Abdulla's view as against Faisal's. But it was still too early for him to act. He had first to consult with nationalists in Syria and Iraq and with his neighbours in Arabia, and elicit the degree of support he could count upon. The distances involved and the care needed to preserve secrecy would mean months of delay. Meanwhile the Turks were pressing for his endorsement of *jihad* and for his active support. He was deluged with letters and telegrams from Istanbul—from the Grand Vezir, Enver, Tal'at, and other personalities. And now Jamal Pasha, commander-in-chief of the Fourth Army in Syria, was urging him to declare himself openly for a holy war, to send the Prophet's standard to Damascus, and to raise an army among the tribes of the Hijaz.

In subtlety and resourcefulness Hussain was more than a match for the Turks, and he acted with consummate dexterity.

To all their appeals to declare *jihad*—war as a duty for the Muslims—he returned enthusiastic answers in diffuse and classic prose. He prayed for its success and gave it his blessing, would support it with all his heart. He felt sure that the Sultan in his infinite wisdom would understand his own difficulties, for on the Red Sea shore the British Navy were supreme, could blockade him, and so starve his people in the Hijaz. Meanwhile he sounded the other Arabian princes and more powerful sheikhs as to their attitude to the Turks, and by the very inquiry raised doubts about his own and their loyalty to them. He corresponded with Sayid Ali al Mirghani, the principal Arab in the Sudan and a friend of the Governor-General, Sir Reginald Wingate, in the same vein.

By refusing or avoiding the declaration of *jihad* Hussain so angered the Turks that his deposition was planned. All that they could do was to pretend that *jihad* had been declared by him and make much out of the sending of the Prophet's standard from Medina to Damascus, but the absence from its progress of Hussain and his sons made it clear to the Arabs that he had not endorsed their demand.

The attitude of the Ottoman Pasha in the Hijaz towards him convinced the Sherif that some plot was afoot, and when the Pasha's papers were stolen and brought to him they went to show that there was a scheme to do away with him. He lost no time in acting. He sent Faisal to Istanbul, nominally to complain to the Sultan and his Government, but chiefly because on his way he would be able to see the leading Arab nationalists in Syria and explain to them all that they did not know about the negotiations with the British through his son Abdulla and the general situation as he saw it.

During Faisal's absence in Turkey the Syrians he had seen on his way concocted a protocol defining the conditions under which they thought concerted action with the British might be taken by the Arabs.

On his return to them Faisal expressed doubt about its acceptability to the British, but he undertook to hurry to Mecca and press its acceptance on his father. The first part of this short document referred to the recognition by Great Britain of the independence of the Arab countries, which were defined as going as far north as Mersin, Adana, Urfa, Mardin, and Jazira ibn Umar; only Aden was excluded in the peninsula itself, and on the west the Red Sea and the Mediterranean was the boundary. It called for the conclusion of a defensive alliance between Great Britain and the future independent Arab State and the grant of economic preference to Great Britain. An oath of allegiance was taken by six of the leaders, by which they bound themselves to recognize the Sherif as the spokesman of the Arab race. The leading dignitary in Damascus gave his signet ring, in accordance with an ancient custom, to be taken by him to the Sherif, as it were a sign of authority and of his pledge.

When the Sherif resumed his negotiations with the British the war was going badly for the British Allies in the East. The attack on Gallipoli had failed and Egypt was still threatened, the Turks in the Yemen had invaded Aden territory, and in Iraq, while the British were advancing still, the odds against them were known to be heavy. It was when he was thus preoccupied with the dangers threatening Egypt that Sir Henry McMahon received a note from the Sherif, part of the correspondence between them, that has been very fully treated by several authorities since the war because of its relevance to the Palestine problem. In May the Sherif telegraphed through Port Sudan asking for Storrs to visit his son Abdulla in the Hijaz.

As a result of that correspondence and of Storrs's visit—whatever the interpretation subsequently put upon it in the various quarters concerned—and because a Turkish expedition was about to march to the Yemen from Medina, and on its way might depose him, Hussain entered the war on the Allied side, on the 5th of June 1916.

The Meccan newspaper *Al Qibla* reported the first action, the throwing out of Mecca of the Turkish garrison. George Antonius gives a translation from that paper for August 14–17, 1916:

> At 3.30 A.M., just before daybreak on Saturday, the 9th Shaaban (June 10), a sustained rifle-fire was opened on the barracks in Mecca and on the Hamidiya building in which are housed the offices of the Government; and a siege was laid on all the Turkish troops in their several strongholds.[1]

The officers telephoned to the Sherif's palace to ask for an explanation and were told that the country had declared for independence and that they were invited to surrender, which

[1] *The Arab Awakening.*

they refused to do. The fighting on Monday, June 12, followed the lines of the two preceding days, but was more particularly intense round the Government offices in the Hamidiya, in which the Deputy Governor-General, himself an army officer, had entrenched himself with a garrison and had been keeping up a reckless fire. A detachment of Sherifian forces made a determined attack and succeeded in storming the place and forcing its garrison into surrender. The Deputy Governor-General and all the officers under him were taken prisoner and quartered in the Sherif's palace. They wrote letters to the officers who were still holding out in the barracks to suggest surrender, but they continued to fire, some of their shots setting fire to the pall of the Ka'aba and falling in the shrine elsewhere. It was not until guns had been brought up from Jedda that they were induced to give in, on July 4. By July 9 the Turks were cleared out of all their posts in Mecca. It was almost exactly four hundred years since they had assumed sovereignty over the holy city.

The news of the revolt caused alarm in Turkey and Germany and was concealed from the public for several weeks. Taif and the Governor-General of the Hijaz, Ghalib Pasha, fell to Abdulla's siege in September. All the other larger towns of the Hijaz, except Medina, were taken during the summer, and even Medina was soon cut off.

In the first of his proclamations Hussain explained his action and appealed to all Muslims to follow his example. He took his stand on the cause of religion and of nationalism. The proclamation denounced the anti-Muslim practices of the Committee of Union and Progress and the arbitrary tyranny of the Turkish Government, in particular of Enver, Tal'at, and Jamal Pasha, who, it said, were responsible for the executions and terrorism in Syria. It ended by calling on all Muslims throughout the world to follow his example, in discharge of their obligations to him as Sherif of Mecca and to the cause of Islamic solidarity.

Jamal Pasha was in a state of frenzy. In January he made a speech in Damascus which showed the extent of his anger, even six months after the revolt had begun. He thundered against

the mean individual who in the very heart of the Holy Land of Islam has allied himself to those Christian powers whose object is to despoil the world of Islam and purloin Constantinople its capital.[1]

The act of the traitor had been primarily to render a service to the British. When the Turkish troops nevertheless crossed the Canal and annihilated the British one of their first acts would be to cut off the head of that scoundrel in Mecca.

A British and French mission, the British under Lieutenant-Colonel C. C. Wilson, of the Sudan Political Service, and the French under Colonel E. Brémond, was sent to Jedda. The duties of the foreign officers under them were intended to be advisory, but some of the officers were later to be brilliantly executive.

The immediate effect of the revolt, militarily, was to frustrate the Turco-German attempt to block the Red Sea from the Yemen, an aspect emphasized by Dr Hogarth, the eminent scholar who was the head of the Arab bureau in Cairo, and by Colonel Brémond.

In September Storrs again visited the Hijaz, travelling in the flagship of Admiral Wemyss, H.M.S. *Euryalus*, which conveyed the *mahmal* to Jedda, the first time it had come with a British naval vessel. The Admiral was invited to ride at the head of its procession through Jedda, but thought it wise to refuse.

In November the Sherif was proclaimed King of the Arab countries. The news was telegraphed abroad by the Sherif Abdulla, his second son, acting as his Foreign Minister; but it was not recognized outside the Hijaz, the British and French Governments informing the Sherif in January 1917 that he was recognized by them as "King of the Hijaz." At the same time one of the last Turkish-held places in the country, Wejh, was captured by the Sherif Faisal's armies and the British Navy. Medina itself held out, but the Sherif Ali Haidar, who had reached it from Istanbul, being ordered by the Porte to succeed Hussain, seeing no hope of success and the probability of capture, asked the Sultan's permission to return to the Levant, where he remained secluded in the Lebanon until the end of the war.

Hussain's sons were playing their full part in the revolt. The diminutive Ali, the eldest, was in command of the forces

[1] G. Antonius, *The Arab Awakening.*

containing Medina; the lively Abdulla, next in age, was harassing their communications from Wadi 'Ais. The third son, Faisal, was mustering forces and attending to their equipment at Wejh, ready for larger operations.

By July Akaba, in the northern Hijaz, had been captured, and the first phase of the revolt was over. The next was the advance on Damascus in concert with Lord Allenby's operations from Egypt. But Faisal's task was far more than a simple military one. He had overcome the canniness of the chieftains whose tribesmen's support he needed. He had to make an alliance with each of them, convince each of them in turn, dissolve the differences between them, encourage with the gold supplied to him by the British and by the faith that was his own. In all this, and in the raiding operations when they began, he was nobly aided by Colonel T. E. Lawrence, of the British military mission. Faisal's emissaries, including Lawrence, travelled far afield and sometimes far behind the enemy's lines into Syria. The Arabs in the Turkish ranks began to desert, and when the British advanced into Palestine they were received as deliverers by the people.

The campaign in the Levant and the connected actions by the Arabs under Faisal have been fully described in books on that phase of the First World War and in particular by Lawrence. At the end of it the Sherif Nasr and some Arab chieftains of the Anaiza tribe were the first to ride up to Damascus, on the evening of September 30, 1918. Their messengers galloped into the main square, the Arab flag flying, as heralds of the two victorious armies. The next day, October 1, a detachment of Arab cavalry rode in followed by Nasr, and two days later Lord Allenby drove into the city just as Faisal and a thousand of his men entered from the desert side. The city is described as being in a frenzy of joy.

Although within two years the French had thrown Faisal out of Damascus, he had been found another throne, at Baghdad, and Abdulla was ruling at Amman, so that if Hussain's full war-time hopes had not been realized he nevertheless directly influenced a great part of Asiatic Arabia, a larger area than any other Arab ruler. He had received about six million pounds in gold from the British Government during the war and he had been accepted by the Syrian Arab leaders as the head of the Arab movement and negotiator on their behalf with the Allies. He had been recognized by the Allies as King of the Hijaz.

Expediency had dictated the later policy of the Allies in supporting Zionist hopes in Palestine and French claims in the Levant; in refusing recognition of Hussain as King of all the Arabs it was only fact that they followed. Ibn Saud had, apart from his treaty with the British, become entirely independent of all external ties; even the Sheikh of Koweit had been recognized as independent; the Sultan of Muscat had long been so, and was in old treaty relations with the United States and France; Bahrain, Asir, and Yemen, too, were independent of Hussain. To recognize him as King of the Arabs was out of the question; to claim to be King of the Arabs was no less than absurd, except as a desperate gesture. And this it seems mostly to have been, and one that was to be repeated.

Ibn Saud, in Central Arabia, had been given arms and money by the Allies during the war, but had not used them except to attack Hashimite forces in Taraba in 1919 and to defeat Ibn Rashid, his rival in Northern Arabia, ally of the Hashimites, after the war. Islam and tradition prevented Hussain from openly allying himself with a Christian Power against Ibn Saud, and the Ottoman Turks, who were the traditional make-weight, had gone down into collapse. The very Caliphate had been abolished by the new Turks, and when Abdul Majid Effendi, with his family, had been made to leave Istanbul hurriedly and for ever, at dawn on March 4, 1924, Hussain forlornly assumed the empty title himself, at Shuna, in Jordan, on March 11, 1924.

Hussain was too proud to compose his differences with Britain and Ibn Saud, or at least with one of them, and in the latter case he was perhaps right in thinking no permanent good could come of it. It was an old feud and a rivalry that nothing could reduce to true amity.

The British asked too much of him, for they sought to buy him openly—as it seemed to him. His sadness and bewilderment at the outcome of the San Remo Conference, at which the Mandates of Palestine and Iraq had been conferred, and of the consequent treaty with him by which Britain offered her protection and continued subsidies in exchange for his recog-

nition of Zion have been described by George Antonius in
The Arab Awakening.[1]

In 1923 and the summer of 1924 negotiations were opened
again and dragged on

> with a tenacity which ended by grating on Foreign Office nerves,
> as he kept protesting in message after message that he was not
> moved by narrow or selfish motives, that his attitude was dictated
> solely by the conviction that there could be no peace for the
> British, Jews, and Arabs in Palestine so long as the latter had
> cause to suspect that the ultimate aim of Zionism was to establish
> a Jewish State in their midst and at the expense of their national
> aspirations.[2]

In August Hussain wrote to the Prime Minister of the
United Kingdom appealing for the putting into effect of
Britain's promises made during the war, but he never received
a reply, for before this month was out the Wahhābis were
marching on the Hijaz, and by October he had ceased to
be King.

His assumption of the Caliphate had given Ibn Saud and the
Indian Muslims, whose spokesman was Shawkat Ali, a handy
weapon with which to impugn Hussain's motives. He was
accused by them of seeking only his personal ambition. The
accusation was untrue, for the Sherif was as pious as any of his
detractors, but his acceptance of the title, although in fact
hesitant, gave an appearance of reality to their charges.

In his isolation he had turned to Britain, but by that time
feeling in Whitehall had hardened against him. As Antonius
says:

> He was regarded as an object of ridicule and a nuisance. The
> fashion had been started of circulating funny stories about the
> old man's idiosyncracies—some of which were undoubtedly
> laughable—and as the stories went round they begat others and
> created a demand for more, as funny stories will. . . . Hussain
> became a laughing-stock. He was no longer taken seriously by
> the Civil Servants.[3]

So they replied to his last appeal, for help against Ibn Saud,
that they regarded the conflict as a religious dispute in which
they could not intervene unless they were specifically asked to

---

[1] p. 331 *et seq.*   [2] *Ibid.*   [3] *Ibid.*

do so as arbitrators by the two parties to the dispute; and, knowing that victory would be his, Ibn Saud wanted no mediators.

So, on October 13, 1924, Mecca was lost once more to the Wahhābis, and Hussain was forced to abdicate, in the same month, in favour of his eldest son, Ali. For a year Ali held Jedda, while Ibn Saud bided his time and continued to correspond with the Indian Muslims, endeavouring to smooth away the fears which had arisen over the news of the massacre by his troops of the inhabitants of Taif, of their intentions to demolish the lesser shrines in Medina and Mecca and prevent all other sectarian practices than those of the Wahhābis. Medina and Yanbu', the ancient home of Qitada, still held out, and so Ali ruled these three beleagured towns as King of the Hijaz—more and more closely invested, with less and less hope, with little or no revenue—until the following winter. On December 18, 1925, he announced to the foreign consuls his withdrawal; the next day the Wahhābis entered the city, and on the 22nd he sailed in a British ship for Basra, and took refuge at his brother Faisal's Court, in Baghdad.

Ibn Saud diplomatically continued to issue conciliatory announcements to the Muslims in general and the Hijazis in particular, to call Islamic conferences, to toy with the idea of installing another Sherif and sound foreign opinion; but in the end he took over, as he doubtless had always in his heart intended, the direct rule of the holy cities and the Hijaz, from Akaba to the Yemen border.

So Hussain was to die a proud and broken exile, in Amman, on June 4, 1931,[1] and Ali, in Baghdad, on February 14, 1935.

It had been the intention to take the body of King Ali by boat, in the evening, along the Tigris through the middle of Baghdad from his house on the river-bank to the Royal Tombs in the suburb of Adhamiya. The soldiers, the black, covered barges were assembled, the populace sadly embarking or lining the river-banks, when a storm began to rise. The sky darkening, the waters rocking the river-craft, and a sudden wind increasing in strength sent the mourners to shelter under any

---

[1] See *The Times* of June 5, 1931, for obituary notice and report of the funeral. He was buried outside the western wall of the Haram-al-Sherif, of Jerusalem. Three of his sons, Ali, Abdulla, and Zaid, were present.

wall or bank, and so the doleful procession to the grave of the last of the Hashimite Guardians of Mecca, the chief mourner his only son, the Emir Abdilillah, went landwise in the haze-hid noon of another day.[1]

[1] See *The Times* of February 15, 1935, for obituary notice and account of the funeral, which was attended by King Abdulla, King Ghazi, and Emir Abdilillah, his son. *The Times* reported that the funeral took place in one of the worst dust-storms for many years, the cortège being accompanied by the wail of thousands of women.

GLOSSARY

AGHA: The title of a Turkish commander, of a Kurdish chieftain, of an illiterate man in a position of some authority, and of a eunuch, whether black or white. In Mecca and Medina eunuchs serve the sanctuary and shrine. The eunuchs of Medina surrendered their communal property in return for a payment by the Ottoman Government to the individuals. The body of Meccan eunuchs declined the offer and have retained the rich and widely distributed properties of their corps, probably one of the oldest unbrokenly continued communities in the world. Formerly more numerous, they are now well under a hundred strong.

ALIM: A scholar, more especially a religious scholar or dignitary. The term is more frequently encountered in the plural form, 'Ulama,' which is loosely used to describe the Muslim ecclesiastical hierarchy.

AMIR: *see* Emir.

ARNAUT: Turkish militia recruited from Macedonians, who practised both the Muslim and Christian religions, or sometimes the Muslim religion only; also, later, Albanian soldiery.

BASTINADO: Origin Spanish *baston*, a stick; known in Arabic and Persian under the name of *falak*. The bastinado was a common form of punishment under the Ottoman Government. Two men supported between them a strong pole, which was kept in a horizontal position: about the middle of the pole were cords with running knots; through these the naked feet of the sufferer were forced and made tight so that the soles were exposed, the victim being thrown down on his back or left to rest only his neck and shoulders on the ground. A third man beat his soles with a tough stick. According to the letter of the Ottoman penal code, this punishment could be inflicted only on men of the fourth and last class of society. The Emirs, or issue of the race of Muhammad, the Ulama, free citizens, and private individuals living on rents or the proceeds of their industry were exempted. The Koran says, "But those whose perverseness ye shall be apprehensive of, rebuke, and remove them into separate apartments, and chastise them."

Beating with a cat-o'-nine-tails was not uncommon in Ottoman territory and habitual in galleys manned by slaves, but this was used less as a punishment than as a daily form of invigoration.

BEY: A Turkish title below Pasha. In Egypt it is still given as a formal title by the King. It is employed as a courtesy title for the sons of Pashas and often as a mark of respect to persons not strictly entitled to it. In Tunisia it is the title of the reigning prince. The title Pasha is no longer used in Turkey.

CALIPH: The word is the equivalent in English of the Arabic *Khalifa*, having in origin the meaning of a deputy or successor, one who follows.

It was adopted as a title by Abu Bekr, the first successor of the Prophet Muhammad. With the expansion of the Empire it came to have the significance of the supreme sovereignty of the Islamic power.

The Abbassid caliphate of the classic era was extinguished by the Mongols in A.D. 1258, but a survivor of the family reached Cairo, where the Mamelukes maintained him and his successors as puppets seldom recognized outside Egypt. With the Ottoman conquest of Egypt, in 1517, the Abbassid caliphal line was finally ended. There had been a rival caliphate in North Africa, and subsequently in Cairo, the Fatimid, but this ended before the Abbassid line. In the latter part of the nineteenth century the Sultan Abdul Hamid of Turkey revived the caliphate in his own person in pursuance of his panislamic policy. The Ottoman caliphate, however, never obtained general acceptance and came to an end with the Kemalist revolt in 1923. The Sultan of Morocco and the Imam of the Yemen have certain caliphal prerogatives and titles in their own territories. The last Arabian caliph was the Emir, later King, Hussain, Grand Sherif of Mecca, but it was a title not generally recognized and was not adopted by his son and successor, King Ali of the Hijaz, the last of the Grand Sherifs. The accompanying title to the Caliph was 'Emir-al-muminin'—*see* Emir.

DAURA: State musicians of Mecca under the Sherifs, customarily playing at guard-changing, probably introduced after A.D. 1517. They were usually four in number, and the posts tended to be hereditary.

DIWAN: In the Arabian sense of the word, the salon or town reception-room of a notable.

EMIR: An ancient Arabic title meaning 'commander' or 'leader'; now often, but not exclusively, used to mean 'prince.' It is, for example, still used in Arabia to mean the commander of any place, or the leader of any body of men, however small, as well as for princes. It is also used in compound titles or styles, as for example, in 'Emir-al-muminin,' or 'leader of the faithful,' applied to the Caliph; in 'Emir-al-Bahr' meaning 'admiral' (which word is derived from it), or 'Emir-al-hajj,' the leader of a pilgrim caravan to Mecca. In the Ottoman capital the leading member of the Sherif's family living there was known as the 'Emir Pasha.'

FATWA: A considered pronouncement by Muslim religious authorities.

FIRMAN: A formal, written order of approval by the Sultan of Turkey or the Shah of Persia.

HAJJ: The pilgrimage to Mecca. Hajj or Hajji, one who has completed the pilgrimage.

HARAM: A reserved and respected place, hence a shrine and women's quarters.

HAREM: Strictly 'women,' but has been used in the text here in its wider, usual English sense—namely, to cover the women's quarters.

HASHIMITES: Members of the family descended from Hashim, great-grandfather of the Prophet Muhammad, but particularly applied to the Hassiniya or Hassanite branch, descendants of Hassan, grandson of the Prophet, ruling Mecca until 1925: the descendants of Amr-Hashim as distinct from the descendants of his brother Abdul Shams, from whom, through his son Umayya, descended the Umayyad Caliphs of Damascus, who were bitterly opposed to the Hashimites, and the Umayyads of Cordova.

HIJAZ: The western province of Arabia, properly speaking the barren country or country between the coastal plain and the plateau of the interior.

IHRAM: The special dress, or rather undress, of a loincloth, without artificial fastening, worn by pilgrims approaching Mecca until they have completed the rites laid down. It may be supplemented if desired by a second piece of cloth which should be worn over the left shoulder and under the right arm. In recent years many pilgrims wear an ordinary bath-towel draped over both shoulders. No headdress is worn.

IMAM: The leader in prayers; literally, one who goes in front, as does a prayer leader among the Muslims, being either an accepted professional dignitary or anyone who leads the prayers of a number of Muslims, however small the gathering. It is used as a title for the ruler of the Yemen, and was in use as a title for the father of Ibn Saud, Abdul Rahman, when Ibn Saud was ruling, although his father was living.

ISLAM: The faith revealed by the Prophet Muhammad.

JAMI OR JAMAA: Literally, the gathering or assembly place—that is, for the Friday noonday prayers and sermon, and hence the great mosque where the congregation meets. In small towns there may be several mosques (*masjid*) but only one *jami*.

JANIZARY: The Turkish military force of that name founded after 1472 and destroyed in 1826. See *Ency. Brit.*, and particularly

F. W. Hasluck, *Christianity and Islam under the Sultans* (Oxford University Press, 1929), vol. ii, pp. 483-493.

JEBEL: Mountain.

JIHAD: Literally, a particular task or effort required of a Muslim, hence a Holy War, especially when proclaimed by the Caliph or sanctioned in a proclamation issued by the Ulama.

KA'ABA: The great Cube, or 'House of God,' in the sanctuary at Mecca, in which, fixed in its outer wall by a silver ring, is the Black Stone kissed by the pilgrims.

KAIMAKAM: Literally, *chargé d'affaires*; it is used to denote district governors and colonels in the army. The title has been in use for the Governors of Jedda until the present day.

KATHUDA: Turkish agent.

KHATIB: The preacher on Fridays.

KHEDIVE: A title formerly used by the ruling house of Egypt. The last Khedive, Abbas Hilmi II, was deposed in 1914.

KHILA': A robe of honour.

KHUTBA: The sermon on Fridays, and the prayers accompanying it in which the name of the Prophet, his family, certain companions, the Caliph, and the ruler of the country are mentioned. To be mentioned in the *khutba* prayers at Mecca became the ambition of the rulers of Muslim states, since it gave recognition of a dominant position in the Muslim world.

KISWA: A robe or covering of honour either for the Ka'aba or an individual. The *kiswa*, or draping, for the Ka'aba was sent in the Middle Ages, at the time of the pilgrimage from the great cities—Baghdad, Cairo, Damascus, Aleppo—from the Yemen, but since A.D. 1472 has been sent only from Cairo, annually, with a few intervals recently.

KORAN: The book of sayings and revelations to the Prophet Muhammad, gathered together soon after his death, A.D. 632. It should be more properly transliterated 'Qur'an.'

LUWAND: Ottoman marines or commandos. They were usually recruited from the toughest young men available, and were in their heyday much feared.

MAHMAL: The carrying of the *kiswa* (see above) for the Ka'aba, and hence the litter and *kiswa* itself while being carried. The procession usually makes a ceremonial departure from Cairo; the *kiswa*, on a camel in its midst, guarded by a military escort, is bidden God-speed by the King and Ulama.

MAMELUKE: Pronounced in Arabic 'Mamlouk'; literally 'possessed,' hence an 'owned' man, or slave, and particularly the slave dynasty of Egypt supplanted by Salim, the Ottoman conqueror, in A.D. 1517.

Masjid: Literally, a praying-place—that is a place of prostration to the Deity, and so 'mosque,' which word is derived from *masjid* via the Spanish. It may be any place for prayers, even an open space selected by travellers, or a temporary mosque, no more than a line of stones with a niche or curve, to denote the direction of praying, towards Mecca and the Ka'aba.

Mejlis: Literally, 'sitting-place,' a gathering, a parliament, a meeting at the coffee-hearth.

Muezzin: A caller to prayers. Properly transliterated it should read 'muadhdhin,' but has passed into English in this form.

Muslim or (synonymously) Muhammadan: Follower of Islam, the faith revealed by the Prophet Muhammad.

Naqib: The Chief of the Sayids and keeper of their genealogies in the great Arab cities.

Pasha: An Ottoman Turkish title, still conferred in Egypt and Jordan.

Qadhi: A judge administering the Islamic law, or *sharia*.

Sanjak: An Ottoman banner or flag of war, hence a superior or flag officer, also a provincial or semi-autonomous district.

Sayid: A descendant of the Prophet Muhammad. In particular persons claiming descent through Hussain, grandson of the Prophet, as distinct from the Sherifs who are descended from Hassan, brother of Hussain. It is now used in Iraq, and sometimes in Palestine, Syria, and elsewhere, without the definite article to denote 'Mr' or 'Sir.'

Sherif: Noble, a descendant of the Prophet through Hassan. "The Sherif of Mecca" was the title of the rulers of Mecca, who were known to Europeans as the Grand Sherifs.

Sultan: The temporal ruler of a Muslim state; not used before Turkish times. It is still in use by the rulers of Zanzibar, of Morocco, and of a number of other states.

Tarawih: Plural, from *tarwiha*, 'sing'; additional evening prayers, used particularly in Ramadhan.

Tihama: The Red Sea coastal plain of Arabia; mostly a salty surface. The coastal province of the Yemen.

Wadi: A gully.

Wali: Literally, 'Guardian on behalf of——,' used in the Ottoman Empire as a title for governor of a province or for an imperial political agent. There was usually an Ottoman Wali in the Hijaz, as an agent of the Sultan. In Iraq the Wali was the governor.

Wazir, or Wezir: Minister or a senior administrative agent, anciently translated as Vezir, Visier, etc.

Zawiya: A lodge of the dervish orders.`

Appendix I

A NOTE ON THE OTTOMAN IMPERIAL ARCHIVES

The ancient Ottoman records, including those of the Sublime Porte, are in the control of the Prime Minister, and through his kindness and the help of his secretary, Bay Adil Derinsu, a friend from the days of the first U.N.O. conference in London, I was able to see and examine them.

Mr W. E. D. Allen, at the time a Counsellor in the British Embassy to Turkey, introduced me to Bay Tahsin Öz, Director of the Topkapı Sarayı Museum and Editor of the Guide to the Archives in the Serail of the Ottoman Sultans, of which two volumes have so far been published covering books.[1] Bay Tahsin kindly gave copies of them to me.

They are arranged alphabetically by authors, down to Hancerli Bey Zade, and no further issues are contemplated for the time being. The library in which the books and manuscript books concerned are housed is the building shown as New Library, on the plan of the Serail facing p. 260 of N. M. Penzer's *The Harem* (Harrap)— that is to say, it is in the north-western corner of the Third Court of the Palace, near the Gate of the Fountain and the Pavilion of the Holy Mantle, or Herkai Serif Odası, in which were kept the relics of the Prophet. Among the treasures of the library, in charge of Bay Kamal Cig, are the Imperial pedigrees and pedigrees of the Prophet's descendants, many of them exquisitely illuminated.

The state of the documents of the Ottoman régime was outlined by P. Wittek (now holding the chair of Turkish in the School of Oriental and African Studies, London) in *Bysantion* (1938) in an article entitled "Les archives de Turquie", tome xiii, pp. 691–699. The writer describes the documents under five headings.

1. The documents of the Sublime Porte, or Bab-i-Ali, were in the building known as the Basbakanlık, of the Grand Wezir's office—that is, near the Palais du Vilayet. These are still in the same place in charge of Bay Kenan Tuna. The total number of documents here and in the depots attached to this section is estimated by those responsible to be in the neighbourhood of five

[1] *Topkapı Sarayı Müzesi-Arsivi Kılavuzu* (Devlet Basımevi, Istanbul; vol. i, 1938; vol. ii, 1940).

million. The Muhimme-defteri and Kanunname records are also in the Baibakanlık. Through the kindness of Bay Nasıf Bülükbaıı, Chef du Protocole of the Vali of Istanbul, I was put in touch with the Director of the Baibakanlık archives.

2. The archives of the former Ministry of Finance were in a house near the old prison of Meterhane, in the Sultan Ahmed quarter; the documents on the first floor were in fair order, those on the second floor in sacks. It was the latter group which suffered in the sale in 1931, which, deplorable as it was, at least brought the attention of the Turkish intelligentsia to the state of the historical treasure in the Government's possession.

The sale occurred through the administration of the ancient property of the Ministry of Finance deciding to clear them out of the building. They were sold as waste to a contractor, who sent them to Bulgaria. Thus, on a certain day in May 1931 a line of lorries carrying 30,000 okes of old papers set off for the station, and now and then some of them fell off and were blown away. A passing schoolmaster retrieved a few, among them dispatches concerning the campaign for Vienna in 1631, deeds about a property of the Ghazi Mikhal family in a village near Plevna, an order about the garrison of Nish, in Serbia, a firman of Sultan Selim II in favour of the poet Sheikh Ghalib, a cook's account for the palace in most splendid calligraphy, and so on. Public opinion was roused, and the remaining documents were placed in safekeeping. They are now in the same area as the documents of the Sublime Porte, in the Palais du Vilayet, but, in common with them, unindexed.

3. Le Cadastre de l'Empire, or Defter-i-Haqani, in the old storehouse, probably of Byzantine origin, situated behind Aya Sofia. These are to-day in the Baibakanlık with the other documents mentioned above.

4. The documents of the Sheikh-al-Islam, or Meseyhat, much damaged in a fire in 1926, and subsequently, in 1933, placed in the Palais de Justice. These documents are now housed in the Library attached to the Mosque known as the Sulaimaniya and are in charge of Dr Mustafa Koymen.

5. The archives of the Evkaf Müdürlügü, which was partly in a school near the Directorate of the Evkaf and partly in a building near Aya Sofia. To these documents of the religious foundation and bequests were added those of the Ministry of Marine and of the provincial Evkaf,[1] although some of the latter had already disappeared—those of Brusa, for example, having been sold as

---

[1] Religious bequests foundation.

waste paper many years ago, and those of the Istanbul Evkaf tribunal having perished in the fire of 1926. These documents, which have no printed catalogue, are said to be in Ankara, but numbers have been seen in the Baibakanlık, in Istanbul. Many documents were removed from the Aya Sofia mosque during the war years and taken into the interior of Anatolia for safety. In addition to the above, listed in "Archives de Turquie" in *Bysantion* (1938), tome xiii, there must be surviving documents of the old Army Command, but it was impossible to obtain a reliable account of them and their present whereabouts.

A state of the libraries in Istanbul was published by Muzaffar Gökmen, of the Directorate of the Public Library of Bayazid[1]. In Section Two of the pamphlet are listed libraries containing a total of over 110,000 manuscripts. The grand total of indexed and unindexed manuscript books is conservatively estimated at 450,000.

[1] Sühulet Basımevi, Istanbul, 1947.

Appendix II

A NOTE ON SOME ASTRONOMICAL PHENOMENA
SEEN IN ARABIA

In A.H. 592 after the pilgrimage a black wind covered Mecca and red sand rained down. The Sanctuary was shaken so that some stones from the Yemeni Corner fell.

IBN ZAINI DAHLAN, in *Khulasat al Kalam*

Author does not quote his sources.

592 Hejira equals, allowing for the event being just after the pilgrimage, the end of A.D. 1195, and probably about the first week in December.

Soon after 3rd Muharram there was seen in Mecca a long-tailed star, like a lance in length [proportion?]. It stayed from sunset to sunrise. The people were irritated by it. Some said that it was an ill omen.

Ibid.

The date given equals September 3, 1770.

On Monday, the 11th of Muharram 1079, two hours after sunrise, a very strong beam of light was seen coming from the sun or from close by it. This beam extended to the west, and whoever looked at it was temporarily blinded. The colours of the beam were blue, yellow, and red. Both edges later disappeared and the centre of the beam became swollen and then burst with a noise like thunder.

After it had burst the remainder of the light turned into smoke and disappeared.

MUHAMMAD HAIDAR AL HUSSAINI, in *Kitab Tandhid al Uqud;*
in events of the year

The date given equals June 31, 1668.

On 19 Dhi al Qada 1146 there was an eclispse of the sun from midday onward. The eclipse was total and the stars visible.

Ibid.

The date given equals April 24, 1637.

In 1091 a star appeared with a tail to the east and remained all the year.

Ibid.

1091 Hejira began on February 12, 1680.

On the 23rd Ramadhan, A.H. 1078, there was a huge blazing of light across the sky in the west and this appeared for three nights, after which it began to disappear, but became longer until it was a third of the sky. It lasted in all fifteen days—that is, until 8th Shawwal.

Ibid.

The first date equals March 8, 1668. There are observations in old records of a comet seen in Goa by a Jesuit father from March 9th to 21st (new style), and there is therefore excellent agreement between the observation in Arabia and that in India.

THE EMIRS OF MECCA FROM THE EMIR QITADA ONWARD

	A.D.
Qitada ('Al Nabigha,' or 'the Genius'; nicknamed Abu Aziz), of Yanbu', port of Medina, *b.* 1132, conqueror and thirteenth dynastic Emir of Mecca; descent—ibn Idris ibn Mutain ibn Abdul Karim ibn Muhammad (Abu Jaafar al Tha'alab) ibn Abdulla al Akhbar ibn Muhammad al Thayir ibn Musa al Thani ibn Abdulla al Mahath ibn al Hassan al Muthanna ibn Hassan ibn Ali, son-in-law of the Prophet Muhammad	1201–20
Hassan ibn Qitada	1220–21
Rajih ibn Qitada	1221–54 (with seven intervals— Egyptian commanders between 1221 and 1229; Abu Sa'ad al Hassan ibn Ali ibn Qitada with Muhammad Abu Nomay; Shiha ibn Qasim al Hussaini, of Medina, in 1240; Jammaz ibn Hassan ibn Qitada, deposed by Rajih's son Ghanim)
Idris ibn Qitada	1253–54 (and in partnership with Muhammad Abu Nomay until 1270)

Muhammad Abu Nomay (nicknamed Abu Mehdi, styled Najm-al-din) ibn Abi Sa'ad al Hassan ibn Ali ibn Qitada	1254–1301 (with intervals—in 1258, when sons of Hassan ibn Qitada ruled; in 1271, when Jammaz ibn Shiha, of Medina, and Ghanim ibn Idris ruled for forty days; and other intervals from 1288 onward)
Rumaitha (nicknamed Abu Arada or the 'strong-willed,' styled Ashadd-al-din) ibn Muhammad Abi Nomay	1301–44 (with six intervals, he and his co-ruler, Humaidha, replaced by Ataifa and Abu Ghaith and restored)
Ajlan (nicknamed Abu Sari'a or the 'swift,' styled Izz-al-din) ibn Rumaitha	1344–75 (co-rulers Thaqaba, Ahmad, Sanad, Mughaimis)
Ahmad ibn Ajlan	1360–86
Muhammad ibn Ahmad	1386
Anan ibn Mughaimis	1386–87 (co-rulers Ahmad ibn Thaqaba, Aqil ibn Mubarak ibn Rumaitha)
Ali ibn Ajlan	1387–94
Hassan ibn Ajlan	1394–1425 (co-rulers Barakat ibn Hassan and Ahmad ibn Hassan, short intervals when Rumaitha ibn Muhammad ibn Ajlan and Ali ibn Anan ibn Mughaimis ruled)
Barakat ibn Hassan, or Barakat I	1425–55 (intervals when Ali ibn Hassan, 1441–42, and Abdul Qasim ibn Hassan ruled)

Muhammad ibn Barakat	1455–95
Barakat ibn Muhammad ibn Barakat, or Barakat II	1495–1524 (intervals when Hazza ibn Muhammad and Ahmad al Jazan ibn Muhammad ruled) (Sultan Selim conquered Egypt A.D. 1517.)
Muhammad Abu Nomay ibn Barakat, or Abu Nomay II	1524–84
Hassan ibn Abi Nomay	1584–1601
Idris ibn Hassan (nicknamed Abu Aun)	1601–24 (co-rulers Abu Talib ibn Hassan, Fuhaid ibn Hassan, and Muhsin ibn Hussain ibn Hassan)
Muhsin ibn Hussain	1624–28
Ahmad ibn Talib al Hassan	1628–30
Masoud ibn Idris	1630
Abdulla ibn Hassan	1630
Muhammad ibn Abdulla	1631 (co-ruler Zaid ibn Muhsin)
Zaid ibn Muhsin	1631–66 (with an interval when Nami ibn Abdul Muttalib pretended to the rulership)
Sa'ad ibn Zaid	1666–71 (with intervals—see following rulers)
Barakat ibn Muhammad	1671–82
Said ibn Barakat	1682–83

| Ahmad ibn Zaid | 1669–71 |
| | 1684–87 |

| Said ibn Sa'ad | 1687–1716 |

(with many intervals—
Ahmad ibn Ghalib 1687,
Muhsin ibn Hussain 1689–
91, Masoud ibn Sa'ad in
1691, Abdulla ibn Hashim
also in 1691, Abdul Muhsin
ibn Ahmad 1704, Abdul
Karim 1693–1704 and again
in 1705 until 1711, and in
1715)

| Abdilla ibn Said | 1716–17 |
| | 1723–30 |

| Ali ibn Said | 1717 |

| Yahya ibn Barakat | 1717–19 |
| | 1721–22 |

| Mubarak ibn Ahmad | 1719–21 |
| | 1723 |

| Barakat ibn Yahya (see above, Abdilla ibn Said, for successor) | 1722–23 |

| Muhammad ibn Abdilla | 1730–32 |
| | 1732–34 |

| Masoud ibn Said | 1732–33 |
| | 1734–52 |

| Masaad ibn Said | 1750–58 |
| | 1759–70 |

| Ja'afar ibn Said | 1758–59 |

| Abdulla ibn Said | 1770 |

| Ahmad ibn Said | 1770 |

Abdulla ibn Hussain	1770
Sarur ibn Masaad	1773–88
(Abdul Muin ibn Said, 1788, for one day)	
Ghalib ibn Masaad	1788–1813
Yahya ibn Sarur (paid stipendiary of Muhammad Ali Pasha of Egypt)	1813–27
Abdul Muttalib ibn Ghalib	1827–28 1852–56 1880–81 (see following four rulers)
Muhammad ibn Abdul Muin ibn Aun	1828–36 (Egyptian Commander 1836–40) 1840–52 1856–58
Abdulla ibn Muhammad ibn Aun	1858–77
Hussain ibn Muhammad ibn Aun	1877–80
Abdilla ibn Muhammad ibn Aun (Abdilla Pasha)	1879–80 1881–82
Aun-al-Rafiq ibn Muhammad ibn Aun	1882–1905
Ali ibn Abdulla ibn Muhammad ibn Aun	1905–8
Hussain ibn Ali	1908–24
Ali ibn Hussain	1924–25

Abdilillah ibn Ali ibn Hussain, only son of the last Grand Sherif of Mecca, King Ali of the Hijaz	The Regent and Heir Apparent of Iraq
Abdulla ibn Hussain, younger brother of the last Grand Sherif	The King of Jordan
Faisal ibn Ghazi ibn Faisal ibn Hussain, great-grandson of the Sherif Hussain ibn Ali (1908–24), the penultimate Grand Sherif, styled King of the Arabs and Caliph of Islam.	The King of Iraq

A NOTE ON SOME OF THE GODS IN AND ROUND MECCA BEFORE ISLAM

Place	*God*	
Wadi Nakhla, near Mecca	Al Uzza	Near by was the cave of Ghubghub. Three trees belonging to the Khozaa and afterwards to the Kinana and Qoraish. Arms might be hung on the trees, for the ground about it was a sanctuary and the devotees safe therein. Votive offerings were brought to Uzza, and at one time human sacrifices had been made. At one time the Bani Shayban division of the Bani Sulaim were caretakers.
		Al Azraki identified it with Venus. Camels were offered as a sacrifice (De Lacy O'Leary, *Arabia before Muhammad*, p. 193).
Hunain	Dhat Unwat	Visited by Qoraish. They used to spend a night there hanging their swords on the trees and making a sacrifice. Belongings might be left there indefinitely and were entirely safe. (Al Azraki.)
?	Suwar	Belonged to Bani Hudhail; a sanctuary.
Mecca	Hubal	Brought from Hit, in Mesopotamia, or Syria. Had one arm broken, which was replaced in gold by the Qoraish. The latter account (*see* Caussin de Perceval's *Essai sur l'histoire des Arabes*, p. 219) says

Place	*God*	
		from Maab, in Belka district. It was made of 'aqiq,' which indicates a red stone. At one time Hubal was the chief deity of the Ka'aba. Ritual arrows were drawn from it. Returning travellers used to visit it even before going to their homes. When an offering was made the donor used to ask the guardian to strike his seven flints. When the arrows were consulted they were identified for meaning as follows: "Pay in blood" (a hundred camels equalled a man); "Yes"; "No"; "One of yours"; "Assistant"; "Foreigner"; "Water"; "Mixed in a sack."
Mecca	Yalil	—
	Madan	—
	Holah, or Allah	Mentioned in Lihyanite inscriptions fifth century. Also in inscriptions found at Umm al Jimal, in Syria, dated sixth century B.C. The Lihyan tribe still exists near Mecca and were troublesomely rebellious in the time of Muhammad. 'Holah' is a bedouin exclamation of surprise and dismay still in use on Hijaz-Nejd borders.
	Yaghouth	'The helper'; mentioned in Koran.
	Yaug	'The preserver'; mentioned in Koran.
	Wadd	Or 'love'; identified with moon-god.
	Aram	Vapour, or spirit, god.

Place	*God*	
Mecca	Khulassa	Necklaces were put round the neck of this female goddess brought from the Yemen, and wheat and barley offered, and liban, or whey, poured over her.
	Nuhayk	Also called the bestower of the winds.
	Asaf	Said to have been turned to stone for adultery with Naila.
	Naila	Feminine, said to have been turned to stone for adultery with Asaf.
		The feeder of birds; possibly connected with the conception that souls went into birds after death.
Qudaida near seashore by Jebel Mushallal	Manat	'Doom' or 'fate,' cf. *Maniya* of *Mana* in Isaiah lxv, 2 (*see* De Lacy O'Leary's *Arabia before Muhammad*, p. 195).
Taif	Al Lat	Owned by the Thuqaif tribe, who strongly resisted Muhammed. A block of stone was still showed at Taif in nineteenth century as Al Lat. Possibly to be identified with the sun-goddess.

Sources: De Lacy O'Leary, *Arabia before Muhammad*; A. P. Caussin de Perceval, *Essai sur l'histoire des Arabes*; Al Azraki; and the Koran.

BIBLIOGRAPHY

Abbot, Nabia: *Two Queens of Baghdad* (The University of Chicago Press).

Abu'l Feda, Ismail Ali Imad-al-din Abu'l Feda, Prince of Hama: *Géographie d'Abu'l Feda*, edited and translated by M. Reinaud (Paris, 1848).

Ali Bey al Abbassi (alias Domingo Badia y Leiblich): *Voyages en Afrique et en Asie pendant les années 1803 à 1807* (Paris, 1814).

Ansaldi, C.: *Il Yemen* (Rome).

Antonius, G.: *The Arab Awakening* (Hamish Hamilton, 1938).

Asqalani, Al, ibn Hujar: *Al Dura al Kamina fi Ayan al Mia al Thamina* (Hyderabad, 1890).

Athir, Ibn al, Izz-al-din ibn Abu'l Hassan al Shaybani: *Al Kamil fi'l Tarikh* (Tornberg, Leyden, 1866–76).

Avril, Adolphe D': *L'Arabie contemporaine, avec la description du pèlerinage à la Mecque* (Paris, 1868).

Azraki, Al, Muhammad ibn Abdulla ibn Ahmad: *Akhbar Mekka wa ma ja fiha min al athar*; published by F. Wustenfeld under title, *Die Chroniken der Stadt Mecca* (Leipzig, 1858).

Baittar, Al, Abdul Razzaq: *Shadha al Zahar fi ayam al quarn al thalath ashar* (manuscript, 1899).

Batnuni, Al, Muhammad Labib: *Al Rihalat al Hijaziya lil Khaidaiwi Abbas al Thani* (Cairo, 1911).

Batouta, Ibn: *Voyages d'ibn Batoutah*, by C. Defremery and Dr B. R. Sanguinetti (Paris, 1874–9). Original Arabic title: *Tuhfat al Nadhdhar fi Gharib el Amsar wa Ajaib al Asfar*.

Bishr Faris, D. L.: "Tariq Lafdhat al Sharaf," in his book *Mubahath Arabiya* (Cairo, 1939).

Bovill, E. W.: *Caravans of the old Sahara: an Introduction to the History of the Western Sudan*. Published for the International Institute of African Languages (Oxford University Press, 1933).

Burckhardt, J. L.: *Notes on the Bedouins and Wahabys, collected during Travels in the East* (Colbourn and Bentley, London, 1829–30–31).

Burton, Sir Richard F.: *Personal Narrative of a Pilgrimage to El-Medinah and Meccah* (Longmans, 1855–56).

Cætani, Leone: *Annali dell' Islam* (Milan, 1907).

— *Stude di Storia orientale* (Milan, 1926).

COURET, A.: *La Palestine sous les empereurs Grecs* (Grenoble, 1869).

DAHLAN, AL SAYID AHMAD IBN ZAINI: *Al Jadawil al Mardhiya fi Tarikh al Dowal al Islamiya.*

— *Khulasat al Kalam fi Bayan Umara al Balad al Haram* (Cairo, 1887).

DHUHAIRA, AL, JAMAL AL DUNYA WA AL DIN MUHAMMAD IBN AMIN: *Al Jama al Latif fi fudhail Mecca wa bina al Bait al Sharif* (F. Wustenfeld, Leipzig, 1859).

DIDIER, C.: *Séjour chez le grand-chèrif de la Mecque* (Paris, 1857).

DIODORUS SICULUS: *The Historical Library of Diodorus the Sicilian*, made in English by G. Booth (London, 1700).

DOUGHTY, C. M.: *Arabia Deserta* (Cambridge University Press, 1888: one-volume edition, Cape, 1926).

DOZY, REINHART: *Spanish Islam*, translated by F. G. Stokes (Chatto, 1913).

ETTINGHAUSEN, RICHARD: "Die bildliche Darstellung der Ka'ba im Islamischen Kultur Kreis," in *Zeitschrift der deutschen Morgenländischer gesellschaft*, Band xii, Heft 3–4.

EVLIYA, CHELEBI (Anliyah Effendi): *Seyhatnamesi* (Government Press, Istanbul, 1935).

FAKIHI, AL, ABU ABDULLA MUHAMMAD IBN ISHAQ: *Kitab al Muntaq fil Akhbar Umm al Qura* (F. Wustenfeld, Leipzig, 1859).

FASI, AL, TAKK-AL-DIN ABI TIB MUHHAMMAD IBN AHMAD: *Shifa al Ghuram bi Akhbar al balad al haram* (F. Wustenfeld, Leipzig, 1859).

FOSTER, SIR WILLIAM: *The Red Sea at the Close of the Seventeeth Century* (Hakluyt Society, 1949).

FUWTI, IBN AL, KAMAL-AL-DIN ABDUL RAZZAQ IBN AHMAD AL SHAYBANI AL BAGHDADI: *Talkhis Majma' al Adab fi al Alqab* (manuscript in the Dhahariya Library, Damascus).

GROUSSET, R.: *Histoire des Croisades* (Plon, Paris, 1935).

GUIDI, J.: *L'Arabie anteislamique* (Paris, 1921).

HAFIZ WAHBA (Sheikh): *Jazirat al Arab fil Qurn al Ashrin.*

HAIG, LIEUTENANT-COLONEL SIR WOLSELEY: *Comparative Tables of Muhammadan and Christian Dates* (Luzac, London, 1932).

HANAFI, AL, QUTUB-AL-DIN AL MEKKI: *Kitab al alam bil alam balad Allah al Haram* (Arabic manuscript, No. 845, in the Bibliothèque Nationale, Paris).

— *Burg al Yamani* (Arabic manuscripts, Nos. 826, 826a, 827, and 828, in the Bibliothèque Nationale, Paris).

HERODOTUS: *The History of Herodotus*, by G. Rawlinson (John Murray, 1862).

HEYD, W.: *Histoire du commerce du Levant au moyen age* (Leipzig, 1885).

HITTI, P. K.: *The History of the Arabs* (Macmillan, 1940).

HOGARTH, D. G.: *Arabia* (Clarendon Press, Oxford, 1922).

HUART, C.: *Histoire des Arabes* (Geuthner, Paris, 1912–13).

HURGRONJE, C. SNOUCK: *Mekka*, 2 vols. (The Hague, 1888).

— *Mekka in the Latter Part of the Nineteenth Century* (Luzac, 1931).

HUSSAINI, AL, SAYID RIDHA-AL-DIN IBN SAYID MUHAMMAD HAIDAR: *Kitab Tandhid al Uqud al Saniya bi Tamhid al Dawla al Hassaniya* (Manuscript copy in possession of Yacoub Sarkis of Baghdad; the copyist was Ahmad ibn Abdul Rahman al Maghribi al Tarablusi, who noted that the author died in A.D. 1750; the copy was made a few years later).

IBRAHIM RIFA'AT PASHA: *Mirat al Haramain* (Al Misriya Press, Cairo, 1925).

'INABA, IBN, JAMAL-AL-DIN AL HASSANI: *Umdat al Talib fi ansab Abi Talib* (Manuscript; part has been published at Nejef and Baghdad by Muhammad Kashif al Ghita, of Nejef).

ISFAHANI, AL, ABU AL FARAJ: *Al Aghani* (Cairo, 1868).

JAUZI, AL SIBT IBN: *Mirat al Zaman* (Facsimile of the manuscript in Antiquities Library, Baghdad).

JOMARD, EDMÉ F.: *Études géographiques et historiques sur l'Arabie* (Paris, 1839).

JUBAIR, IBN, ABDUL HUSSAIN MUHAMMAD IBN AHMAD AL KINANI AL ANDALUSI AL VALANSI: *Rihalat* (Leyden, 1852: second edition, edited by M. J. de Goeje, Leyden, 1907).

KAMMERER, A.: *L'Abyssinie, la Mer Rouge, et l'Arabie* (Royal Geographical Society of Egypt, 1935).

KHALDUN, IBN: *Kitab al 'ibar wa diwan al mubtada wa al khabar fi ayyam al Arab wa al barbar* (Reprinted, Cairo, 1867): in particular "Al khabr an dowlat al sulaimaniya," vol. iv and v.

KIERNAN, R. H.: *The Unveiling of Arabia* (Harrap, 1937).

LAEMMENS, H.: *Le berceau de l'Islam, l'Arabie occidentale à la veille de l'hégire* (Rome, 1914).

— *La Mecque à la veille de l'hégire* (Beirut, 1924).

— "Les Ahabis et l'organization militaire de la Mecque au siècle de l'hégire," in *Journal Asiatique*, Paris, November–December 1916.

— "Les Competitions des puissances en Arabie à la veille de l'hégire," in *Extrait du Bulletin de la Societé Sultanieh de Geographie*, Nouv. Ser.T. viii conference II, 2. 1916.

LANE POOLE, S.: *The Mohammadan Dynasties* (Constable, 1893).

LAWRENCE, T. E.: *Seven Pillars of Wisdom* (Cape, 1926 and 1935).

MAQRIZI, AL: *Al Saluk li mirafat Duwul al Muluk* (Reprinted, Cairo, 1934).

MARGOLIOUTH, D. S.: *The Relations between Arabs and Israelites prior to the Rise of Islam* (Oxford University Press, 1924).

MUIR, SIR WILLIAM: *The Caliphate; its Rise, Decline and Fall*, edited by Dr T. W. Weir (Grant, 1924).

— *The Mameluke or Slave Dynasty of Egypt*, A.D. *1260–1517* (Smith, Elder, 1896).

NIEBUHR, KARSTEN: *Voyage en Arabie et en d'autres pays circon-voisins*, translated by F. L. Mourier, 2 vols. (Amsterdam, 1770–80).

O'LEARY, DE LACY: *Arabia before Muhammad* (Kegan Paul, 1927).

— *A Short History of the Fatimid Khalifate* (Kegan Paul, 1923).

PERCEVAL, A. P. CAUSSIN DE: *Essai sur l'histoire des Arabes avant l'Islamisme, pendant l'époque de Mohammad et jusqu'à la reduction de toutes les tribus sous la loi mussulmane* (Paris, 1847–48).

PHILBY, H. ST J. B.: *Arabia of the Wahhabis* (Constable, 1928).

— *The Background of Islam* (Cairo, 1947).

PITTS, T.: *A True and Faithful Account of the Religion and Manners of the Mohammadans* (Oxford, 1704).

POOLE, S. LANE: *The Mohammedan Dynasties* (Constable, 1893).

RALLI, A.: *Christians at Mecca* (Heinemann, 1909).

REINAUD, M.: *Extraits des historiens Arabes relatifs aux guerres des croisades* (Paris, 1829).

REY, E.: *Les Colonies franques de Syrie* (A. Picard, Paris, 1883).

RIVOIRA, G. T.: *Moslem Architecture; its Origins and Development* (Oxford University Press, 1918).

RUTTER, E.: *The Holy Cities of Arabia* (Putnam, London and New York, 1928).

RYCAUT, SIR P.: *The Present State of the Ottoman Empire* (London, 1687).

SALE, G.: *Preliminary Discourse to the Koran* (London, 1734).

SCHOFF, W. H.: *The Periplus of the Erythræan Sea* (New York, 1912).

SNOUCK HURGRONJE—*see* HURGRONJE.

STORRS, SIR RONALD: *Orientations* (Nicholson and Watson, 1943).

TABARI, AL, ABI JA'AFAR MUHAMMAD IBN JARIR: *Tarikh al Umam wa al Muluk al Hussainiya* (reprinted, Cairo, 1908).

TAMISIER, M. O.: *Voyage en Arabie. Séjour dans le Hejaz. Campagne d'Asir* (Desessart, Paris, 1840).

THOMAS, LOWELL: *With Lawrence in Arabia* (Hutchinson, 1925).

TOYNBEE, ARNOLD J.: *Survey of International Affairs, 1925*, vol. i, "The Islamic World since the Peace Settlement" (Oxford University Press, 1927).

— *A Study of History*, 3 vols. (Oxford University Press, 1934).

VARTHEMA, LUDOVICO: *Travels in Egypt, Syria, Arabia Deserta and*

Arabia Felix, Persia, etc. A.D. *1503 to 1508,* translated by J. W. Jones and G. P. Badger (Hakluyt Society, 1863).

WAVELL, A. J. B.: *A Modern Pilgrim in Mecca* (Constable, 1918).

WEYGAND, GÉNÉRAL MAXIME: *Histoire militaire de Mohammed Ali et de ses fils* (Paris, 1936).

WOLLASTON, A. N.: *The Pilgrimage to Mecca* (Leyden, 1880).

WOOLLEY, SIR LEONARD: *Abraham: Recent Discoveries and Hebrew Origins* (Faber, 1936).

WRIGHT, T.: *Early Christianity in Arabia* (Williams and Norgate, 1855).

WÜSTENFELD, F.: *Chroniken der Stadt Mekka* (Leipzig, 1857).

YOUNG, MAJOR SIR HUBERT: *The Independent Arab* (John Murray, 1933).

ZAEHRA, IBN, TAJ-AL DIN IBN MUHAMMAD IBN HAMZA: *Ghayat al Iqtisar fil bauytat al alawiya al mahfoudha min al ghubar* (Bulaq Press, Cairo, 1892).

INDEX